T0072463

ALSO BY LORIAN HEMINGWAY

Walk on Water: A Memoir
Walking into the River: A Novel

A WORLD TURNED OVER

A KILLER TORNADO AND THE LIVES IT CHANGED FOREVER

LORIAN HEMINGWAY

SIMON & SCHUSTER

NEW YORK   LONDON   TORONTO   SYDNEY   SINGAPORE

SIMON & SCHUSTER
Rockefeller Center
1230 Avenue of the Americas
New York, NY 10020

First Simon & Schuster trade paperback edition 2003

SIMON & SCHUSTER and colophon are registered trademarks
of Simon & Schuster, Inc.

For information regarding special discounts for bulk purchases,
please contact Simon & Schuster Special Sales at 1-800-456-6798
or business@simonandschuster.com

Title page photo spread courtesy of AP/Wide World

Designed by Paul Dippolito

Manufactured in the United States of America

1   3   5   7   9 10   8   6   4   2

The Library of Congress has cataloged the hardcover edition as follows:
Hemingway, Lorian.
A world turned over : a killer tornado and the lives it changed
    p. cm.
1. Tornadoes—Mississippi—Jackson. 2. Tornadoes—Mississippi—
Jackson—Psychological aspects. 3. Jackson (Miss.)—
History—20th century. I. Title.
QC955.5.U6 H45   2002
363.34/923/0976251—dc21   2002073346

ISBN 0-684-85634-4
0-7432-4767-1 (Pbk)

THIS BOOK IS DEDICATED TO THE LIVING
SPIRIT OF THOSE WHO PERISHED IN THE
CANDLESTICK TORNADO ON MARCH 3, 1966;
TO THE BRAVE FAMILIES OF THOSE WHO WERE
LOST THAT DAY; AND TO ALL WHO SHOWED
SUCH COURAGE IN THE AFTERMATH.

AND IN LOVING MEMORY OF MY MOTHER,
SHIRLEY JANE RHODES.

ACKNOWLEDGMENTS

The generosity of so many has made this book possible:

For her tireless help, exhaustive research, and unfailing encouragement, I am forever indebted to Jo Barksdale. With respect and in deep appreciation for those who suffered so greatly that day in March 1966 and in the years to come, and who so kindly agreed to talk with me at length more than thirty years later, I wish to thank the Hannis family: Sharon, Darlene, Donny, Mae, and W.T.; Meland Smith, Eddie Jones, Linda Flowers, Karei McDonald, Fred, Mary, Fredna, Gloria and Tony Hudgins, Larry Swales, Larry Temple, Jimmy Bradshaw, Bobby Grant, Shorty Wells, Peter Boulette, Carla Boulette, Donna Durr, Valeta Pafford, Jennifer Faircloth, and Homer Lee Howie. And for their help in obtaining vital information, my thanks to J. C. Patterson, Bert Case, Clarice Bridgers, Thurman Boykin, John Hopkins, Bob and Sylvia Hubbard, The Eudora Welty Library, and Wright and Ferguson Funeral Home.

For his keen intuition and remarkable editorial eye, my thanks and gratitude to my editor, Bob Bender, and to his assistant, Johanna Li, for her good help and good humor.

For her belief in writers, especially this one, my thanks to Nicole Rowland.

For a friendship that has endured and transcended much these last twelve years, my thanks to Susan Crawford.

For Cousin Hubert Grissom, always, always my love and abiding respect.

For Dolores Baer, thank you once again for seeing me through.

For her good words, cheerfulness, and encouragement, my thanks to Valerie Hemingway.

For Tamara, wherever you are, once again, thank you.

And to my dear husband, Jeff Baker, my gratitude and love for always believing in me and for never being too tired to read.

"Behold, a whirlwind of the Lord is gone forth in a fury."

—Jeremiah 23:19

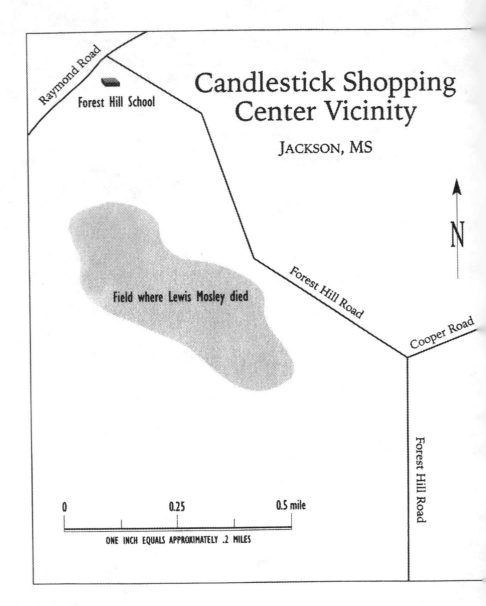

Candlestick Shopping
Center Vicinity

JACKSON, MS

Raymond Road

Forest Hill School

Forest Hill Road

Cooper Road

Field where Lewis Mosley died

Forest Hill Road

N

0   0.25   0.5 mile

ONE INCH EQUALS APPROXIMATELY .2 MILES

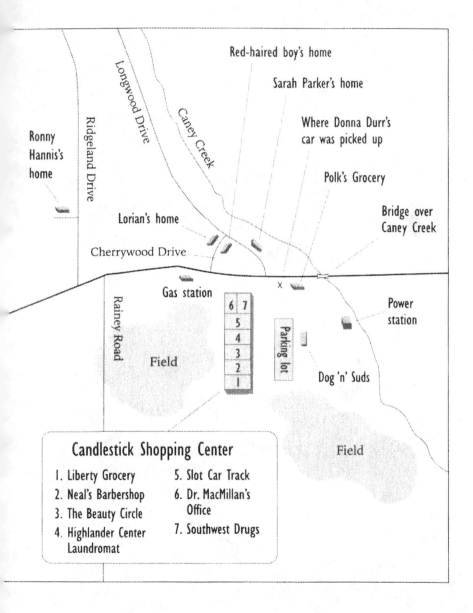

Red-haired boy's home

Sarah Parker's home

Where Donna Durr's
car was picked up

Polk's Grocery

Bridge over
Caney Creek

Ronny
Hannis's
home

Longwood Drive

Ridgeland Drive

Caney Creek

Lorian's home

Cherrywood Drive

Gas station

Rainey Road

Field

6 7
5
4
3
2
1

Parking lot

x

Power
station

Dog 'n' Suds

Field

Candlestick Shopping Center

1. Liberty Grocery
2. Neal's Barbershop
3. The Beauty Circle
4. Highlander Center Laundromat
5. Slot Car Track
6. Dr. MacMillan's Office
7. Southwest Drugs

PART I

HOW IT WAS

CHAPTER ONE

*"People were massacred up real bad. It was like war. They was
people that had been hit, and part of they head taken off, not all
they head, just part. Bodies in every form of mutilation. They
hands cut off. They legs cut off. Some of 'em cut half in two."*

—Karei McDonald, firefighter on the scene
of the Candlestick Tornado

IT WAS A WILD PLACE ONCE, the Civil War battlefield at
Vicksburg, so wild you could imagine that the dead here still
spoke, that from beyond the long curtain of kudzu draped and
twisted on the old trees, someone watched, the ancient sentry
for the ghosts of all wars past. The entry to the winding, steep-
valleyed road that turns at rolling angles through the fields of
graves and monuments and battle sites was a lowered archway
of kudzu when I was a child, a green porthole through which the
mirage of the past widened and became defined like an image in
a diorama. You knew then that this had been a battlefield, the
trenches still marked along eroded slopes, rough with rock and
brambles, the trees bound together in the sheath of tightly knotted vines, the granite monuments rising above the neglected
fields like tree-high tombstones in this place of interminable
stillness and heat. Without these markers, I was certain, you
would still know upon which ground you trespassed because, as
one Civil War historian put it, "It is the land that remembers
bloodshed," takes it deep into an elemental consciousness, sep-

arates guilt from righteousness, honor from pride, and distills what is left into an abiding remembrance of the horror of things past. Which is to say that hallowed ground has its genesis in pain and treachery, and what we come to remember afterward, what we come to honor on behalf of those who have fought in such a place is the overwhelming silence that is the aftermath of all war.

It was a place of silence when I visited there as a child, beyond the steady high-voltage hum of cicadas hidden high in the oak and sweet gum trees, a sound perfectly pitched in its ability to numb consciousness and make it all the more easy to imagine the shoeless footfalls of the Rebel army under the siege here in winter, dug into the cold and dampness of the clay hills, provisions nonexistent, starvation imminent. Vicksburg surrendered on July 4, 1863, a day that for Mississippians created a form of psychological independence that went deep. Defeated and dishonored, many refused in the coming years to celebrate the independence of a nation, choosing instead, on the Fourth of July, to remember Vicksburg and the men who had fallen here. More than a century later some still mark this date in silent vigil—no firecrackers, no backyard barbecues, no American flags—with a thousand-yard stare into the past, and sometimes with a pilgrimage to this battlefield that is now combed clean, polished, and spit-shined, just another roadside attraction.

When I have returned to the wild place of memory, it has been familiar only by the contours of the land and the heat that rises from it in a fog. The once overgrown battlefield has been weeded and pruned and mown so that it now looks like a manicured estate, the old trenches still there, but now they are gentle slopes sown in fescue, a broadening lawn that would appeal to the romping instinct of a child and would not, by the most liberal imagination, call forth the image of bodies decomposing beneath a July sun. It had been easier to imagine war when this place was forbidding, when its roughness forced you to stop at the edge of a weed-choked depression for fear of snakes, black widows, an ankle turned in the jaws of a land still angry. It was the very wildness of it that gave it sanctity.

Forty-five miles east of Vicksburg, along the low bluff of the Pearl River where the water runs red with clay, lies Jackson, burned four times during the War Between the States so that all that was left along the blackened bank when Sherman's troops pulled out was the chimneys of homes and public buildings. For a while Jackson was called Chimneyville. There are trenches, still, in Battlefield Park, where children play on the cannons, Civil War generals and soldiers are buried in Greenwood Cemetery, and Fortification Street is named for the Confederate fortification built along its course. On Terry Road, which runs from the heart of Jackson out into what for years was country land, there was once a fine plantation where Confederate troops would stop for food and a bed. The plantation home was never burned. The troops kept vigil. The home still stands today, the land that surrounded it now divided into suburbs. For years the neighborhood that the plantation became was a wild place, too. There were woods still, and acres of pasture, acres of cotton and corn and soybeans. A tributary of the Pearl River, Caney Creek, made a natural boundary in the deep backyards of the modest homes that would be built here, winding its way beneath new bridges, bearing its floodwaters in spring, drying to a pockmarking of deep potholes in summer. Far into the woods the source of Caney Creek lay, a deep trench of water where albino catfish swam, a mystery long before I came here.

This sprawl of swamp, woods, and fields, the sun hard and hot on the dirt in summer, the air wet with the steam off the gulf waters that rolls north and spreads like a shroud, this would be the place that I, as a girl, would come to know indelibly as home. No matter that there were places before and after. I would pledge allegiance to none of them. This was a place, too, where natural wars would fall, in the spring when the gulf burned with a fever and the territory north pushed its cold air into the buoyant balloon of Mississippi. Spring storms, floods, lightning bolts, hail,

fire, and brimstone. A wild place where North and South still col-
lided, where atmospheric wars would lay out the fields with the
dead again. And again. It is a place that would remind me always
of the look and feel of the old battlefield at Vicksburg, where the
green world rose up to cover the past, and where you could still
see the mark of it in the creek bed littered with arrowheads, and
in the redness of the dirt, and in the sound of the cicadas when
the wind was still. And for all the time I came to know this place
and what happened here, there is a dream that comes, always the
same, always a dream unwelcome because it can never be undone. It can never be just a dream.

In the dream I see the yellowing Mississippi sky in distinct parallel bands that are broken by the broad green canopy of pin oaks,
pecan, and sycamore, strips of sky the shape of banners, a cartoon
wash of color that threatens rain. In the dream rain is welcome, not
a thing to fear, and as I walk quickly toward the small shopping
center beyond the trees, at the end of the black ribbon of road
where I live, the rain starts up, defined, too, by the gutters of
houses along the road, by eaves that catch the quick unleashing of
water at an angle and force it momentarily skyward. Rain that rains
upside down. I look away from the wet and heavy sky, afraid of
what I might see. But I know. I know this because this is the one
dream where it does not matter what I do, it will happen the same
way, and I know that in this dream, familiar above all others, I will
not look up to find the sunlight fractured in an enameled bowl of
blue that holds everything suspended in calm. I will not look up to
see snow falling. Snow is cold and slow and hypnotic. Safe. You
never have to hide from snow. This dream is about the world rolled
onto a spear, of the sky punctured at its heart. But still I look up
because it would not be the dream if I did not.

The yellow awning of the grocery store, the color of the sky, is
close enough now that in a moment I can be under it, dry, ignorant, pretending that I will not see again what I am about to witness for the hundredth time. It has come that often in these
dreams, maybe more, so many times that I can only guess at how

easily my unconscious slides into the world of the haunted and conjures up what it knows I fear, feared before the fear had substance. I look and there it is, the veil of yellow gone, its relative brightness swallowed up now in black webbing, and at the core of this pockmarked darkness there begins the gyroscopic tightening of clouds, a Luciferian sleight of hand I will turn my back to once, to gain courage, before I look at it dead-on. It is a spiral, thin at first, barely discernible on the heavy gauze of the horizon, a wisp that could be mistaken for hallucination if I did not already know the pregnant way the turning needle will begin to swell until it becomes what I have suspected all along, the four winds twisting in combat, the Wizard of Oz cyclone poised above the store, ready to fall.

All light is gone now but for the sulfurous burn of streetlamps that blink on suddenly, their sensors tricked by the curtain drop of clouds.

Where to run? I know what happens here, at this overhanging of eave in the dark in this too-familiar place. People die here.

And they do not die in an ordinary way, in clean-sheeted beds, their fingers pulling at the satin trim of blankets, their eyes fixed and waiting and ready. They do not die knowing someone else is near. They do not die having time to think there is a chance not to die. Here in this dream of darkening skies, on this killing ground, they die by punishing force, against their will, and long before their time has come, so those who gather afterward to gaze at the tumult of bodies say, as if it were a mantra, "dead before their time has come," "dead before his time has come." Dead. It is the last word that will be inescapable, no matter what the context of the life, no matter how poignant the lament, and it will remain unto itself a proclamation of what is and can never be undone.

I feel the edges of the wind, quick and rough and nearer than I ever believed it could be, cutting an undertow in the now-unbreathable air. It is close now, stealing by degrees across the pasture that spreads like a dark lake behind the store, its black belly bulging straight out as it begins to feed on scrub pine, then on the girdered steel of the supermarket, on the cars once parked in even rows, on living tissue pliant as clay. If there is time, there is nothing to do but run.

I push my way through the spinning plasma of air, my body the shield that splits the heightening current into two rushing streams that meet at my back, shoving me as if it wants me gone. I ride the whip of wind halfway to a building that has not fallen, a home built high and narrow in the green of the pasture lake, and I know that I will make it inside because I always do, but it is not until that halfway mark where my feet strike some magical, memorable place on the heaving ground that I remember that this time I will live. Though not until I close behind me the door that is heavy as a vault, as the wind sucks in around the edges, bowing it so it strains and the walls shudder and then explode and the roof lifts clear, rising like an arrow into the maelstrom of dust and steel and wood, do I know for certain that I am alive. The rain begins again, but black now and steaming, melting the outline of my body against the dim light as I pull myself up to the broken world by a ladder of splintered boards and twisted rebar, the hollow place where the house had been filling with dark water.

In the dream I turn to look from where I have come, no further than three hundred feet, to the place where the wind has scoured a pit, where now stand spears of metal in the shape of crosses, and then beyond the pit to where the trees once stood, a level field of busted ground now, the color of mercury in the dawning light. At a point between the crosses and the field the bodies lie. Thirteen of them lined up heel to head, and I can see by their faces that I know them all. And I wonder for a moment, in the psychotic way of dreams where all that is surreal has a crossroads in reality, how a wind so brutal and so without conscience would take the time to lay out the dead row on row. But even in the dream I know that this is not the way these bodies finally rested, that instead they were smashed and broken, decapitated and scored, pulled like sacks of water and bone into the sky and left to drop and splinter and burst. I know how they really died, but still in the dream, where the unconscious will not even own to this treachery, I see them quiet and unmarked and so near to one another that maybe they are just resting from the drain of the wind.

I turn from the bodies and the waste that is beginning to grow and spread around them, back to where the shattered store has now re-formed itself, new and gleaming, lit from inside like a warming oven, no mark of the wind left anywhere, and even in the dream I think of Vicksburg, of the battlefield bright and clipped and sterile, of the lie that it is.

CHAPTER TWO

"Why do I stay here? I don't know. I guess familiarity. I guess, you know, you get used to something and then the anxiety of it is relieved because you're so accustomed to it. Refuge is really nothing more than what you can make yourself live with."

—Linda Flowers, Candlestick Tornado survivor

ALL DREAMS HAVE THEIR ROOTS in the corporeal, all dreams gather up shavings of fear and form from them something recognizable that the psyche can live with. This dream of a twisting wind, a sky that darkens on cue, and bodies splayed like scarecrows in a field has its real-life reason, its own circulatory system that exists in the objective: the memory of a place, a time, an event, of people, all of these pulled from the holding pens of ordinariness by catastrophe, all of these forged into memory because of one day, one hour, thirteen deaths, and because memory is as impressionable as clay when you put a hard fist to it.

I used to live across the road from that shopping center in the dream long before it became the reality of South Jackson builder Homer Lee Howie, a man given to praying aloud over the mercy of God, Mississippi born and raised. When Howie did begin to build, my friends and I had watched as bulldozers leveled the pastureland where horses had once grazed, tearing loose the clumps of buttercups and wild onions, the big tires catching in the thick braid of honeysuckle vines. It seemed to me at times that honeysuckle covered the entire state of Mississippi, threading its way across counties, lining the ditches of old roads, the splintery fences of rutted pastures, the thick sweet scent of it part of the mystery of Mississippi air, air so thick sometimes in the bloated heat of summer that it, like a handful of the pale yellow blossoms, crushed and bruised, gave off the very scent of wildness. It is a smell that lingered even as we watched the dump trucks pour fill dirt into the marshy areas, the red dust bubbling on the surface and then exploding in miniature volcanoes, and then as a rectangular pit was dug for the concrete foundation of the new Liberty supermarket. It was a word that had not long been in use in the American vernacular—supermarket—much less in the vernacular of Mississippians, and a word that by its very grandiosity suggested the miraculous. For the town of Jackson that lay north of this country land in a neat grid of public buildings and parks and antebellum homes, the old streets still bearing names from the Civil War, a town made nearly extinct in the early part of the century by yellow fever epidemics, prosperous for a time in the thirties and then, in the sixties, regarded by much of the nation as a proving ground for the annihilation of reason when Medgar Evers was shot in the back outside his Jackson home and the civil rights of blacks in Mississippi were scrutinized for what they were—virtually nonexistent—the shiny and the new and the well-stocked were things of quiet glory. The year was 1964, and watching common structures take form was still something of a pastime, and if you attached the word "super" to the work in progress, it had a galvanizing effect. So we watched, the adults joining us, too, day in, day out, as the humidity calmed the dust of the cinder blocks that made up the southwest wall of the Liberty store, and then the smaller businesses laid along beside it, a neat little train of wood and concrete and rebar.

It is the smell of that place, even today, that hits me first, a smell like a rusted-out pickup after a rain, the air sharp with oxidized iron, damp and thick with the weight of humidity. I remember it from the first time we walked the land where our new house would be, on a diagonal from where the shopping center would be built, on the south side of Jackson, in a rural sweep of flat, soggy bottomland with nothing more than a clapboard store called Polk's and, up the rural run of Cooper Road, tiny Marble's store, to mark the area as civilized. In between Polk's and Marble's was a nursing home whose grounds were choked with kudzu that trailed the length of the long dirt road up to the quiet bungalows where the old and the infirm and the simple slept their days away. And there were churches. There were always churches.

It was an outing peculiar to my family—I still wince when I use the word that suggests a unit, that in the best of all possible worlds we would have been content to live together under one roof, which in our brief time together was never even remotely true—walking through the boot-miring red clay of a subdivision site, in a place where the word "subdivision" was regarded as vaguely communist, in a town where my mother never wanted to be. Her idea of Heaven was California: dry heat, white beaches, West Coast culture, not, as she referred to it, "this cesspool" she reviled once she'd had a taste of grander places. My stepfather would be making choppy gestures with his arms, indicating where the picture window of the house would face, where the sidewalks would end, the height of the redwood fence he would build to keep the neighbors from prying. I stared in doubtful silence, pondering the insanity of such a scheme given the swamplike expanse we gazed upon. And beyond the swamp we would call home lay the hardwood stands and the cows and the chickens and the snakes and the chiggers—the true country—former land of broadening plantations, of slavery and civil war and blood in the dirt.

We were not alone in our surveying. Others walked among us and off into the steaming distance on sludgy clay paths where the bulldozers had just begun to make inroads. There were couples, and entire families, too, some with dogs that bounded off into the thick sweep of pines beyond the muck, others with small children carried low on their hips, and they all wandered with purpose, deep in the poisonous snake territory, for a reason. This would be their home, their neighborhood, the stamp of Mississippi deeply on it, and they dreamed about it as they walked the rough land, in a way that the uninitiated dream, without fear, and what they, and we, pondered was the unimaginable, that from this morass of woods, brambles, water-laden fields, and clay could be carved the thing most desirable in that era in America: a suburb to the Mississippi way of thinking, lavishly wild beyond the winding streets and still forbidding in an untamed way. And past these unthinned woods, not forty yards from where our house would be, ran the dark water of Caney Creek, on to where it fed into the even darker water of the Pearl.

It is the creek we would all remember, even as adults, our bodies no longer lithe, rubberized, unbreakable, no longer certain enough to cross the narrow black pipe that spanned the tumbling run of water. It was the pipe that the fearless among us would walk in flood season, when the water pushed below in a tide of debris, and in dry seasons when the drop to the potholes and rock islands beneath was far enough to kill. We would take the walk on weekly dares, our arms held out for balance. It was a rite of passage, a mark of courage that led not only to the other side of the ravine but to the respect of those who waited on shore, and they remembered when they were older that you had been that brave. It is where we would take our baptism, all of us, no matter how afraid, no matter how sissified, no matter whether our mothers told us not to, no matter whether snake skins lined the shore, the drying, cast-off sleeves of cottonmouths that could slide unseen into water the very color of their skins. No matter. Its tide would bear us from childhood to adulthood. It would form us all.

This would be a place of the Jackson blue-collar middle class, of country people come to a kinder way of living. It would be, too, a place with country values still intact—revival meetings, vacation Bible school, county fairs, and trips dressed in our good clothes to the streets of downtown Jackson—and we would spill from these

single-level homes without basements, from this secure place
with deep backyards thick in tall pines, from kitchens complete
with garbage disposals and sliding glass doors and carports and
California redwood fences tall as a man. We would have the
amenities that said we were not country anymore, the lying comfort of central air, the cool-tiled kitchen floors, as would the new
neighbors who roamed these thickets with us, smiling, anticipat-
ing. And there would be, too, a big picture window, just as my
stepfather had planned, a window that in time would become the
most important part of the house to me, an expanse of glass that
once in an errant while makes its way into the tornado dream, a
fractured portal that frames the bodies laid end to end. It would
face the southwest and define the ever-changing Mississippi sky, a
point of reference from which I would learn to gauge the speed
and direction of storms. That is the part they did not tell us as we
walked the land that day, and perhaps the developers did not even
know that this wild, sprawling patch of dirt where hundreds of
houses would bloom had been historically a tried-and-true tornado run, a track into which storms slid as easily as a foot onto a
beaten path. Whirlwinds. Devil spouts. Tornadoes. There was not
one mention made.

Not that we would have listened. Fate is not a notion that settles easily amid the luster of new Formica and parquet floors. It is
instead a notion with which only those who contemplate the
dark side on a daily basis are familiar. And so it was that I, per-
petual doomsayer, child misanthrope, dark seed, was the one,
eventually, who worried, gazing out that perfectly bright window
as if it were a crystal ball. It seems foolish to say that I always
knew it would happen, that somewhere in the genetic imprint of
my forebears there existed a memory of death long before it became a memory. But foreknowledge can be a thing no more com-
plicated than instinct, perceptions rooted not in the gauze of the
cosmos, but in the dirt. A thing of terror had passed here before.
A thing of terror would pass here again. In the days I spent digging in the dirt here and deep in the clay-walled canyon on Caney

Creek, I came to know it. *Here* was memory, scarred into the walls of the old tributary that feeds into the Pearl River at the Hinds and Rankin county line. This place, from the first time I stood upon its bed rutted with potholes, strewn with what the floodwaters did not want, became lodged deep in me the way old dreams are, and every moment spent here, in the heat of summer, far into the ravine or deep in the woods that ringed our world, was like the very edge of a dream where the conscious and unconscious bind together in peculiar alchemy and at the moment of fusion there is one bright, hard, narrow beam aimed at the future. But you have to look quick.

The throbbing heart of the homeland is as distinct as the rhythm of a human heart, recognizable as no other, syncopated to reveal one life rooted in one place, and it was here in this chlorophyll world where all was green but the dirt that I first heard the faint drumming of that beat separate from all others, and I knew home when I saw it. I knew home when I heard it. I knew home when I smelled it.

I have thought, in these later years, about the promises inherent in the notion of home, of what my parents and all the other new families might have expected that first day we walked the land outside Jackson. It must have been a dream of something different, better, than what they had had, these grown children with the heritage of dirt farmers still close enough to smell, people with the bright dream of their own "bidness" someday, and people like us, hard out of Louisiana, who needed a place more rooted and fitting than the small blue trailer we had lived in in Lake Charles, nicer than the two-room shack with a flower box out front in Dubach; a place free of arguments and tensions, a placid haven cooled by central air, closed off from the burn of summer, germless and odorless and safe. A refuge we could live with.

The others, too, must have kept sacred and mighty that vain hope that is timeless and inevitably disappointing, the belief that by creating a place unmarked by the past, an eternal newness is

achieved and, with that newness that reinvents itself with each
rising sun, a perspective untainted by failure. It is a common
enough mistake.

I still dream of the house the concrete foundation became,
the dream image open and haunting, the light that streams
through the big picture window my stepfather wanted so badly,
always muted, never that odd yellow light that falls before a
storm, and it is within those dim grays and pastels of the dream
house that once was real that I often return on a pilgrimage
home, never able to release what this one place became to the
sharper eye of reason.

CHAPTER THREE

*"There was a dark cloud like night, and there was two storms,
one light and one black."*

—Eddie Jones, husband of Juland Jones,
Candlestick Tornado victim

EVIL, AS WELL AS GOOD, can be a creature of habit, rising out
of a place from which it has risen before, traveling a familiar
path, defining for all time a tract of land, so that when the winds
rise again they will spill without effort into the old channel. The
land of South Jackson was marked territory. Tornadoes had
passed this way before, most never quite making it to the
ground, forming in the southwest out by the old Forest Hill
School, then moving on a northeast diagonal across the expanse
of woods and farmland, deepening the gully of Caney Creek,
bearing down on the low wetland that would one day be Candlestick Park, and often on toward Jackson along the river bluff.

Mississippi knows well the death blow of tornadoes and has
given up the lives of thousands to this natural war. The number
of tornado deaths is second here only to that in Texas, and of the
ten most lethal tornadoes in the nation's history, Mississippi has
borne three of them. Two have claimed over two hundred lives
each. The Natchez Tornado, May 17, 1840: 317 dead in an afternoon when a tornado hit seven miles southwest of the city, on

the Mississippi River, "stripping the forest from both shores," killing 269 on the river flatboats and then moving into Natchez itself, where "the air was black with whirling eddies of walls, roofs, chimneys and huge timbers from distant ruins, all shot through the air as if thrown from a mighty catapult." And there were even more deaths than the final count would tell. In slave-era Mississippi, the deaths of blacks were often ignored. The Tupelo Tornado, April 5, 1936: 216 dead. The massive tornado struck at nine in the evening. Entire families were killed in their homes, as many as 13 in a single dwelling. The young Elvis Presley was unharmed as his mother lay with her body covering his in the back room of their tiny shotgun house on the outskirts of Tupelo. A movie theater was converted to a hospital and the popcorn machine was used to sterilize instruments. Again, the black deaths were not counted.

In Mississippi, tornadoes often come in the night, when sleep owns all fears. At times this quirk of fate can seem almost kind, for people to die in their beds never knowing the precise face of death, because then they have been spared the anguish of a conscious fear and those who live on can comfort themselves with the knowledge that whatever dream belonged to those they loved at the moment they died was the dream that claimed them. And they will pray that the dream was good.

Long before cotton spread in widening plains of white across the Delta, there were tornadoes. Long before slavery and the moral war that issued from its containment spilled blood in those fields, there were tornadoes. Cherokee and Choctaw had once ruled great portions of the southeast territories, mythically bound to a land they would in time be driven from, and as that time approached they watched the skies for signs, and when the tornadoes came they feared for what this could mean. Devil winds, they called them. Winds of evil.

Wind is a conjured thing, made of nothing more substantial than air, invisible but for what it moves and carries and destroys. And tornadoes are nothing more than the empirical physics of air, the atmosphere's need to stabilize when the buoyant, helium-light heat of the gulf fans out like an alluvial plain across the southern land, the source and fuel and sustenance of multiplying columns of cumulonimbus clouds that at their most volatile can reach eighty thousand feet into the sky, a nuclear breeder of charged atoms and unstable air. Moving anvils of cold push down hard from the north, the cold air heavier, more stable, drier. When hot and cold collide along the demarcation lines, strong convection currents form, the hot air continually rising in sharp updrafts, the parallel downdrafts of cold air plummeting, an atmospheric pas de deux that achieves equilibrium in the violent rotation of current within the clouds. But then physics has a mutable logic oddly at one with the mystic, wherein anomalies and feats outside the realm of natural order occur—straws propelled through windowpanes, a two-by-four driven through a steel girder—so when a tornado strikes, there arise not thoughts of physics but of God instead.

And if those who bear witness to the storm survive, they say it is by God's grace. If they die, those left behind say it is by God's will. Yet within the unconscionable vastness of obliteration, where row on row in common houses the living are felled, there can rise up an anger as great and as potent as the storm itself, and at its core is the question all those who have watched a benign sky turn malignant ask: Why? And if they are still on speaking terms, then it is: Why, God?

There are seasons that are memorable in the history of deadly storms, there are dates fixed forever in memory, there are patterns, similar paths of ruin and survival stories that are eerily familiar. Nearly half a century before Homer Lee Howie built Candlestick Park, on June 6, 1916, an F-5 tornado originated in the same rural South Jackson area as would the Candlestick Tornado of March 3, 1966. By the Fujita scale of tornado intensity, an F-5 is a wind that causes "catastrophic" damage. From the F-0 to the F-6, descriptions of the breadth of damage done evoke a growing sense of disbelief. From mild to moderate to significant to severe to devastating to catastrophic to inconceivable, human comprehension of wind speeds that begin at 40 mph and can exceed 350 mph dissolves.

But in 1916, it was not called an F-5 tornado. No scientific scale had yet been developed to measure the ferocity of storms. It was only what the eye could see and the degree to which the heart could break that measured the level of loss. In the broken aftermath of their passing, tornadoes were often given the names that defined a particular destruction. They were named not for individuals but often for the buildings that were supposed to keep people safe. In 1916, the tornado that hit downtown Jackson became known as the Deaf and Dumb Tornado.

They had lain asleep in their dormitories, their beds together row on row, dozens of the mute and the deaf, impervious to sound and to its meaning in the lives of those who had come to rely on it, ignorant of the calling card of the tornado, a relentless pounding that gained in depth the nearer it moved, a sound some say is just like a train, a hundred trains, a thousand trains—a sound that must be described again and again so that it may be gotten right, so that it may be believed, until out of this similar experience of sound there surfaces a description like no other— "It was as if the world rolled over," one survivor said—one that throws the whole train comparison out of kilter, so that we know from this anomaly, from the heightened perception of one who listened hard, that it doesn't really sound "just like a train" but more guttural, more alive.

What, then, of the deaf who lay in their beds in the old building, those who for years, deprived of sound, had learned to detect motion by the frequency and depth of vibrations beneath their feet? Did they, in a sense, hear? Did they, as they slept, absorb and quickly come to understand the vague rumbling that intensified beneath the splintery floors as the storm boiled nearer in the darkness, disturbing the ground with such might that the thin metal frames of their beds must have acted as conduits, jarring them awake? Did they, then, in immutable silence, with the world still trembling around them, run to the straining, bowing windows to behold the master of sound, almost tangible now in a turning fist beyond the glass? Did they know enough to be afraid as they felt the boards beneath them pull free, as they watched the glass crack and shatter, or was there something like pleasure in a sound so huge that even in deafness it could not be denied them? Or perhaps they hoped that within this one irrevocable surge of wind, what they had known in silence all these years might be borne away and replaced by something keener.

And what did the survivors think after the hammering had died away and the story was told to them in whirling hand gestures that this midnight wind had been given the very name of their affliction, that here, by circumstance, was spoken the true meaning of such storms, an atmospheric beast deaf and dumb to all but its own internal drumming, its own preordained path?

Across town the 1916 tornado moved toward Bell Street, where the white people lived. A boy died in his bed there. His mother had heard the wind come up and above the noise she called to her son to get up, to please get up, but it was so great that he, in sleep, was as deaf and dumb as those the storm had just left behind. She saved the child she could, a daughter she pulled screaming from the house as it gave way above the boy who still lay in his bed. "He had never risen from his bed," wrote a reporter for the Jackson *Clarion-Ledger*, Mississippi's oldest newspaper, "but was pinned beneath the wreckage with his head mashed and neck broken." It is an old southern term, a "mashed" head, and one that is both graphic and final.

From the afflicted to the rich to the poor, the storm spared no one—if not death, then the fear that this was its signature scrawled high in the sky and then suddenly at their doorstep. If not this time, they worried, then perhaps next time. The storm struck finally in the shantytown neighborhood of the black residents, along the river near the railroad tracks that led to Vicksburg. In some blocks not a house was left standing, and along the ruined streets the dead lay beneath timbers that not long before had been airborne. Beneath the debris of one house a black woman was found dead, a baby in her arms, also dead. When the spiral of wind, the color of the night, died away, there were fourteen people who would no longer walk the streets of Jackson, thirteen of them black. The paper did not identify those thirteen by name as it did the dead one who was white. It was the way of Mississippi in 1916. It was very nearly the way of Mississippi in 1966.

CHAPTER FOUR

*"On this side of Highway 80 is country people, tied to the soil, the
great-grandchildren of Indians, the grandchildren of farmers, and
I'm not talkin' Delta plantation farmers, I'm talkin' grub farmers,
dirt farmers, the ones who had cows and chickens and they didn't
have them to sell, they had them to feed their children, the children
of the men and women of World War II, the people who saved the
world, and we were taught pride in that, and it stuck."*

—Linda Flowers, Candlestick Tornado survivor

THE MAGIC WAND OF THE SUBURB DEVELOPER was put to
the muddy, snake-wild thicket we had trudged that day, and
when we and the other new families moved in there were winding streets where the mire had been, wide ribbons of black tar
smooth and perfectly edged where they fell away to the deep gutters where the yards sloped down, each street flanked by what
would later be called by those who reported the destruction as
"modest middle-class homes," oaks and sweet gums left in great
abundance to shade the borders of this brave new world. Our
street had been named Cherrywood, and given the broad poetic
license of those who conjure up Shangri-la on a blueprint board,
there was, of course, not a cherry to be found along the new
street. Still, the name evoked visions of pale blossoms held suspended by a pale wind, of the black street littered with white con-
fetti, of bushel baskets of fruit in early summer. More than a
dozen streets now wound within a grid of tarred gravel with
names like Woody, Longwood, Woodview, Woodcrest, Norwood,
and Heatherwood, so that there could be no mistake, even if you

hadn't bothered to look, that we had woods in these parts, the newly poured labyrinth making up what was now known as Oak Forest, because once a neighborhood has a name and an identity, especially one rooted firmly in the dirt, it is easier to fool yourself into believing it is somehow invincible.

Cherrywood Drive was a gently curving spoke off Cooper Road that connected with Terry Road, which bisected Highway 80, the road that scored the town in half, elite to the north of 80, the red-dirt tribe to the south. Beyond Cherrywood and the squared-off, newly leveled yards yawned the gulf of brambles, potholes, and red-clay water that was Caney Creek, the eroded and forbidden place that lured all the new neighborhood kids from their comparatively boring, freshly seeded lawns, tempted them from the flimsy, candy-striped swing sets that had sprung up in backyards before, it seemed, the foundations of the homes had even had time to set.

Linda Flowers, a long-muscled whip of a girl with broad hands and wild dark hair who lived on another stretch of Caney Creek, in a neighborhood older and more established than ours, spent her tomboy summer in the gully, straining guppies from the rusty-smelling opaque water into mayonnaise jars, and when the sun would rest orange on the horizon and the scalding day gave way to a dusk backlit by fireflies, she would gather these up in jars, too, watching the glowing thoraxes of the creatures through the convex portal of the jar, always amazed, as we all were, by the living light trapped between our burning palms.

Linda was a girl we would have envied had she been known to us then and not living in a far neighborhood away on another stretch of Caney Creek, only a few miles but to kids a distant land. She had a horse of her own and a war hero father and an independent tomboy mind that attracted her to rougher things, to what she called the "gumbo mud" of the creek and the leeches that bound themselves to fresh pink skin when we waded in deep where the water was still.

"It was fun to find them all over your legs and pull them off," she would say when she was grown, remembering, and by that admission she would have claimed the crown of Queen of Caney Creek, and we would have followed her the long length of the gully just to witness her bravery.

It was a wide, untamed run one hundred feet across at its most untraversable point, its sheer red-clay banks choked with blackberries, honeysuckle, and poison ivy. We had seen it in spring while wistfully inspecting the final stages of the house in progress and had regarded with caution the roiling channel it had become after a steady downpour of hail and rain, the hail still rolling white in the brown waves. I remember my mother eyeing the torrent as she would a snake, one foot poised ahead of her, ready to run, as we stood on the banks of the ravine, watching as the waves rolled from the churning center of the flood up over the lip of the bank.

The water that splashed us was warmer than the air, a liquid volcano that filled me with a morbid delight as I watched a tree trunk roll past, an old car part, a tangled fist of rusted barbed wire. I stood rapt before the fluid onslaught of junk, watched the eddying, swirling current build momentum as it pushed past, and imagined what a wild ride it would give. But people would die here, too, a girl caught in the spring flood within a year after we moved in, and the new kids and I watched in horrified silence along the crumbling edge of the ravine, our jaws slack, mouths open, as she floated past, the blue arrow of her body clad in a torn print dress, moving fast down the channel, her eyes wide open, her arms held straight out, a young Ophelia borne upon the tide.

Still, from that first moment of witnessing spring's purging, the creek became Oak Forest's version of Mecca for grubby kids loose on a summer day, the artery from which radiated all things of value, and despite my own mother's warning that day and a score of similar ones that echoed through the neighborhood— "Now, once we move in, don't you *ever* set foot in this hellhole"— we would spend a dedicated part of each afternoon in the belly of the monster. But I had remembered the word—*hellhole*—and though it had been an idle description, it had conjured up images of a thing that would not let you loose once it had grabbed hold. And there was, from the very beginning, something both eerie and seductive about the ravine, not just a kid's take on the forbidden but a certain darkness that seemed as old as all of us put together.

We came to know one another quickly, unavoidably, our world defined by the outlying edges of new construction, and beyond that woods and farms and water. And because here in newly carved South Jackson suburbia each family came bearing at least two children, with more on the way, kids with names like Jimmy and Debbie and Danny and Laurie, interchangeable at times but for their specific house numbers and whether or not they could stay out past dark.

There was one lone child, fortunate, we would come to believe, not to have siblings, a peculiar red-haired boy with freckles all over and horn-rimmed glasses thick as the bottom of a Coke bottle, a boy who lived across the street from my house, the son of a portly and strange-talking couple from Pennsylvania, a land that to the Mississippi-born-and-bred was as foreign as Antarctica. It would be this boy, though, whom we teased and taunted and tried to maim on a regular basis, who, one dark and unsettled day not long after I had moved away would issue the agitated, unbelieving cry of warning from his sissy-pink lips and become, for that one moment in time, the bellwether of South Jackson.

Along the crest of Cooper Road where it ran beyond the neighborhood out into the country toward the old consolidated school we would all attend, near where the Crawford Nursing Home sprawled in gothic decay beneath live oaks hung with kudzu, Ridgeland Drive ran back toward Caney Creek. Here W. T. Hannis and his wife, Mae, lived with their four children, Sharon, Darlene, Donny, and Ronny. W.T. worked at the Colonial Bakery and Mae at a local bank. They were Mississippi natives,

W.T. born in Pattison, where his family raised cotton and owned a couple of sawmills, near the town of Port Gibson, where there is a church with a golden hand atop the spire, the index finger of the hand pointing heavenward. Mae, one of seven girls in a family of ten children, was born in Jackson. She had met W.T. in high school, in the small town of Byram, south of Jackson. When Mae, petite and pretty with wide eyes and a lilting singsong voice, had first seen W.T. in the library at school, she had not liked him because his hair was red. It was, though, something she would forget about entirely because even in his youth W.T. had an uncommon kindness that drew people. It was a trait that he and Mae shared and one they would foster by example in their children.

Like most people in Oak Forest, the Hannises were a Christian family, and each Saturday evening after they had moved to tree-lined Ridgeland Drive with the four children, W.T. would sit on the living room floor of the new home and polish four small pairs of shoes and two big pairs for church on Sunday. Sharon Hannis would say later that she believed this was what every father did on Saturday night. When Sunday morning came, he would tie the sashes on Sharon's and Darlene's dresses and Mae would put a roast in the oven to cook for Sunday supper after church. They made homemade ice cream together on the back porch in summer. Mae taught Sunday school. The household was, said Sharon Hannis, "a safe, loving home."

Those of us whose homes were less than safe, whose homes were places where tensions were still untempered by the bright new floors and the air-conditioning and the garbage disposals and all the polished things that should have made us happy, were drawn like pale-winged moths to the light beyond the Hannis home, where we would play softball in the deep backyard and watch in envious disbelief as the four Hannis children laughed openly with their parents. For those of us who did not know this sort of ease at home, the Hannises were fair-haired gods, and we were drawn, too, by the way we were included in the laughter and by Mae's pretty, brown-sugar voice, and by their boy Ronny, the one we would all remember because he was, even as a teenager, a boy of infinite fairness. No matter if you were the sniveling, snot-nosed runt of the pack, no matter if you had funny glasses and red hair, no matter if you had ugly parents from Pennsylvania, the boy would still smile at you in an open way that could never be forgotten, he would still remember your name. His favorite song was "Sherry." He had a girlfriend named Sherry and an old car W.T. had given him, and when the nights were warm Ronny and Sherry would drive the back roads of South Jackson with the windows rolled down, the radio on. He had wanted to play football, but he was not a strapping boy, so he played cornet in the Forest Hill band instead, going to all the games. When he got a job as a bag boy and then as a checker at the new Liberty supermarket, he would buy his own clothes and pay W.T. for insurance on the car. But he wouldn't work on Sundays. Sundays, he told his boss, Webb Jones, were for church. He smoked like all the other boys and wore his shirtsleeves rolled under. Beneath the cash register drawer at Liberty, Ronny kept a bag of suckers for those of us who'd blown our allowances at Polk's grocery on sugar straws and Cokes, and we would wait in his long line for the handout, mud-caked and greedy, not just for the suckers but also because the boy noticed us. Sharon Hannis would say when she was grown that Ronny was the one who got all the "good genes" in the family, that he had been born to enjoy life and to enjoy people, and that the first thing that always comes to her mind when she thinks of her brother is his smile.

I was part of the creek urchin pack of kids who adored the boy, who remembered the easy way he smiled and laughed and teased. We were still scab-pocked kids who were rounded up each summer for vacation Bible school and made to sit in tiny wooden chairs, sullen and recalcitrant, eating, when the teacher wasn't looking, the uncooked alphabet macaroni with which we had been trusted to make Bible verses, drinking our grape juice in horselike gulps, dribbling lemon cookie drool down our chins, and later croaking out the song "The B-I-B-L-E, that's the book for me." We were not refined like Ronny and his buddy Larry Swales. We weren't old enough to wear our hair slicked back, we didn't roll our shirtsleeves up, we didn't smoke, we had bicycles and scooters instead of cars, and we were too chicken to swim the rough trough of Caney Creek in flood season.

Larry Swales, who would later say of his friend Ronny Hannis that "God didn't make 'em any better," was, even to the prepubescent sensibilities of girls my age, a golden boy, handsome and slender with wolflike eyes, oblivious to the damage his smile did as we watched him swim the rapids of Caney Creek, a brown-skinned boy in the brown water. For his unawareness of the power he held over the emotions of young girls, he was escalated all the more in our eyes. Though he was a boy who had the look of the Devil about him, he was the son of parents who did missionary work, and faith was something that kept close to him like a shadow. When the new shopping center was completed, Ronny and Larry would work together at the new Liberty, a parking lot's distance away from the old Polk's grocery, where bottles of Coke and RC Cola still chilled in ice in the deep metal soda bins.

I remember, too, another boy, my own age, in a way that childhood affection gives staying power to the perfectly ordinary. Which is not to say that the boy was ordinary, but only that he might have been, because it was then that I knew him and not twenty years later, so there is no way of reckoning how he would have become defined in the world. Still, I see him clearly now, forty years later, unmarked by time. I remember his crew cut, the way you could guess even then how he would look when he was older. He was a cute boy, but more than that, he had the sort of face that certain children are branded with, one that shows a promise of maturity that may or may not come to pass, freckles across the wide bridge of his nose, his mouth the wide and generous mouth of a bad boy pretending to be good, his brown hair oiled with Vitalis. In time his mother, Sarah Parker, would take a job folding clothes at the new Laundromat at Candlestick. A

mother who worked was exotic in South Jackson, and when I
learned this about the boy's mother, his importance grew for me.
I never knew the details of his life, although I tried to know,
wanted to know, because this was the boy I had my eyes set on,
the boy who in my childhood fantasies walked alongside me in
the close, firefly-strobed dusk, and for this reason I came to care
how his life turned out.

By degrees we began to claim the new territory as our own,
pulling at its wild roots, carrying pieces of them home—leaves,
sticks, birds with broken wings, snake skins, arrowheads—believing that once we owned a part of this place it would never
turn on us, an illusion we held to within the lush summer nights
when you could feel the green even in the dark, the gardens
growing in the moonlight and beneath the stars whose light stuttered dimly beyond the haze of heat that rose wet from the cool-
ing land. In the platinum wash of light the white faces of
gardenias opened, the honeysuckle bloomed, and the lightning
bugs were brighter than the stars. When morning came, the dew
fell from it all like rain.

And there were those among us whom even the green nights
could not heal, the girl who would become my best friend, a dark
honey-haired beauty from Kentucky, a rebel of a girl who wore
torn sneakers to school and seemed to know about sex long before the rest of us. We would never have known, seeing her in
school, what the nights were like in her house on the other side
of Caney Creek, nor could we have guessed that in time her
mother would aim a gun at her father and kill him in self-
defense, and that before she did, the girl would strike him with
her fists and scratch him deep enough to draw blood, so that
when he died, as she would say later, "it was with my marks on
him." It was a thing she would be proud of all her life.

On the outskirts of our new homes set secure within the
trees, along the banks of the ever-changing creek, lived a protector, a firefighter named Karei McDonald, who had been born in
the country, and whose heroes, as he would always say, were

"Mother and Daddy, and older people, down-to-earth people, dirt farmers and cotton farmers and people who make do." McDonald lived with his wife and two children near the new power station that abutted the shopping center, and he was a man who, early on, had no concept of fear. To Karei McDonald fear was an emotion misplaced, because, he believed, at every turn there could be something to fear, and a career could be made of that fear if you let it. So he had never let it get a foothold, he had never really given it a name. When he was not on duty at the fire department, waiting for the bell, he watched the new neighborhood beyond his kitchen window, the slow, sparse traffic along Cooper Road, the children on their bicycles, the turning sky. He watched out for the fearful and for what might give them cause.

God lived here, too, in the old churches that had been here before we came, in the new ones whose tall, modern spires caught the sun and beamed it back into the warm air in small, fractured rainbows, and beneath the heavy canvas revival tents that ballooned in the wind in empty fields where the revivalists set up camp overnight. By noon, a crowd of men in work shirts and women in shirtwaist dresses would arrive, bearing pies and coffee and fried chicken. And the preachers would preach, beneath the hot balloon, of a God who was both merciful and cruel, but cruel only to infidels. And then the songs would rise up, the hymns that were haunting to a child, of salvation at the hour of death, of salvation in the hour of need.

There was a school waiting for us, too, long before this new place came to be. In the mornings we would wait along the curb at designated stops on the new streets, a jumble of kids of all ages dressed in the still dumpy style of the early '60s; the girls in collared print dresses with stiff nylon half slips beneath their skirts, glasses that swooped to points, bows stuck in our teased hair; the boys in jeans with the cuffs rolled up, button-down short-sleeved shirts and crew-cut hair. We would watch, our schoolbooks held tight against our chests, our feet scuffing the pavement, as the bright yellow bus rounded the corner and moved along the black street, a contrast of colors that seemed ominous, like a yield sign or the tropical-looking bees the size of small birds that sat heavy on the gardenia blossoms. We rode the bus to school, first-graders and twelfth-graders alike, for this was an old country school in the truest meaning, along the wide, looping curves of Cooper Road, through pastureland and woods and the scabs of new construction, past Wayne Bowlen's house, a '60s churchlike sweep of wood and glass with a steepled roof and wide front lawn that sloped to the rutted road. It was a house that spoke of our new refinement and of all things modern and good, and we studied it each morning and each afternoon, never tiring of it because it let us know that where we lived was not exactly country anymore. Wayne was the seventh-grade heartthrob, a boy my own age, and his reputation carried him at least through middle school. Even as a preteen he wore his hair slicked back, his shirtsleeves rolled.

Forest Hill School rises up monolithic in memory, far nobler in my recollection than perhaps it ever was in its decades as a stronghold on those few acres of country land. They tore the old buildings down a few years ago and built a new school with bright new brick and inlaid mortared seams, a cold building for all its architectural aspirations and a place immediately recognizable as a school. The old school was old in the way of the classic, three stories of dark brick rising up from the beaten-down red clay that held fast to clumps of grass and turned, in spring, to a white lake of wild onions. On the south side of the school a huge amphitheater-like depression gave way to another field of red clay where basketball courts were designated not by official markings but simply by a backboard and a hoop, a court hard-packed by hundreds of feet at recess when we could push and shove for our turn at the net, a dozen basketballs dribbling at once and sailing aimlessly through the dusty air. And beyond this huge and seedy and ultimately beckoning plane of dirt lay a greening football field where the Forest Hill Rebels met rival teams, and where we would, on the still close autumn nights, screech deliriously as our pint-sized players pulled themselves up wearily from the turf, their uniforms stained bright green.

Donna Durr was the blond angel of Forest Hill School, the seventh-grade science teacher who moved like a goddess through the long dingy halls because boys on the cusp of puberty paid attention to blond beauties, behaved well for them, studied hard. The girls did, too. We wanted to be like Donna Durr with her pale, flawless skin and full lips. She was young enough to be an older sister, smart enough to make us think that education was not a bad idea. She taught us Earth science, and it was a natural bridge from our work in the classroom to the outdoors that fell away from the school and our neat little homes in such abundance that, given a field trip in which to study it, we barely knew where to begin. We gathered moldy leaves for Donna Durr, rocks and dirt samples and poison ivy and locust shells, and carried this elemental detritus into the classroom, beaming, proud to please her because she inspired shameless display. We named the leaves, studied intensely the various shapes that fell from the hardwoods that ringed our homes—oblongate, spatulate, ovate— pressed the leaves between waxed paper, ground our brothers' and sisters' Crayolas on top and took a steam iron to the mélange, blurring the leaves in a molten display of autumn color rare in Mississippi.

Mrs. Durr taught us ingenuity, patience, and on occasion, morals. We made miniature replicas of dinosaurs traversing volcanic fields and Styrofoam models of molecules, incubated chicken eggs still warm from the nest, turned our work in always on time, and sought her blond benediction. She once sent me from class into the dark hallway as punishment. Even if you were sick and flushed with a deadly fever, spending time beyond the spell she cast was torment. I had brought a copy of Somerset Maugham's *Of Human Bondage* to class, and when she spied it on my desk, so out of place among the frayed textbooks, the rocks and leaves, so begging to be noticed in its shiny plastic library book sleeve, she snatched it up and regarded the cover with a look of disappointment that is still palpable today. Then she turned to me, concerned but decisive, stated flatly, "You are too young to be reading this," and locked the book in her desk, which meant, by her qualified proclamation, that there might be a time when I would not be too young. I figured that time would no doubt come when I reached her lovely, golden age of twenty-four. I loved Mrs. Durr. We all did. She does not remember me.

But I remember her, a woman as close to the real-life version of Glenda, the Good Witch of the North, as Forest Hill could produce. None of us would have been surprised if one day she had touched a magic wand to charcoal, turning it to diamonds. Her real-life habits—shopping at the new Candlestick Park, raising a family while teaching school, fixing supper for her husband— might have been as ordinary as those of the rest of us, but the day would come when our suspicions of her otherworldliness would be justified. The day would come when we would learn that Mrs. Donna Durr could fly.

So we, clean from the woods of Oak Forest, Forest Hill Rebels, the infantile and the nearly mature, rode each day except in summer to the old school that was really just an extension of the neighborhood. And here we saw the same faces we saw after school, at first in the blossoming yards, the gully of Caney Creek, the Hannises' backyard, and then at the new place of congregation, the place we would come to call, with delighted familiarity and irrepressible naïveté, just "Candlestick."

CHAPTER FIVE

*"I was just sorrowful for all those people that got hurt and killed
and everything. I was just real sorrowful for that, and I guessed
the Lord just didn't want this place here anymore."*

—Homer Lee Howie, owner, Candlestick Park

TODAY HOMER LEE HOWIE'S DREAM CENTER would barely
qualify as a strip mall, a fact he admits when he recalls the then-
unimaginable vastness of a 12,000-square-foot supermarket and
the train of small shops beside it, all of it built on spongy land
that had once been half swamp, half pasture.

Howie liked the image that the name "Candlestick Park"
brought up and admits to some magical thinking when he had to
name the new shopping center. Howie, a Jackson native and an
old man now, remembers how "we were working on it, and it was
during the World Series, had the game on the radio, and they
were playing at Candlestick Park, and I just thought how that
would be a wonderful name, what a wonderful name, and then to
be able to put a big ol' sign down there with candles on it. Caney
Creek spilled out through there then and just sort of went over
the whole field, so we dug a ditch around the back end of it and
put all the water in there and filled it in a little bit, and, uh, you
know, just put the shopping center right in there." Magic.

Swamp mud had been turned to glitter. It seemed that one

night we had gone to bed and the next morning there had risen
Candlestick Park in all its glory with Howie's inspired sign of
wax-yellow candles with red flames and beyond the sign, spread
pristine upon the dimple-free concrete, a thing of newness and
hope and unadulterated fun. There was the new Liberty supermarket with its yards of blazing plate glass, strung corner to corner with balloons and multicolor vinyl flags, with free sacks of
flour and cartons of eggs given away for the grand opening inside
the clean sweep of wall-to-wall linoleum and refrigerated meat
cases, anything you could possibly want stacked in neat rows on
the long shelves, the cash register checkout a bay of orderliness
where Ronny Hannis and Larry Swales now worked, wearing
clean white aprons that hung from their necks and tied in back.
There was the new coin Laundromat with shiny galvanized steel
washers with portals through which you could watch the soapy
water turning, a place of clean smells and the steam-iron scent of
dryers tumbling, where Sarah Parker now worked washing and
folding clothes for women who wanted luxury while they
shopped for baked goods.

Next to the Laundromat was a beauty shop where girls and
their mothers would sit with damp hair in jumbo rollers beneath
space-age hairdryers while they read worn copies of *Photoplay* and
listened to the warm wind from the dryers. There was a drugstore with an elderly pharmacist named Theodore Gaetz from
Fitchburg, Massachusetts, who measured out medicinal saffron
for the housewives to make saffron rice, a barbershop where the
young barber Bobby Grant worked, the first decoration in the
small shop a Miller Beer clock with a scene of moving water.
There was a small hobby shop where young boys took their
model cars and raced them on an indoor track, and a five-and-
dime, and at the very end, near the gas station that sat a few
yards back from Cooper Road, was the office of Dr. McMillan.

Across the wide parking lot, now filled with cars and kids and
parents and delivery trucks that came regularly to keep every
shelf stocked, was the beacon that drew us all in slavering

hordes, a small chalet-type building off the main complex called Dog 'n' Suds, a hot dog and root beer joint that put out the smell of Fred Hudgins's soon-to-be-locally-famous "char-burgers," which settled so heavy in the neighborhood that the evening smells of supper riding on the humid air could never compete.

We beheld Oz with instant loyalty from the polished windows of our new houses, looking out across Cooper Road to the trio of candles that glowed yellow and red deep into the night, and we pledged allegiance silently, promising never to forget.

Candlestick Park was now the axis of the neighborhood, where dreams of successful businesses, brought from the dirt-farming heritage of the country, would be tentatively made and then ruined beyond recognition so you could not tell what the dream had ever been or if it had been a dream at all. Fred Hudgins and his wife, Mary, knew clearly the dimensions of their dream. Hudgins, in his thirties at the time—diminutive, ambitious, philosophical within his own perception of how the world worked, and a World War II veteran—had long wished for his own small operation, a business that would be the seed of bigger things. It was he who had built the burger and hot dog stand called Dog 'n' Suds, a piece of impractical architecture straight out of the future-gazing fifties, a peaked roof jutting skyward over the eaves of the tiny building. On the sign outside the Dog 'n' Suds was a picture of a Goofy-like dog, red tongue hanging wet from his mouth as he clutched a bright red hot dog and, in the other paw, a mug of foaming root beer. We would sometimes stand in single file outside the restaurant simply to gaze at the sign.

Fred Hudgins was no fool, and within the pared-down scale of South Jackson he was something of a visionary. He knew what kids wanted. We craved a place to hang out where we could satisfy our need for meat and fat and starch and sugar, listen to the tinny jukebox, and gawk at one another. We hoarded our allowance, refusing to spend it at Polk's grocery anymore. What were a sugar straw and a Coke when we could have real hamburgers from Hudgins's well-oiled grill, french fries with watery ketchup, and root beer served in icy mugs heavy enough to break your foot?

This was the way, we figured, kids who lived in bigger cities in finer neighborhoods spent their afternoons, within the Formica-and-chrome heaven of bebop joints, with the shiny jukebox blaring and the red leatherette stools spinning, this world within filled to bursting by us who wore the bloom of what would later be acne scars, and by Elvis and Bobby Darin and Dion singing just for us. At Dog 'n' Suds we were suddenly somebody, on awkward display to classmates we might have a crush on, the girls with their hair teased up high or pulled back in long ponytails, the boys' hair slicked back smooth with Vitalis, a glowing, greased, and shining crowd of self-conscious kids always posing for a snapshot. We lived to be noticed. We lived for the afternoons, when we would drop from the yellow school bus and descend like the swarm we were on Candlestick, drawing a bead on Dog 'n' Suds after we had cruised each shop and inspected each possible crack in the new sidewalk outside the stores.

Yet beyond our self-absorbed crowd that sucked down root beer as if it were the water of life, just beyond the door where the kitchen steamed and spat, there was another world entirely, and it belonged to a black woman. Ms. Juland Jones, Hudgins's cook, sometimes traded shifts with her twin sister, Meland, but most often it was Juland who worked the kitchen. Meland was the smaller of the two. They had been born in Prentiss, Mississippi, in a family of sixteen children. Meland wrote songs about her family, songs about herself and Juland. Juland was tall, athletic, opinionated.

"Somebody say something mean to her," Meland would say, "she have no use for that person. She would just discard them." Juland was twenty-seven. Her husband, Eddie, worked at a fertilizer factory downtown, and they lived with their four children, not in bright new Oak Forest, but away on the black side of Jack-

son, on a street named Booker T. Washington, and you knew
what kind of street Booker T. Washington was just by the name.
You knew the houses were small and narrow and tilting, and that
each had a low front porch because it was always too hot to stay
indoors. There was no central air on Booker T. Washington, and
on the porches entire families gathered on the stoops, colors
bright against their dark skin, and you could see the dust from
the road lying up like snow in the corners of the porches. The
yards were mostly dirt, no Saint Augustine grass, no fescue,
some swept clean and packed down hard, some littered with old
car parts, broken washing machines, and crates and boxes the
children used for forts. There were no candy-striped swing sets
here. And there were always lots of children, their skin darker
still from the Mississippi sun, their skin blue-black against the
backdrop of the dingy houses and the brittle yards, running
loose, absorbed not in the strict rules of their poverty but in the
common games of children.

In Oak Forest we did not know Juland Jones's world, and
not until the deaths of Goodman, Schwerner, and Chaney,
names we would remember because they were always spoken in
this same order and because of why they died, for no good reason, and not until Medgar Evers was shot in the back outside
his Jackson home one hundred years after Vicksburg fell, and
not until the rolling boil of Freedom Summer were we driven to
attention. Some of us understood the meaning of atrocity because of these things, and some did not. Yet no matter what we
might have understood, Juland still returned to that dark, delin-
eated part of town each evening, listening to the songs Meland
would sing about them, eating their leftover lunch from a paper
plate placed between them on the car seat, a lunch their mother
had made so they could eat, as Meland said, "Good food, and
not no char-burger."

Ronny Hannis would not order a hamburger at Dog 'n' Suds
unless Juland Jones was there to fix it. On his way to work at the
Liberty store, he would stop in to play the jukebox or to have a

Coke with his girlfriend, Sherry. We, who knew nothing yet of romance but for the pale, tentative reflection of it we saw here at Dog 'n' Suds and read in the grimy *Photoplays*, watched the always smiling Ronny with his handsome cleft chin and steady eyes holding hands under the table with the gentle-looking, dark-haired Sherry, she with the boy's heavy class ring on her finger, filled with wax to make it fit, he with his shirtsleeves rolled under instead of up, looking vaguely like James Dean. We envied them, imagined them marrying as soon as they graduated, the way Larry Swales and his high school sweetheart would, and toward that end we gave them our collective naive blessing and played the Dixie Cups' "Chapel of Love" on the jukebox in celebration.

And while we sat up front, spinning on the stools until we grew dizzy, Juland Jones danced in the back in the kitchen with Fred Hudgins's daughter Gloria, and we would slip from our perches when we heard them laughing and peer curiously through the door's small porthole, greasy fried food clutched in our fists, and watch the two girls twirling dangerously close to the grill where the heat rose up in waves, and wish that we were old enough to work in the kitchen at Dog 'n' Suds and dance in back with a black girl.

The new Liberty supermarket gave out Green Stamps with each purchase, and a small staple-bound catalog that displayed pictures of exactly what those stamps could get you. To those of us still too young to work, who now haunted Candlestick, Green Stamps were free money, and amid what appeared in the catalog to be a lot of useless junk—dishes, pots and pans, flatware— there was a cheery picture of an army green pup tent, complete with stakes and poles and a loop hung from the center of the tent for a flashlight. Suddenly we collected Green Stamps, pawed through our mothers' purses for the sticky decals, begged the always obliging Ronny Hannis for one or two extra when we bought a Fudgsicle at Liberty instead of Polk's, crawled beneath the checkout counter and searched for some stray patch of green that might have fluttered from a housewife's open palm, beat other kids into submission for their horde of stamps, and when the edge of summer came nearly every backyard in Oak Forest bore the crouching specter of a dull green tent illuminated dimly from within, and from each canvas portal there was hung a crayon-etched sign with the words KEEP OUT! Within the broad, continuous wooded backyards there now thrived an urchin tent city. At night we would crawl into the tents still pulsing with heat, where mosquitoes lined the sloping cloth walls, and watch through the tent flaps as heat lightning stuttered above the thick canopy of oak and maple leaves, and then feel beneath us, as we fell to sleep, the thunder of an approaching storm.

We in our squatters' camp loved this world that was green at every turn and rode our bikes together fearlessly at dusk behind the fog machine, a truck with a rotating cement mixer belly that sprayed, in a sulfurous and deadening swath, mosquito poison, and the nearer to the source of the spray we rode, racing one another, breathing in the toxic fumes, the more daring we believed ourselves to be and the more we believed that ours were untouchable lives. Through the streets waist deep in water we walked in spring, diving beneath the muddy tide, feeling the tarred bottom with blind fingers, our breath held in tight. From the houses our mothers would scream out into the streets to come inside, that there were snakes in that dirty water, but we heeded no voice but the alluring newness of freedom that pulled us on to the ravine where the flood raged mighty, and beyond the ravine to the new houses that were being built, their concrete foundations and two-by-four shells open-air playgrounds where we would carve our names into the new wood still sweet with sap.

Sometimes we would wonder about the new families who had yet to move here, how many children they had, what they looked like, what their names would be, but never once about how long they would live or how they would die.

CHAPTER SIX

"Yellow Hell. That's the only way I know how to describe it, as yellow Hell. I have never since seen that particular color yellow except the day my daddy died."

—Linda Flowers

YOU ASK, AND THEY WILL TELL YOU they never thought it would happen, the good people of Oak Forest who have remained since that day in March 1966. Who ever does? Who calls fate to themselves on a dare? Who but a fool tempts it, in the old way of saying, by putting their mouths on it? Who conjures up thoughts grim enough to keep the hopeful sleepless? And who but those in the habit of dark prophecy would point a finger to the future of disaster, at the blown-out, heaving patch of dirt and concrete South Jackson would become?

I am no prophet, but a broad fault line of doom bisects my ability to look reasonably to the future. I was the doom-saying child of the cow pasture suburb, the one who said one day it will get us, someday when we're digging trenches around our tent city, stalking the creek bottom for arrowheads, eating ham sandwiches with mustard in the shade of oak trees and poking at our scabs, that will be the day it comes, when our mothers are making grocery lists, checking the clock so they make it to the Liberty by five, having their hair done at the beauty shop, while our fa-

thers are at their desks or mowing the yard or sneaking over to
Rankin County to the bootleg shack, that day when all things ordinary and predictable occupy us, that will be the day when the
extraordinary happens. And before that day we will not have read
a passage in Revelations to which we could nod and say, "Yes,
here we are, this is us, and here is our day of reckoning. This is
the day God turns on us." And there would be no prophet on our
block, nor in the whole of Jackson. There would not even be a
tornado siren. There would be nothing but the dead-on yellow
calm before the storm.

I knew, but did not know when. It is a sin of omission that
haunts me still. Yet it seemed more than innate negativity, more
than just a lucky guess that what finally happened was what I
feared would happen all along. A woman named Gussie Mae, the
ample, sagelike maid my mother had hired, who lived in that broken section of town where years before the tornado had come
just after midnight, had her theories about me. Season after season she would watch me with her great owl eyes as I stared
through the big picture window my stepfather was so proud of,
out of its southwest-facing frame, my eyes trained on the often
darkening horizon. She called me "weather bird" for this neurotic
habit of sky watching, in triumph, as if she had finally managed
to pin down my particular psychosis.

She would call to me in a singsong, almost playful voice, "Oh,
weh-thah bird, hey, girl, what you see? Them skies growin' dark?
Whachu see?"

"Tornado," I would say defensively, wishing that studying me
wasn't her fondest pastime.

She would roll her eyes then, shake her head so that her
steam-pressed curls fell loose. "Ain't no tornado," she'd say, dis-
believing. "Lemme look." And then she would pull her round,
full-to-bursting body from the dinette chair and roll toward the
window, staring past my outstretched finger.

"There," I'd say with conviction. "Right there."

"Fool," came her response, always. "Thas jus' a ol' scraggly tail on that cloud. Ain't no tornado. You got tornadoes in yo' head."

There it was, Gussie Mae's theory, tornadoes in my head. She was right. But they were in my blood, too.

My grandmother, the granddaughter of a Cherokee chief, read the sky as if it were an open palm, and her gift for knowing when the sky would fall left its mark on me early. For most children weather was of little consequence, the bearer of rainy, housebound days, the giver of golden summer skin. For me, a nervous witness to the violence of Mississippi skies and a student of my grandmother's atmospheric prescience, it was always an edgy shop of horrors, a contrary, moody, deadly gamble. I never came to trust a benign-looking sky, knowing what could rattle its cage just out of sight, waiting for a drop in the barometric pressure, a rise in the dew point, a prayer from a farmer.

Her name was Muriel, but everyone called her Big Mama out of respect and a fair amount of fear. She, wild-haired, dentured, afflicted with phlebitis, her legs wrapped tightly in flesh-colored rubber stockings, was openly ecstatic to have me as her prisoner for the one week I visited her each summer on her small farm outside Memphis. There she would shroud perfectly sunny afternoons in tales of weather doom. In the midst of her stories she would sip coffee from a busted saucer, eat sugar on her tomatoes, dip snuff from a rusted Red Man tin, spit obsessively at no particular receptacle, and often remove her dentures just to scare me. Pressed against her right calf she wore an extra bandage beneath the rubber stocking. A black widow spider had bitten her once as she had walked through the tall grass of her land, and ever after there was a rotted place that would not heal. Her little white house with green plastic curtains sat on thirty acres in a belt of Delta where the summers steamed and the storms that cooled them were violent, and I often wondered if she lived there simply because it must have resembled, in the crashing, rolling peak of an electrical storm, the very mouth of Hell. It is what I have forever associated with Big Mama—hellish things—storms, black widow spiders, toothlessness. Her caution of what might befall me, that possibly, even eventually the sky would pull me into its turning vacuum, paired with her missing dentures and venom-rotted leg, branded Big Mama in my mind as a witch of uncommon power. I came to see her as a mental sorceress whose cold, bloodless heart made her the exact kind of wicked it takes to experiment with the minds of children. In time I believed that everyone should have a grandmother named Big Mama as a penance of sorts, because by the very nature of the name you knew that she would deal you wrong. So I blame it on the old lady, what I said I knew would happen.

What Big Mama knew best was a tornado sky. It was her religion, the holiest of the holy, and long before I ever heard one spiraling from the belly of midnight, I knew it from her description alone. The sound, she said, would be familiar. Light turned strange before a tornado hit, she told me, a sick, pale green the color of spring grass shoots or yellow as a lemon skin, and as this odd cast opened along the ridge of the horizon dogs would grow quiet, their tails tucked low, and search for a place to hide. It was a light, she told me, like no other, unmatchable in its eeriness, reproduced exactly in no other medium. In fields flooded with sulfurous yellow, cattle would lie, heads bowed to the ground, massive bodies hulked together. Birds roosted in dark clots low in the trees, and sometimes hail would come, fists of ice that lay the field grass flat. Within the growing vacuum of the now-still air, the strange light would grow even stranger. If you were lucky, the old witch told me, you would see it before it hit. Within the black anvil of the wall cloud the spinning would begin, slowly at first, with wisps of clouds caught in the rushing updraft, and then would come the dimension of the thing itself, and darkness as it began to pull the immediate world from its pinnings: barns and houses, cows, birds, tractors, telephone poles, sod, sand, people, and it would look, from the untroubled distance, like a flock of birds banking on a current.

"But on toward evening," Big Mama had said, "when you

can't see the sky, you listen for it." As the deaf could not do, I thought years later. "Just listen. You'll know it when you hear it."

I heard it once as my mother pulled me from the deep breath of sleep one wild spring night in Jackson, forcing me to lie curled within the bright walls of the bathtub as she lay her body over mine. There had been lightning when we had gone to bed, and I had watched from my bedroom window, studying the black gauze of the Mississippi night, the moonless sky above that shuddered with light, illuminating for an instant the high and boundless walls of cumulus clouds, threatening even as we planned to sleep. To my question of why I had been forced, barely conscious, into the bathtub, my mother had answered "tornado," the terseness with which she spoke enough to frighten me, but had I waited just that fraction of a moment to ask before I heard it hammering aloft, rising above our house in an act of grace before touching down in a place less fortunate, I would never have needed to ask again. Beyond the creaking sound of shingles pulling free and roof tiles spinning into the air was a rhythm unmistakable in its meter, amplified a thousand times beyond the familiar. As I lay with my ear against the cold enamel of the bathtub I heard it as clearly as the pulsing muscle in my own chest. It sounded like a heartbeat.

CHAPTER SEVEN

"South Jackson is like a good ol' quilt, and for the people there,
their quilt is where they've been, who they know, who's your
daddy, who's your mama, where'd you go to school . . . and it's a
lifetime of good ol' quilts."

—Linda Flowers

WE MOVED AWAY IN THE WINTER of 1966, out of the house
with the big picture window, beyond the beaten red clay and the
long, shadowy yards of South Jackson, far away from the steep
banks of Caney Creek and the dark floods that would come in
spring. On the face of it, it was a thing common enough, this move
from Jackson to Nashville, a nothing sort of thing to those whose
world was bigger than Mississippi, defined by a greater consciousness, by expectations of more than any of us had beyond the Bible
Belt that held in close the green dimensions of Oak Forest.

I had thought it would be the place where we would stay. I
had thought it would be home because it felt like home, it
smelled like home. I had thought that what had begun to form
me there would be an abiding thing that I would wake to each
day, a sense of myself measured by the circumference of this
community, by an allegiance with kids who knew the dirt the way
they knew the spelling of their own names, by an allegiance to
the slow drumbeat of the sky that grew louder and more reso-
nant as the days passed on.

I did not want to leave, ever. And I would remain loyal to this place formed from the mire and the dust and the clay the color of a sunset. "It's the dirt, girl," Linda Flowers would say to me years later. And so it was. The same dirt that bore the bootprints of Confederate soldiers, the same river of dirt that gave way to a sea of cotton, the same dirt studded deep with arrowheads, the same dirt I carried in a small box when we pulled out of the driveway, traitors all, the same dirt I would smell at night, my face held close inside the box, as I lay awake in the new bed in Nashville, by the new window that looked out on stars that were not the same, the same dirt I held tight in my fist so it molded to the shape of my palm, and in the morning when I woke the sheets would smell like rust and water and heat, like Jackson.

I left, but I carried it all with me, for years never understanding that I could return and for years feeling the anvil weight of guilt for having gone away mere days before the wind came in.

I thought of them often, the kids in the neighborhood and the heroes of Forest Hill, Ronny Hannis and Larry Swales, who were, in my eyes, better than children, better than adults, because they lived in the realm of the untouched, not yet defined by the ordinary world, gilded in their last glory days of school before time would claim them, in an era of black leather jackets and blue jeans and slicked-back hair and church on Sundays. There was always church on Sundays.

I left behind, too, the girl who had become my best friend, the girl whose mother killed her father and who would, on a March third six years later, send a small gold ring in the mail to me in Seattle, a gift for my newborn daughter, her birthday the anniversary of a day no one in Jackson would ever forget.

I could not have told them the hour or the day, nor even the season when it would come. Knowing this now, despite faint claims to prescience, I tell myself there was nothing to be done, no voodoo spell to be had that would push back God, no quieting hex that could change the wind to water and instead lay the doomed place over in a thin veil of liquid, something harmless, something that could be undone.

I have dreamed of it all these years, before and after, and each time I escape into the dawning winter day as I did the day we drove along the rutted arrow of Highway 49 to Nashville. Who could have said that I, harnessed by the will of dissolute parents, would be the lucky one who would no longer stare into the southwest sky from that house on the corner ringed in woods, fearing what would come but needing to be there for the mark it would put on me, the mark of the blood brotherhood, the mark that said forever, you belong to this hour in time and to Mississippi because of it. And like a man who longs for battle and never sees a war, I felt as if I were a coward for leaving. But I walked away. Intact.

CHAPTER EIGHT

"Oh, it was so dark, so eerie, so very, very dark."

—Mary Hudgins

THERE IS AN EXALTED ANONYMITY that surrounds the man who first reported the Candlestick Tornado to WJTV in Jackson. He is the Paul Revere of that dark afternoon, the man who sounded the warning to those who sat far away, safe and unaware. No one remembers his name, not even veteran newscaster Bert Case, who took the call that Thursday afternoon in 1966. Case is a man Jackson has been watching and listening to for more than thirty years. He has the voice, the educated good-ol'-boy baritone, deep and measured, easygoing and assured, an airline pilot's voice. It is a voice that calms you just to hear it. It is a voice of authority. Of the man who called him at the station that Thursday afternoon, Case said, over thirty years later, "I've laid up nights thinking about who that guy was who called me. I think it was maybe Easley. Like I said. I laid up nights. What *was* that guy's name? It haunts me. Was it Easley? He flat-out yelled, 'It's comin.' It's comin' right across Candlestick Park and right up Cooper Road right now. You need to get somebody down here— *Quick!*'"

And then the phone fell—or was torn—from the caller's hand and dangled at the end of its cord in a phone booth somewhere off Cooper Road. What Case heard through the receiver he will not forget, a pummeling, hammering whine that intensified as he listened, and for an instant he was held in his place by the sheer volume of it. There came then the sound of things being wrenched free, and it was only then that Case understood the magnitude of what he was hearing. He hung up the phone and put a temporary silence to the storm that had begun to kill on the other side of town. A news crew was sent out, but it would be nearly twenty-four hours before Bert Case himself would make his way to Candlestick. As news was fed back to him, Case went on the air in an emergency broadcast. As it would turn out, WJTV was the only game in town that day. Out in rural Hinds County, near the small town of Raymond, where the funnel had formed, WJTV's competitor, WLBT, lost its 1,600-foot tower when the winds tore it free and laid the massive structure out across a cow pasture, its apex pointed like a finger toward the northeast, toward Candlestick.

The tornado hit at 4:33 P.M. The time is not a matter of dispute. Young Peter Boulette, watching from his backyard in Oak Forest, heard the wind coming, closed his eyes for an instant, and then tried to open them again but could not. His mother pulled him inside, where he ran to call his friend Lloyd. He looked at the clock, and at that moment the power went out. 4:33 P.M. The small homes of Oak Forest fell into darkness, and clocks that had been marking time until this hour suddenly stopped, leaving no doubt in the minds of those who glanced up as to the hour and the minute when Hell arrived.

CHAPTER NINE

"It was like the anteroom to Hell."

—Linda Flowers

MEMORY IS THE HUMAN RELIGION, the church of the subjective, the vault and burial ground of the past upon which we perform the mutable ritual of scrutiny. Perspective, a thing gained not by longing but by the simple, clear mark of time, grows by degrees until, if we are lucky, it becomes the one thing central to memory, perception. And it is, then, memory and perception that hold the past as a pure distillate, a thing not of compromise and inevitable death, but of what has truly formed us. It is, on the corporeal plane, God.

What happened that afternoon in 1966 is a matter of a hundred memories, and there is no one memory the same but for how the tragedy has marked the people of South Jackson with a brand so deep and distinctive that perhaps sometimes they can spot one another in a crowd, know one another by a look, a turn of the head toward the window when the sky grows dark. To some it is the color of the sky that will never be forgotten, a cast of yellow so unnatural that it had to be a warning. For others it is the sound, a roaring so immense that it was, as Fred Hudgins's wife, Mary, put it, "as if the world had rolled over," the timbre and crash of a living thing gone mad, but unto itself a unique madness, indefinable.

There are those, to a person, who remember what they were wearing because it was their clothes that gave way first: ripped from them, lifted off, stained with their own blood or someone else's, and it is the impermanence of clothes that they recall, how silly almost, in the face of what happened, to remember this at all, but remember they do, down to the details of whether or not the clothes were freshly laundered, new or old, a color that looked good, a favorite jacket, a dress worn on a date the Friday before. And then there is the realization made indelible that nothing more than a thin sheath of cotton became the demarcation line between flesh and sky, and the horror of this registers on their faces as they talk, as they remember throwing the clothes away, never wanting to see them again, never wanting to be reminded that death had stained them.

And they remember the time. No one gets it wrong. If the time had been recorded to the second, they would have remembered that, too. They will not forget because in the collective memory of spring afternoons certain things happen at 4:33, and they are often ordinary things, often pleasant, and so, ever after, this time of day can never be fully trusted again, nor can the month of March, nor the third of March, nor any Thursday in tornado season.

They remember, too, that it was the kind of early-spring Mississippi afternoon that you come to know when you live there. The air was waterlogged, heavy and wet like cotton in the fields after rain, and the smell of the clay was strong in the air, rusty and old and undeniably organic. It was a smell that, if you have been accustomed to it, can take you places in memory fast, back to other years, other spring afternoons, because it has a certain scent at different times of day and in different seasons. In the early heat of morning, as the dew rises from it, the smell is renewed and comforting. At night, as the land cools and the clay

holds on to heat deep down, it gives off an aroma rich as pork frying. In winter it is clean with frost tightening the edges of it, and
in autumn the deep, dark color of summer begins to fade and
give itself over to the leaves. But in spring it owns the air.

THE YELLOW SCHOOL BUS, the same color as the sky, dropped
off the kids from Forest Hill School, one by one, taking the winding road flanked by woods and gullies thick with honeysuckle,
past the new Oak Forest Elementary School, where the field had
been burned off and hundreds of rabbits had fled across the open,
burning land. It continued past churches and farms and on into
the open maze of tarred streets, past Caney Creek, onto Wood-
lawn, Ridgeland, and Cherrywood, where the red-haired boy got
off, right across the street from where we had moved the month
before. In half an hour he would be across Cooper Road at Candlestick.

It was still, the kind of still that comes when the air holds its
breath and the pressure begins to build. The barnyard sounds
from nearby farms were quieting. No dogs roamed the streets.
The birds were silent, and the cicadas gave off a low whisper of
wings against the leaves as they settled in. There was no wind
now, and Karei McDonald noticed this when he got home from
work at the fire station and looked out his kitchen window onto
the trees that lined Cooper Road.

"I looked to see was they one leaf movin' anywhere," he
would say, and there was not. In the pregnant heat, the close-
together trees that lined each street grew heavy, the dew point
rose, and it became hard to take a full breath.

Some people noticed that the sky had started to go yellow in
a slow, sulfurous burn that arced from the southwest horizon and
was slowly taking over the sky. But they did not know that at that
moment, when the cast of the sky turned hellish, the tornado, in
a cloud blacker than any they had ever seen, was beginning to
form, its currents rising violently and falling violently, the air

within colliding, mating, beginning to turn. Had they known, had they been able to put a finger to the embryonic pulse, they would have knelt and said their prayers in a rush of sins to be forgiven, pleaded, all of them, to retract the event that was at hand.

It is difficult to say at which point, exactly, it took its first unbroken breath and formed a towering, counterclockwise spiral. The tornado came from out near the small town of Raymond, not far from Forest Hill School, where an hour before the yellow bus had rolled out of the parking lot and followed the blueprint of the path laid out fifty years before, trailing its miniature twin, and as it headed on the northeast diagonal toward Candlestick, it became the most feared of all tornadoes, an F-5 that gathered strength.

Within the center of the storm, deep in where human eyes rarely gaze, there can be a hundred tiny vortices, twisting within the belly of the mother column, spinning in a crazy pinball run along its length, feeding on the tight, pregnant surface of the inner wall. Other, smaller tornadoes form from the same huge, anvil-based cloud that spawns the parent tornado, and it becomes a matter of aerodynamic survival: the weaker, smaller columns of wind must seek the rotating balance and mass of the bigger tornado, and when they do, disappearing into the shaft of wind in a moment of eerie sorcery, the original funnel, having swallowed up its own, grows before the eyes of those who wait, wordless, on the ground.

It leveled the inanimate first, the 1,600-foot television tower out near Raymond. It was now, in shape and form and darkness, the Wizard of Oz tornado reborn, with a smaller spiral dancing at its flank as it lifted up and then slammed back down into the woods off Siwell Road, and when it came out at Cooper Road, on the high end nearest Forest Hill, the skies over South Jackson were black and boiling.

The clean, cathedral-like house where Wayne Bowlen lived, the one we stared at each day in envy as the bus rolled past, was pulled apart. Next door, in the house of a family named Bradshaw, the mother broke the windows with a chair and pulled her children under a table and sang to them. Her son Jimmy said to her, above the grinding noise that made the children cry, "Mama, God will take care of us, won't he?" Next door they heard a neighbor scream. Her child had been thrown into a field of broom sage, its leg broken. Across the street a house was lifted from its foundation. A teacher at the new Oak Forest Elementary School, a pastor named Lewis Mosley, was killed in his car as he drove into the tornado's path, his body thrown into a low ditch. A church was destroyed; the pastor's wife and children in the parsonage were spared.

There was no way to place the sound within the realm of common sounds. A thousand freight trains bearing down. Night came fast and hard along Cooper Road, and the green fields glowed neon in the strange yellow light.

From his kitchen window Karei McDonald still watched, waiting for a leaf to move.

The red-headed boy, the soft-skinned, freckled child from Pennsylvania, saw it first as it lifted above the green, enclosed world of Crawford Nursing Home, and his voice, ordinarily meek and defensive, always bordering on a whine, became, for the first time since anyone could remember, the one they listened to. The boy had sat in front of me in class for two years at Forest Hill, and I remember the freckles on his head through his close crew cut, and how the stiff collar of his checked shirt pushed up against the bristles, and when he turned to look at me, there would be the thick, horn-rimmed spectacles on his Pekinese face. We had called him sissy, baby, chicken. But it turned out he could scream.

"Tornado!" The meek voice became a cylinder of hollow panic. "Tornado's comin'!" It gained in volume as midnight fell on Candlestick and the red and yellow candles flickered to life.

"Tornado!" He ran along the clean sweep of sidewalk that fronted the stores linked all in a row, stores filled with people, a shotgun run you could fire a bullet through and have it come out clean on the other end. Quickly the yellow sky gave way to black.

Streetlamps blinked on. Past the hobby shop, the beauty shop, and the pharmacy he ran, crying his unbelievable news, and at first they believed him to be what he had always been, the boy who cried wolf, the brat who would get them all back for all their teasing with one good scare they would not forget.

At first Larry Swales did not believe him, but he had noticed the odd light, the stillness. He stood in the parking lot of Candlestick with a bag of groceries in his arms, about to bend forward and put them into a woman's car, when the light rolled away like a tide and he heard the red-haired boy. He thought to himself that it was just the kind of thing the kid would pull, yell fire when all around the world was wet, watch the panic rise and then skulk off giggling. Larry Swales turned to look.

"Tornado's coming!" The kid would not shut up as the queer stillness of the afternoon began to unravel and give way to the outer edges of the vacuum. The vortex neared in a grinding pulse, and as it did, things began to shift. Cars rocked in the parking lot; the smooth tar beneath them, the tar that we would, in the melting summer heat, dig out with our fingernails, began to vibrate. Beneath the shroud that had fallen, the red-haired boy would not be quieted, would not be denied, and when all turned to look, it was more than the color of the sky that held them for a moment, paralyzed, before they ran.

Linda Flowers had watched the alien light dawn as she drove down Rainey Road in her bright red Corvair, on her way to Candlestick to buy orange juice for her mother. The light had bothered her, but she was still a high school girl, on her way from seeing a new horse at the stables, driving her shiny car. But when she looked back again to the southwest as she stopped at the crossroads, something unconscious pulled at her, a sense that she was being stalked, and she saw it then, what that eerie yellow light had spawned. She says that she thought, almost idly, "Why, that looks just like the tornado in *The Wizard of Oz.*" And then she drove on as the wind picked up and the sky grew darker. Not even then, she says, did what this mean register with her.

"I blanked it out," she says. "All these years I just blanked it out, refusing to believe that it had even happened, refusing to believe that into my ordered world of horses and Caney Creek and Mama and Daddy, that something like this would even *think* of touching me. I just looked at it and thought, Oh, a tornado. But there was a point, and I can't tell you when that point was, that I knew, consciously, that it was trying to get *me*. That it was coming for *me*."

Yet when Linda Flowers pulled into the nearly full parking lot at Candlestick, she was not thinking of the tornado she had seen. She took a five-dollar bill from her purse for the orange juice, got out of her new car, locked it, and turned around. A woman still in curlers was running from the beauty shop, screaming, "Oh my God, my children! My children!" And beyond her, along the sidewalk, the red-haired boy still ran.

"I heard him," Linda says, "yelling to the top of his lungs, 'Tornado! Tornado!' and it was then that she, too, ran to the Liberty store before all she had seen around her was changed forever. Instinct told her that by closing her eyes and burrowing as deeply as she could, what now threatened would not see her. But in truth there was no place to hide without its knowing, no corner and no cubbyhole in all of Homer Lee Howie's dream center, where the noise would not come and the world would not be shattered.

Inside Liberty, still bright and clean and orderly, but where now people began to hide and scream and pray aloud as the jackhammer sound drew nearer, Linda Flowers "assumed the position."

"You know," she says, "the one we were taught since grade school, your back against the wall, knees tucked up, head down, arms folded behind our heads. They always said it was for a tornado drill, but we knew they were trying not to scare us. We knew better. It was practice for when the bombs came from Cuba."

I remember when the alarm would sound at Forest Hill as we

sat in the old classrooms, the high, multipaned windows filtering the afternoon sun through decades of dust. We knew enough to fear what it could mean because the news was inescapable. Cuban missiles were aimed right at us, and we often watched the sky, not for tornadoes, but for massive silver-bellied missiles descending. The lucky ones had bomb shelters. We had the long, echoing hallways with planks worn and swaybacked by thousands of feet scuffing to and from class. The bell would ring, not in a short burst but in a building crescendo that did not stop, and within its duration fear had time to form and grow, and by the time we were tucked against the wall in the hallways, heads down, we were certain that this time it was for real. We thought not of the evil of tornadoes, but of the evil of Cuba.

Larry Swales moved away quickly from the car where he had placed the bags of groceries neatly inside so they would not topple and fall, so there would be no mess for the woman to worry over when she got home. He believed the red-haired boy now as he ran to the end of the sidewalk by Liberty that looked onto the pasture filled with wild onions that seemed to rise up white and glowing in the surreal light. And there it was, immense and undeniable, holding aloft in a sickening spin the remnants of roofs, strips of road, trees, and a young boy who would be dropped in the pasture as the tornado took its mark on Candlestick.

Larry Swales did the only thing he knew to do. Thirty seconds before impact he ran into the store and hollered for people to get down, and when they did not he ran to them and pushed them to the floor and up under counters.

Composure, dignity, decorum—passwords for entry into the secret world of the South, a world where hardship is borne with grace and fear is kept under lock and key—disintegrated as quickly as did the cinder-block walls and the wide windows of Liberty supermarket. Panic took the place of nobler emotions, and God was called upon as people cried their prayers aloud.

Moments before, women had been pushing carts along the brightly waxed aisles of Liberty, the shining, well-stocked gift of

Homer Lee Howie to the people of South Jackson, the store that said they were important enough to have freshness and convenience and a place where they could see their neighbors, and here, as the day beyond the big windows darkened, they had leaned over to inspect through the tight, clean cellophane the cut-up fryers and spare ribs.

The grubby, creek-bound kids who had been my friends had searched the floor for green stamps here, thinking of the summer to come, of the green army tents and flashlights and sleeping bags that the stamps would buy, and on this afternoon in March some had stood patiently in line with candy and gum turning soft in their palms, waiting for Ronny Hannis, hoping he would show up soon and maybe give them an extra sucker. He had not come in yet, but they were patient. They liked the way he teased them. They liked how important he looked in his white over-the-neck apron. Someone had said earlier that Ronny was over at the Dog 'n' Suds playing pinball, and that he would be in soon. So they waited. The artificial, comforting world of lights and linoleum and the sound of cash registers ringing up change was dissolving. The wolf the red-haired boy had cried about was at the door.

Larry Swales heard the screaming as the wind poured in and the world above him began to turn. "Help me!" came a voice, and it was familiar. Swales turned to look from where he crouched beneath the checkout stand as he heard the whining suction of the wind begin to take apart the building, and watched in horror as his friend Ronnie Clark, a bag boy at Liberty, held tight with bloodless fingers to the double handles of the supermarket door. It was as if he were watching a cartoon. The boy, still holding tight to the handles, was being blown straight back by the wind and whipped through the air like a flag.

"And I knew then that it was gonna happen," Larry says, "that we weren't getting out, and it was at that moment that the tornado hit the building."

And the big door, with Ronnie Clark holding on to it with all his strength, slammed shut with a finality that Larry Swales remembers to this day. Those who watched the boy, terrified, knew that once it closed they were trapped, and suddenly they did not want to be inside Liberty supermarket. They wanted to be out in the low ditches that surrounded the fields, inside the massive drainage pipes that ran through Caney Creek, in a bomb shelter dug ten feet underground, anywhere but inside the vibrating, barnlike walls of Liberty, where the dazzling flash of lights had now snapped out and the once-clean air was choked with cinderblock dust.

They have changed their theories, weathermen have. They now say that buildings do not explode when a tornado nears and the pressure outside drops so fast that the structure, filled with buoyant, pregnant air, blows out the windows and the doors and the plywood shell. They say this is a myth, as if all these years those who have borne witness have been fools. They say now to believe what isn't true. But Larry Swales will swear they are wrong.

"It pulled a vacuum on the whole building," he remembers, "a suction like you wouldn't believe. My ears hurt so bad. My head felt funny."

The pressure drops so fast that eardrums bleed, sinuses bleed, vessels in the body rupture, confusion sets in.

Massive plate-glass windows lined the front of Liberty with shoppers' specials fixed to them along thin skeins of wire—advertisements for whole roasting chickens, hot dogs, gallons of milk, tomatoes—and as the vacuum grew, those inside watched the windows swell and bow and then suddenly blow clear of their metal frames. The glass, airborne now, glittering in the maelstrom of wind and dirt and metal, moved at speeds incalculable and hit Larry Swales full in the back, driving him, with his hands outstretched, the length of the supermarket, straight down the recently polished aisle that had now become a shooting gallery of flying glass and baseball-sized chunks of cinder block. He remembers the sense of flying and of being shoved by the brutal fist of wind until it rammed him headfirst into the meat compartment.

"If the meat counter hadn't been there," he says, "I would never have stopped."

Swales, bleeding but still conscious, pushed himself back with great effort from the meat counter and pulled himself, on his hands and knees, inch by inch, against the wind, back to the front of the store. Here were the screwed-down counters that held the heavy cash registers, and he managed to pull himself beneath one. From this vantage point, his body slashed and pricked with dozens of shards of glass, he watched as the roof lifted clear, as if nothing had ever held it down, and as it was pulled free into the vortex, he could see the sky above filled with all the things it had taken, high up into the column that now owned them all.

The twisted metal frames where the plate-glass windows had been moments before was now a bizarre portal through which Larry Swales watched as the wind pulled cars from the parking lot as if they had no weight at all, some with people still inside, hurled and smashed and crumpled them, dropping some straight down and carrying others away. Linda Flowers's red Corvair was crushed, her purse gone into the vortex and inside it her driver's license, which would be found a month later in Florence, Mississippi, ten miles away. Ronny Hannis's jalopy that W.T. had given him would be found upside down in Caney Creek.

The tornado was louder than anyone had ever imagined it could be, deafening as it relentlessly tore and severed and wrenched anything, everything. It took up the pavement in the parking lot, pulled boards free, and then drove them seven feet into the ground. Cars became unrecognizable, bristling spines of steel and glass, radiators hissing, gas leaking out, windows splayed in diamond patterns and busted out of their frames. And still, above the noise, Larry Swales could hear people screaming. He says that the sound of those screams seemed to last forever and that hearing them, knowing what they meant, that someone's arm had been torn loose, that a leg had been cut free, left him feeling helpless as he lay with his long legs drawn up beneath the counter. He says that he did not think or pray and that he heard the screams not really with his ears, but with his body. It was all instinct now. He knew that people were dying. There was no way they were not.

Beneath another counter Linda Flowers was folded into the defense position and remembers the noise as a "guttural growl. It was alive. It was like something from the bowels of Hell." Her head and body vibrated with the sound, and above her glass rained down as if from a hundred broken chandeliers. There was a child crying nearby, a boy who began to scream inconsolably, and when he would not stop Linda reached her hand out from beneath the counter where she hid and grabbed a candy bar that still sat untouched on a display rack near the aisle, unwrapped the candy, gave it to the boy, and said, "Now go find your mama." The boy looked around. There was no roof. There were no windows. There was nothing but pummeled scraps of glistening metal where the cars had been, and the boy kept crying.

As the noise edged away, Linda Flowers stood up to run, but her legs were wrapped in the wire that had hung the advertisements, and as she pulled at the wire to free them, it sliced through her legs and blood began to run down her torn stockings and onto her shoes. She ran, then, in the blackness of rain like she had never seen before. Rain so heavy, it was as if a river had changed course and now ran from the sky. Still, she says, even in the rain that made her blind, there was dust everywhere, clogging the air, "live wires everywhere and absolute chaos and debris." The sound of live wires popping now replaced the sawing, burning sound of the wind, pure voltage streaming from the downed lines along the wet ground; live wires wrapped around the heaped scrap metal of cars, spitting and arcing in the ditches full of water from a rain that now fell from the faraway land of a God who might yet drown those he had not yet killed.

She ran as if running were the one thing she had been born to do, north through the parking lot in the false midnight to the service station at the edge of Cooper Road. In a ruined car outside the station a woman and her young son lay dead, while another son sat crying on the broken pavement, his clothes torn from his body. A black man who worked at the station stood staring straight ahead, his arms limp at his sides, as Linda Flowers ran to him. Blood poured from his head and covered his face. She asked him if she could use the telephone to call home, she screamed the question, and the man stared back at her in shock and said, "Everything's gone." She asked him again, and he said, "Lady, we don't have no phone. There's been a tornado."

She ran now in the direction from which the tornado had come, west on Cooper Road, lifting her legs high over the live wires. She remembers hearing them crack and snap in the downpour.

"I could hardly even breathe," she says. "And it was very black. So black. It went from yellow straight to black. And live wires everywhere, and I shall never forget what I had on. It was a sleeveless beige, like a little slip dress, the simple A-line scooped-neck thing that you wore in the sixties, and a pair of Weejuns, and my stockings—and I remember I had on my stockings and they were shredded, and the blood all down my legs, and I just started jumping over those wires. I ran seven tenths of a mile without stopping, all the way to the Woodville Heights Church parking lot, and the church was destroyed, too, and what was in my mind was getting back to the stables and finding my brother, and I was hysterical by then."

As she stood in the parking lot of the Baptist church, her heart slamming in her throat, Linda watched as a car approached through the downpour and the gritty dust that was still being washed from the sky. Other than the man who had stood with blood covering his face, the man and woman in the car were the first living people she had seen.

"I was screaming at them as soon as they were out of the car. And I kept screaming that I had to find my brother."

The man was from the old school that says a witless person must be shocked back to his senses. He stood in the driving rain before the hysterical girl, raised his hand back as she opened her mouth once more to scream, and slapped her hard across the face. Linda Flowers stopped screaming. And then the man and his wife drove her home, back to Savannah Street, along a part of Caney Creek where no one had even heard the wind.

THE STORES THAT HAD BEEN linked up end to end were gone. Where the Laundromat had been, the place of chrome and purposeful sounds and the clean soap smell, Sarah Parker, the mother of the boy I had wanted to walk with in the damp, firefly-lit evenings along Caney Creek, lay dead, her body crushed.

The friendly druggist from Massachusetts was dead, too, buried in the rubble of his pharmacy, a place that had once been intimate, with a small run of shelves stocked with rubbing alcohol and aspirin, foot powder and Epsom salts, that had aimed toward the back where Mr. Gaetz had stood on high behind the counter in his white lab coat, where he would dip a small metal scoop into the jars of yellow saffron the color of the tornado sky.

The indoor slot car track where all the boys had gone with their race cars each afternoon, and where the girls had gone to watch, had just finished up a race ten minutes before the storm hit, so many had gone home in time, but where the hobby shop had been a young girl lay with her arm severed at the shoulder where the flying glass had cut through.

The red-haired boy had run into the barbershop where Bobby Grant was cutting hair, still crying his warning until the force of the wind took the walls down. He had run to a corner and curled up with his hands over his head. Others had pushed into the shop's small bathroom. The red-haired boy lived, and it would come to seem as if his life had been spared as a gift for the way he had come through, the way he had forgotten how we had treated him.

THE DOMED METAL HAIR DRYERS from the beauty shop lay amid the crucifixes of rebar and metal frames and two-by-fours, locked together by a steel bar, the absurd helmets tipped upside down where they caught the pouring rain.

There were others dead, others mutilated and dying, but for a very long time no one moved.

Across Caney Creek from Cherrywood, the girl whose mother killed her father had watched the tornado spin up the creek.

"I remember standing in that window that looked back across the creek," she says, "and I saw the funnel with tires and concrete blocks and big chunks of tree." And she says that she remembers wondering if I were alive, so familiar was her habit of gazing across the creek to where I lived. But I was gone, long gone.

CHAPTER TEN

"Juland was the onliest black person to die at Candlestick."

—Eddie Jones, husband of Juland Jones

IT WAS JUST A SIMPLE A-FRAME hut with fancy eaves, but reinforced with steel rebar and a solid concrete foundation. Fred Hudgins and his family had carved their initials in the cement slab of the Dog 'n' Suds café before it had set because they wanted to remember that this was where the dream of better things had begun and that whatever prosperity came after, this one place would always be the cornerstone. Like Homer Lee Howie's vision of Candlestick, Fred and Mary Hudgins had put what money they had into a root beer and burger joint that would, from the day it opened, become hallowed ground where we, harnessed by the awkwardness of youth, felt braver among our own kind, nearly invincible when the jukebox played loud.

On the afternoon of March 3, 1966, Fred Hudgins left Dog 'n' Suds around four o'clock to pick up an adding machine. His wife and their teenage daughter, Gloria, often went over to the restaurant at this time, but this day they were late. Gloria, seventeen, had had a Coke the day before at Dog 'n' Suds with Ronny Hannis. He had told her about his plans for college.

Ronny pulled people to him, caught them up in his world filled with light, smiled at them and talked to them in such a way that years later, decades later, they would remember him. He was no Goody Two-shoes, his sister Sharon says, but he was honest and fair and his optimism was uncommon, an optimism of substance held in place by what seemed to be a secret knowledge that the future dawned bright and ample and that all he had to do to move through the world in equanimity was to lock his finger around the gold ring and pull.

The morning of March 3, his mother, Mae, had watched him carry the garbage to the curb to be picked up, balancing the can on the shoulder of his blue shirt that he wore with the cuffs rolled under. In the other hand he carried an envelope with his college application inside. Ronny planned to go to college, and his brother and sisters had teased him about it, asking what he was going to be when he was done. He told them that he didn't know yet, that he might end up digging ditches, but that they would be the prettiest ditches anyone would ever see. Mae Hannis, with her pleasing voice, had called to her son not to get his shirt dirty, and he had laughed and handed her the envelope with the application inside, saying, "Don't you worry about this old shirt. You just worry about mailing this for me." And he had waved his hand high in the air and laughed as he walked away. Mae had gone to work at the bank that morning, and Ronny had driven the '56 Oldsmobile that W.T. had given him to school.

Ronny played cornet in the Forest Hill band and had practice that afternoon, but he would miss it that day and go to Candlestick early.

It was a slow afternoon at the shopping center, perhaps because of the weather. All day the sky had looked unsettled, and there had been tornado warnings, but there were often warnings in spring that amounted to nothing more than lightning and rain and a quick wind. Ronny had a Coke at Marble's grocery store, down Cooper Road from Polk's, with his best friend, his cousin Doyle Moore, a few minutes after four o'clock, and then went on to Dog 'n' Suds to play a game of pinball before his shift began at Liberty, driving the Olds down the short stretch of Cooper Road beneath the low sky in the odd afternoon heat. A young married woman named Doris Freeney was working the counter at Dog 'n' Suds that afternoon. She and Juland Jones, who lived on Booker T. Washington Street with her husband, Eddie, and their four children, were both twenty-seven years old. Juland's children were at home with her mother, her husband was working downtown at the fertilizer factory, and her twin sister, Meland, was working in another part of South Jackson. It had been Meland's turn to cook at Dog 'n' Suds that afternoon, but the sisters had traded places that day. A little girl, nine-year-old Pamela Pace, had come in to order something for her mother.

They say that Ronny saw it first as he looked up from the pinball machine, out the wide windows toward Liberty, the windows that would sometimes frost up on the inside from the air-conditioning. It would have been no more than a few hundred feet away as the wind at its center, with a rotating velocity that some will forever believe was as great as 500 mph, began to undo every pinning and every post, every mortared seam and every nail, grinding concrete to dust and wood to splinters and driving the splinters and the straw from the field through pane-sized planes of glass, and the glass through damp flesh and the flesh through glass. The path was too wide. The cloud was too big. They watched from the tiny room as Candlestick went down, and Ronny cried out that they should go, and Doris Freeney said, "There's no time."

Juland Jones, with her purse held tight in her long fingers, ran into the small bathroom. Ronny and Doris and the girl fell behind the counter, where Ronny lay his body on top of the child.

The building, no bigger than a two-car garage, was hit dead-on as the three lay on the floor and Juland braced herself against a corner of the bathroom. It was the wall she leaned against that took the full blow. Cruel and without conscience, calculated in its killing, the wolf at the door was deadlier than the red-haired boy could ever have known. The world rolled onto its side, the ground was pulled into the sky, the prayers for mercy given up were given back, and up into the dark column rose our sense of place and those who had made it so: Juland, Doris, the child, and the boy we all loved. When the tornado cast them off, two were dead and two were broken, and what had once sat bright and engaging before us, the place where we had marked time by the degree of our naïveté, not looking forward or back, became now a busted-up, blown-through memory, the way it is when you go back home and everything is smaller, the way it is when you go back home and everyone is dead, and it is then that the past hits you full-on, and you understand, finally, what time is, moments strung together marked by rhythms—heartbeats, drumbeats, thunder, a river changing course—and that the only thing that binds you to it always is the memory that has become a religion, and one thing, just one, that looks the same. And so it was that the past, the present, and the future were pulled from their holding ground all at once, and when the tiny building broke heaving into the air, all three points in time became forever final, and this one place was nothing but a killing ground where trust had been lost.

"Hit by tornado," Juland Jones's death certificate would read. They say she was decapitated. Her sister Meland does not speak of this, only to say that looking on from above, as Juland lay in her casket, she was "just herself, like she always was. Wadn't nobody like her."

Beneath the wreckage Doris Freeney lay buried with one hand exposed. Fred Hudgins knew it was Doris because he recognized the watch and rings she wore. For months she would lie in a body cast, one lung severed by a spear of glass, the deep wounds in her body filled with rocks and gravel and glass. But she would live.

The warm cushion of Ronny's body had saved the girl.

And for an hour, as bright as the sky would dawn the next morning, there was a miracle, and if it could have been sustained, if Caney Creek had run not with blood but clear and cold and emptied of the bodies that fell there, we might all have believed again. From the wreckage Ronny Hannis rose, Christ-like, and walked forth. There were dozens who would later say that they had seen him, bleeding, the clothes torn from his body, his head with two wounds, the skin flayed from his leg, helping to load the others when the ambulances came. But first he pulled himself free and stumbled across the wasteland toward the Liberty store as he had remembered it. Someone stopped him and asked where he was going, and he said he had to get to work. And then he looked around him and saw the cars with the roofs ripped back and the concrete gone beneath them and the live wires burning, and he saw that beneath what was ruined the dying lay, and he helped them, carried them across his shoulders, and when he collapsed, they put Ronny in the ambulance, too.

At the hospital W. T. Hannis found his son in a room where doctors were working to sew the boy's leg back together and cover the deep wounds in his head, and as his father asked aloud, first God, and then the doctor, if his boy would be all right, Ronny Hannis died.

CHAPTER ELEVEN

"Lord, it was a mighty thing."

—Donna Durr

ON THE AFTERNOON OF MARCH 3, the angel of Forest Hill, the fair-haired science teacher whom we never believed lived a life as ordinary as our own, was down at Cook Center, a shopping area that had been in place long before Homer Lee Howie built Candlestick. Mrs. Durr and her two-year-old son, Derryl, had gone to buy groceries for supper.

It was her habit to shop at Candlestick on Thursday afternoons. She does not remember why she decided to go to Cook Center that day. Her green Volkswagen, a car she and her husband, Bill, had bought when they were first married, had just been paid off. They had no insurance on it; it was just a car to get Donna Durr to school and to the store, and it suited her. In Mississippi, in 1966, Volkswagens were exotic, and almost suspect because they were German-made. Driving a Volkswagen meant you were a rebel of sorts, a freethinker, someone who understood California. It was the way we thought of Donna Durr.

When the shopping was done, she headed back up Cooper Road, toward Candlestick, to her home on Branch Street, and as she neared Candlestick she noticed the sky for the first time. "It was getting very dark," Donna Durr recalled, and she thought to herself that she needed to hurry and get home before the rain set in. She had seen a hundred skies that promised rain, but this one was far darker than those, so she sped up, and as she drove faster she looked up again, made uneasy by something, a sense, she says, that things weren't right. What she saw in the sky above, as dark nearly as the clouds but moving and turning, was what she thought at first were buzzards, "just kind of gliding, you know, above my car, and I thought, well, that's kind of strange."

By the time she was in front of Candlestick the buzzards were still there, but thicker now, sailing and looping and diving, and she thought again that it was even stranger to have buzzards over Candlestick. She now sought some logical explanation, the way she had taught us to do in class, some reason to explain why birds that were drawn to the dead on the road and in the fields would have come like locusts, their numbers so great that they seemed to fill the sky, just in this one spot, right here, right now. She looked toward Candlestick again, and then back up the road in the direction of Forest Hill, and it was then that she saw the funnel, how massive it was, and that it was not bearing to the right or to the left or lifting up, but moving on an unwavering path toward her car. She knew then that it was not buzzards at all that she had seen, but large planks and bricks and shingles that were being pushed ahead of the winds.

Donna Durr says she knew what she was supposed to do but did not do it. She says that the thing she had been taught, to get out of the car and not to try to outrun a tornado, never entered her mind. Behind the wheel of a car there is at least a fleeting sense of invincibility, of having the power to move away from what threatens. In a dark parking lot, with a stranger coming near, the instinct is to roll up the windows, lock the doors, and gun the motor—move away fast without looking back. And it was dark now and something was coming for her, so she tried to outrun it. She wheeled into Candlestick to turn around, to head back down Cooper Road as fast as she could. She pulled into a large unpaved area that lay between the parking lot of Candlestick and the parking lot of Dog 'n' Suds. But the rain had come by then, falling so hard and fast that the triangle of clay turned to quicksand and her little Volkswagen got stuck. Her back was to the vortex now, so she could not see in the false night that had fallen that there was no way out, even if she had grabbed her child and run.

The laws of physics have a loophole clause, a divine addendum that explains the uncommon, the unlikely, and the impossible with the vast and patient silence that wells up later in the lives of those who witness it, which is to say that to the question of *Why?* there is no answer more revealing or more beneficent than *Why not?* And for those who balance God and science on a scale that rests upon a plane infinite in its capacity to disprove, there are times when you get your money's worth for having borne out the scorn of others. That afternoon at Candlestick, Donna Durr got her money's worth, and she was given the better part of mercy, too.

The wind that reached from the ground up to a destination unknown, that carried trees and cars and the pliant bodies of the dead, hit her car hard. The drumming roar of the storm itself was overwhelmed by the sound of bricks and rocks and glass slamming against and penetrating the body of the Volkswagen.

"It was just like brickbats," Donna Durr says. "So many, so many, I mean, everything coming at us."

The tires of the car were stuck deep in the rain-sodden clay, mired to the hubcaps, and she knew with a peculiar finality that she was in the center of the storm. Her young son sat terrified on the car seat next to her, and she began to talk to him, never stopping, she says, saying again and again and again, as she looked him in the eyes, "Oh no, we're in it, we're in it. We're in it."

It is a happening rare even in the bizarre files of freak tornado experiences, rare in that those who feel the crushing pressure and high-velocity winds of the storm's interior ever live to tell about it, rarer still that they are conscious when it happens. The little green Volkswagen began to rise into the air with Donna Durr still at the wheel, her child beside her.

"We just started being lifted up," she remembers, her voice still filled with wonder more than thirty years later. "We were just lifted and we were bouncing, and you know, all this sounds so crazy, the more I think about it, the more I tell it, just asking the *whys* of it. *Why* weren't we blown with the rest of what was blown away, and *why* didn't we swirl? We bounced and bounced and got lifted higher and higher."

Once they were deep within the vortex, the assault by the debris became constant. Her little boy began to cry and then to scream. Donna Durr pulled her son to her and lay his head in her lap, she says, "to shield his little face and eyes and all." She thought then about her own eyes, of the hard contact lenses she was wearing, and whether she might be blinded. And they rose still higher, seventy-five feet straight up, a man who had been watching on the ground, watching from afar, would later say, above the tops of the old oaks and the sycamores, far beyond the telephone wires that were being stripped from their moorings. And then Donna Durr dared to look down.

"It was like I was in a cartoon," she says. "I was just way, way up there in the air looking down, and Derryl was just screaming, and then all of a sudden we were right by the two-story electric power building, and I saw that thing just explode. It looked like you would have a little toy block house on the floor and just kicked it. Bricks went everywhere."

The explosion of bricks that blew out from the power substation heralded the hour and the minute that the clocks stopped in South Jackson and all fell into darkness. As Donna Durr watched the airborne bricks being sucked deep into the center where she still rode high, she says that there was one phrase, and one phrase only, in her mind. "I thought, 'Oh, no, *this is it.*'" She says she thought there would be some rush of wisdom that would form itself in her mind and offer up, perhaps, a Bible verse or the words of a philosopher or her own words that spoke of who she had been, and what her life had meant, but there it was—*this is it*—unadorned, brutal almost, the most succinct euphemism for a life about to be taken, when you hadn't had time to prepare for it at all. But instead of the knowledge that she hoped would fill her, what she felt was peace, she says, and she still cannot explain the depth of it or how suddenly it visited her while she was rising above the parking lot of Candlestick, all the cars below her destroyed in a heap of tortured metal and busted-out glass.

"I wasn't even thinking about dying and going to Heaven," she says, "and I wasn't callin' out to Jesus. I wasn't. I don't know why." Perhaps, she thought, because Jesus most likely knew. "Those are the kinds of questions I'm still asking myself now, why didn't I call out, other than, I guess, I just had a peace that He was in control, even though I wasn't consciously saying it."

And at the moment that she became conscious of that unbidden peace, with the remnants of houses and the power station bricks and the pieces of Candlestick Park hitting the car from all sides, Donna Durr and her small son began to descend through the cloud.

"About that time, as I felt this, we just started comin' down, just as gently as we went up, and that tornado blew every brick off that concrete foundation of the power station. There was not a brick left. It was like you had taken a broom and just swept it off. The Lord just put us right back down. I mean, just as gently as you would put a toy car on the floor. The only way I can visualize it is that the Lord just picked us up and blew that thing right under us, and set us right back down. And when I got out, once I realized we were down, I picked my baby up and I just stood there and looked. By that time it was just pouring torrents of rain, you could hardly even see. But I looked around and the whole shopping center was flat. And there was not a person moving. Not one. And it was like the movie *Last Survivor on Earth*. And there were power lines down everywhere. I mean, the whole parking lot was one big power line, but I wasn't even aware that they might be live. I took my boy and ran all the way across the parking lot, and I looked back over to Candlestick and it was just so still and people weren't movin'. I mean, there was nothin'. No life. Nothin'. And then, after some minutes, after a time, people started comin' and gettin' out, and there was a little boy who was screamin' over there lookin' for his mother, and there was a lady with a gashed head. Just people surfacing, but all so quiet then in the rain."

SHE GOT A RIDE HOME with a couple of high school boys who were carrying one of the injured to the hospital, and when her husband found her she was standing with her son in the driveway of their home, her hair matted with glass and dirt. Donna Durr had a small stick embedded in her arm, and her son Derryl had a trickle of blood at his temple. That was all. She asked her husband if he had seen the Volkswagen, and when he said he hadn't, they walked back over to Candlestick.

"By that time," she says, "there was so much congestion, with ambulances and all, that you couldn't drive over there, so we walked, and there sat my little Volkswagen. The top was just as rounded and pretty as you ever would imagine, but the rest of the car was just beat to a pulp. The windows were cracked out, the hood was ripped, best I remember, from where the hinge is, from where you pull it up on the back. It was just ripped right in the middle, like you'd tear paper, ripped clear through. And inside the car were shingles and bricks and all kinds of colored glass, big old pieces, some were twelve or fifteen inches long, and jagged. Any one of them could have cut us in half. All of this, all in our car, and that's all the injury we had, just a little stick in my arm that I could almost scratch out and a little blood on Derryl's temple. There were about seventy-five cars in the parking lot, and I just stood there and looked at them, oh yes, front tires in the backseat, every one of those tops crushed, every single one, all kinds of unimaginable damage, worse than you could *ever* imagine, and there sat my little car with the top just rounded right over. One man told my husband that he saw us about seventy-five feet up in the air, and then another man told him that he saw us above the treetops. But as high as we went we didn't move a distance of about fifty feet from where I got stuck in the mud to where the Lord lifted us up and then set us back down on that foundation. Why were we not blown away? *Why?*"

WAR TURNS ITS BACK ON THE QUESTION of *Why*. If Donna Durr had been a man who had seen war, she might have made the connection between the leveled spread of ground and war's immediate aftermath. She might have thought that you know it is war only because you have anticipated the things of war, even if you cannot know beforehand how incomprehensible it might be. The difference here, as Donna Durr stared, unbelieving, as the rain drew the dust down from the sky, as the wounded crawled out of the foxholes the wind had made, was that no one knew there was a war. No one believed that in two minutes' time—for this is all it took—their home would become the front line, the bombs would fall, and what had once been retrievable would be pulled beyond their grasp forever.

This place that stood in ruin now, that vibrated and hummed not with the familiar sound of cicadas but with live wires sparking in the rain, seemed to have come to know what we needed, through the daily rhythms that spoke of that need. Candlestick had been something constant, and the changes that had been no-ticeable over the years at the Liberty store, the hair salon, the bar-bershop and Dog 'n' Suds were that the help changed when the kids graduated from high school, the linoleum floor grew dingy, the tiles cracked along the edges, the paint needed freshening, new tunes were played on the jukebox, and maybe Juland Jones became pregnant with another baby, and maybe Ronny Hannis won another heart. But on this day, in a shorter span of time than it takes to fully conjure up the fear of death, death had come.

The linoleum was stripped from the concrete slab, the concrete slab from the ground. The jukebox was taken, broken, into the rotating sky. Ronny Hannis didn't work at Liberty anymore, not because he had graduated and gone away to a life where he would dig the prettiest ditches you would ever see but because he had died, and Juland Jones would never have another child, would never dance in back of the hot kitchen with Gloria Hudgins, would never make it back to the farmland in Prentiss, Mississippi, where she'd been born. And whatever was put in place of the ruined world would be nothing but a spook, a ghost, a haint, a specter to remind us that the ground bore the blood mark here, and it bore it deep.

THE CANDLESTICK TORNADO was not done. It only grew stronger as it rose above the Pearl River, emptying its belly into the dark water, and then fell to earth once more, moving on a long, unbroken run across Rankin, Scott, and Neshoba counties. By nightfall fifty-seven people would be dead. Fourteen at Candlestick—thirteen white and one black—a bizarre reversal of the Deaf and Dumb Tornado toll fifty years before.

A Democratic candidate for U.S. Congress named Joe Bullock would die as he drove along the rutted macadam of Highway 13, head-on into the funnel. Five more members of Mae Hannis's family would die in Rankin County. Mae's cousin would open the door of her home to look out at the storm, and the wind would pull the child she held from her arms.

In Neshoba County a man named Shorty Wells would say this about what he had found after the storm had passed:

"As I got closer to my homeland, I could hear grunting sounds. It was one of my sisters laying flat on her stomach, badly hurt. Someone put her in a car and took her on to the hospital. We found out later that every bone in her body was broke. As I looked around, all I could hear was women and children crying. I found my baby brother beside a tree. His neck was broken, and there was a deep puncture wound in his arm. Two hundred yards from the house my Aunt Rose Dean was wrapped in a barbed-wire fence. Wasn't no one who saw her could ever forget how she looked. I noticed later they was thirteen big trees down in our yard, and thirteen left standing. This was a sign from God."

CHAPTER TWELVE

"That place was flattened. That place was just obliterated."

—Karei McDonald, firefighter

ON THE GROUND THE WORLD is far different than when viewed from above—closer, tactile, immense. What lay destroyed and scattered and forever unrecognizable as what it had been before had a vastness to it as the black cloud lifted and moved toward Rankin County. Those who began to work their way from beneath the debris were confronted with the hugeness of the lost world.

There is an aerial film of the tornado path that shows row upon row of pecan orchards laid flat like sawgrass after a flood, each tree blown on its side in the same direction by the force of the wind. At first they look like logs floating in a muddy river, but the nearer plane and camera move, the more the eerie symmetry begins to take shape, until the misperception is gone.

In the air the volume of the world recedes: the long, wide roads that take time to travel, time to cross, become nothing more than dusty black ribbons; pigs in a barnyard look like chickens, houses like different-colored cardboard boxes. From the air what is mortal and what is not remain defined by gravity, and all the cheap, insubstantial things gravity holds in place look just as insignificant busted up and broken.

The finality of what it means to be earthbound is not apparent from the air. But knowing what sat put together that is now unhinged places a broad thumbprint on the territory below. Knowing that the gutted, blown-down pile of boxes is the exact spot where dozens lie buried suddenly makes real what the stuttering camera records. As the plane hovers and bumps over the bygone area of the shopping center and then drops lower, it looks as if Homer Lee Howie's bulldozers have come on the wrong day, in the wrong season, and as if they were in the process of returning what he had built to pastureland. All walls are down except for those of the Liberty store, and it is hard not to think of Ronny Hannis, on his way to work, that if he had not stopped to play pinball and had made it to the relative safety of Liberty, he might have lived. The camera does not record what-ifs, but they abound. There are rough fragments of the west walls of the pharmacy and the beauty shop and Laundromat still evident, but that is all. There are ragged scraps of Polk's grocery store, of the service station. Where Dog 'n' Suds once stood, there is heaped in its place what look like balled-up pieces of foil, mangled cars whose fenders and hubcaps throw light back at the camera. In the aerial view the long rope of tar that was Cooper Road is interrupted where the bridge once was that spanned the deepest part of Caney Creek, and even the road itself is gone in places, stripped back to the red clay like bark torn from a tree.

But what the camera cannot show, no matter how low the plane flies, are the bodies. The camera does not pick up the form of Lewis Mosley splayed in a field where the rabbits used to run. It does not show his blood against the green of the grass. It does not show Theodore Gaetz, the pharmacist from Fitchburg, Massachusetts, or the marks in the rubble and the dirt that his body made as Larry Swales and the other boys dragged him out. Nor can it show Mrs. Carpenter and her young son David beside the bent steel and fractured glass of the car from which their bodies were pulled, nor Juland Jones, struck down and buried where she lay, the strap of her new purse still clutched in her fingers.

The plane flies on, leaves Candlestick behind, rolls on the air over the river that is filled with trash, over the football-field length of industrial waste that was the Continental Can Company at Flowood, over the worn-out thread of Highway 13 where Joe Bullock died, over the field where scores of cattle lie, looking like nothing more than small blisters on the landscape. It flies over the gray stone faces of foundations blown clean, over the matchstick trees, and then flies back again, in case it has missed some incongruous fleck that might be recognized as what it was before. From this distance a body looks like nothing more than a dirty rag, but when the plane lands and the camera encompasses a distance it can clearly record, no substitute can be made, no trick of the light will change what it is.

ON THE GROUND the worst is true. The frangible nature of what has been hidden from the camera's eye broadens, spilling to the horizon that has gone yellow, not with the storm's light but with the sun that is setting as the close air begins to cool, and those who can still walk and speak do so with reverence because what is heaving and bending at jagged turns all around them is a burial ground they must undo.

There is footage taken at Candlestick of Lieutenant Governor Carrol Gartin standing on the clean slab of what had once been a store at Candlestick, looking out at the level pasture beyond the wreckage. Wrought metal and broken wood flank him, and after a time he bends over and picks up something out of the camera's view and then brings it into view, a piece of clothing, a shirt, ripped and dirtied. For a long time he stands still, looking at it, turning it over in his hands. If the context were not there, the shot would be absurd, a grown man pondering a scrap of clothing, but in this view the question goes begging: Whose shirt, where are they now, did they live? He holds it out to the camera, an offering. Evidence at the scene of the crime.

THERE ARE THOSE who resented the politicians coming in, tiptoeing through the wasteland with their white shirtsleeves rolled up, assessing the situation, saying, *What a tragedy.* Some thought they did it to get votes, so that when election time came near, their compassion would be remembered. Joe Bullock, one of their own, had died. It looked good for them to be there, but the only ones who were truly welcome were those who had come to work silently side by side.

The first film footage was shot only forty-five minutes after the tornado struck. It is a silent film but for a brief narration at the beginning, the voice of an older man with a rolling, sonorous Mississippi accent, overlaid with somber disbelief, an Edward R. Murrow voice grown in a cotton field. In the first frame, and at eerie times throughout the film, there appears the almost translucent, ghostly outline of the words "Jackson, Mississippi" at the bottom of the screen. When the camera pulls away and the screen goes blank for a moment, these spectral words still waver below, fading in and out, and the effect becomes disconcerting, more so when the deep-voiced narrator abruptly stops and never resumes.

In time there are ambulances from far away that look like paddy wagons with rounded tops and flanks. They came from the funeral homes—from Mobile, Alabama; Copiah County, Miss.; Louisiana; and there is one from Vicksburg, where the war dead once lay in the battlefield that then still looked like a battlefield.

There are men and teenage boys in the foreground of the first shots, among them Karei McDonald, the protector of Oak Forest who looked out for the fearful, who had watched out the window of his house that afternoon, waiting for a leaf to move and had seen the two funnels high above move together and become one. He had watched them drop, filled with debris, and he could tell by how the cloud had grown steadily darker how bad it was. "I told my wife I'd go see if I could help somebody," he would say later. It was what he did for a living, watched and waited until it was time to help. He studied things hard, and when it was time to act, he acted. There had been no way in at first, so he had crossed a wide pipe that spanned Caney Creek, the pipe that we had dared each other to walk over in flood season, balancing unsteadily, our bare feet burning against the hot pipe as the water rolled beneath us, and if we lost our nerve we would fall to our knees and crawl, impervious in our fear to the cries of "sissy" that came from shore, grateful always when the red clay bank rose up to meet us. Karei McDonald had taken the pipe in a run and was the first one in. Now, as the news crew on the ground filmed him, he was among the others who were up to their knees and shoulders in the morass of concrete and brick and metal sheared at angles. No one smiles in this silent film, no mouth moves to speak, no one looks at the camera. The faces to a man and to a boy look drawn, and the sense is that they comprehend on a level that troubles them deeply that there is no other way to do what they are doing, that if this were ordinary rubble they would use pitchforks, backhoes, shovels, but that here and now, everything is at risk. A shock to a body still beneath the trash, a shovel pushed at a damaged lung, could kill. So they lift, they sift, they pull boards away cautiously, but still they do it quickly, two or three working together at a time to drag away the heavier lumber, the pockmarked pieces of cars, the broken cinder blocks, the shards of roof and eave, the lances of rebar, the knotted pieces of clothing that binds something they cannot see. There is no sound, not metal against metal as they drag away car parts and aluminum flashing, not the grating sound of debris settling in on itself. No move is punctuated by a reverberation that tells the senses what to recognize. There are just the movements of the men, the focus in their eyes.

Prisoners are there, too, a line of them bending and digging, rising and falling within the camera's range, dressed in striped chain-gang canvas, clothes meant to mark them in the free world, but as they dig it is strangely apparent that they are freer than the ones they search for and it is not hard to imagine that their faces show this. They look embarrassed even at being so lucky, for being out in the air, no matter what has brought them here. The loose uniforms with the wide, two-toned wales are cartoonish against the backdrop of waning light. These men are the only ones conscious of the camera; you can see it when they look from the corners of their eyes, quickly, and then back down. No matter what the crime, no man wants to be filmed in prison stripes.

If there are bodies found, the cameras do not film the dead. Sacrilege is understood here. But the camera continues to record in a jerking sweep the totality of the destruction, and the mind makes the bridge naturally, yet unwillingly, from the parking lot overlaid by ruin to the bodies pinned beneath it, and it is the inevitability of this knowledge that infuses the twenty-seven minutes of film.

The light fades, and the floodlights come up. By dark the wind from the cold front that brought the tornado begins to blow, and the men are in jackets now, their faces and hands filthy. They gather around the makeshift Red Cross canteen, eating sandwiches quickly, drinking soup from shallow cups, still not talking, still not meeting the camera's eye, as the Red Cross flag snaps in the breeze behind them. It is easier now to see their hands as they cradle the cups and hold the sandwiches awkwardly, as if somehow it is disrespectful to be eating at a time like this. Karei McDonald will say later that it took him days to scrub the blood from beneath his fingernails and to free it from the deep cracks and callouses in his hands. It is blood and clay, both red, that cover the hands of these men, but in the washed-out color of the film, you cannot tell for certain where one ends and the other begins.

The last frame of the film shows the dawn, pale above the wasteland, the men still digging.

*   *   *

ALL NIGHT LONG the sirens sounded. Trucks with steel cables attached moved in to pull away the downed walls, and ropes were strung along the periphery of what had once been Candlestick.

"It was all you heard," said Karei McDonald, "si-reens in and si-reens out. All night long." There were four places where the people of South Jackson could be found that night: home, the hospital, church, or the morgue. In Caney Creek lay the adding machine from Dog 'n' Suds, Ronny Hannis's '56 Olds, Fred Hudgins's office chair, a car, crushed, with a couple still alive inside.

AT HINDS COUNTY General Hospital the injured were brought in by the score. There was only one doctor on duty when the radio call went out across the city for all medical personnel, and there were only four emergency beds. More than 150 people would be treated that night. The small hospital opened all floors as the casualties streamed in. Blankets and mattresses were brought from the National Guard armory so an unfinished wing could be used. The tiny chapel was used to treat patients, the labor and delivery room was used for surgery, and an X-ray room was converted into a morgue. Emergency treatment extended into the hallways, and before the night was over the hospital would be filled beyond capacity.

A nurse who had tended tornado victims before would remember the most disturbing injury she had ever seen, a young boy with a two-by-four through his chest, still alive. Now there was a boy with a Coke bottle through his leg, young Larry Temple, who had worked at Polk's grocery. In the rush to save those who could be saved, the boy was mistakenly covered up and left for dead on a gurney in the hallway. There were those with missing limbs and those with glass and rocks driven deep beneath their skin, heads gashed from the neck to the crown, missing ears, a little girl with an arm torn off, the injuries of war. The first patient in was a twelve-year-old boy, not breathing. He was given mouth-to-mouth resuscitation and survived. From out where the tornado had first hit, near the 1,600-foot television tower that was now laid out in a cow pasture, a woman was brought in on a car seat used as a stretcher. A nurse on duty said that no one there would ever forget the woman's screams. "Her body had shut down from shock," the nurse would say. When they tried to get her vital signs, there was no blood pressure, no pulse, no heart rate. When they tried to insert a needle for an IV drip, they were unable to find a vein. When they made an incision to insert a catheter, there was not a drop of blood. Yet the woman kept screaming. Narcotics, usually kept under lock and key, were laid out on a table in the hallway. A brown tag was pinned to each patient brought in, with notes on how much medication he or she had been given.

On into the night the ambulances loaded and reloaded. "They brushed off the glass splinters and slammed the blood-splattered stretchers into the back end of the ambulance and had the motor running before the doors were shut," one witness said.

Outside the hospital the people of Jackson stood on State Street and directed traffic into the emergency entrance. Many of the injured came in private cars, some with their windows shattered. On the run back to Candlestick from the hospital an ambulance attendant suffered a heart attack. In the confusion his death was at first blamed on the tornado.

At Mississippi Baptist Hospital the switchboard was flooded with calls from people whose relatives hadn't come home that night. Often the words they hoped for were not heard. "No one by that name" the answer would come. Or "We don't have him listed, not on the records yet." And it would be the word "yet" that would resound.

But help, brought by critical need, came in abundance. Pediatric head nurse Clarice Bridgers was a patient herself at Hinds General that night and was called to duty from her hospital bed. Blood donor cars were volunteered across the city. People called in saying they had spare room for the homeless to stay in. Food was cooked and carried in—to the hospitals, the disaster site, the funeral homes, the churches. Those waiting to hear prayed aloud in the waiting room. "What else do you do?" asked one woman who waited at the hospital to hear news of her husband. "When people are busy doing God's work, it's only God that's got time to listen."

As the wounded and the dead were excavated and driven toward the heart of the darkening downtown, where the power was still out, people moved, without a thought to the day that would follow, in the direction they were needed.

CHAPTER THIRTEEN

"If I ever build a house, I'm building a storm shelter. I'm building an inside-access basement, concrete, steel-reinforced, that I can hide in if this ever happens to me again."

—Linda Flowers

THAT EVENING, AS A COOL, DRY WIND blew from the north, carrying on it the muted smell of spring, raising it up from the gully of Caney Creek, the flashlights from the field by Candlestick cut the shadow of the night into triangles that narrowed and widened with the direction of the beams, the floodlights spilled out like stage lights, and the sirens sang.

Linda Flowers was at home with her family, her mother, father, and brother. A boy she knew came to the door that night, and when Linda answered, the boy turned pale. "I thought you were dead," he said. She threw away the torn clothes she had worn. She forgot about her bright red car that was gone. She listened to her hero father tell her to suck it up and go on. She does not remember going back to school with her arm in a sling, nor does she remember the bruises on her face, only the wire wrapped around her legs and how it had sliced through the skin like a cheese cutter. She had feared her father would have a heart attack when he heard she had been at Candlestick, but he did not, not this year. Though he had told her to shake it off and go on, he was sympathetic, and in the years that followed, when the sky would grow dark and the tornado warnings would come, he would call his grown daughter and tell her to come over and sit with him so they could watch the sky together. Most of that afternoon Linda Flowers does not remember. Just in freeze frames, she says, the way you see an afterimage when lightning flashes in the night. She does not remember that evening spent with her family, only that she was there, and safe.

Karei McDonald returned to his wife and children very late on the evening of March 3, his clothes flushed with blood, a sheath of it covering his hands and forearms. He was in a trance, he says, what he came to understand later as shock, and he would often think in the years to come of the survivors and would say with conviction, "It was *traumatic, very* traumatic, seeing the debris and destruction at Candlestick. I would like for some doctor or somebody to do a study of those people and see how they made out afterward. I never got any sort of feedback from that at all, how the people that were in shock tolerated it later on and how they came back to a normal attitude later on, or if they ever did come back at all. The more I study the little bit of medicine I do, the more far-reaching effects I realize that shock has, and that shock *will* kill." And Karei McDonald would talk about it with his wife that evening, and later the two of them would track the storm's path through the ravaged counties so he could study, close in, the habits of a killer.

Bert Case, the newscaster for WJTV, dreamt that night of the man who had called him from the phone booth, anonymous in his dream, anonymous still in life. The next day he would ride in a plane over the blitzed terrain, wondering out loud about the exactness of the storm's path, how it had kept on a zero-degree point along a northeast line, unwavering. He would study with unconcealed awe the downed trees laid out, he said, like matchsticks in a box, and would remember how old trees could often withstand the wind, and that sometimes they were the last thing to give.

The pregnant angel of Forest Hill School, Mrs. Donna Durr,

was at home with her husband and young son that night, washing the glass and concrete from her hair, checking her boy for injuries, unable to retreat from what she had seen that day, the
bricks and stone and wood and glass beating at her car windows
to get in while she sailed and lurched ever higher until she saw
the world below explode in a shower of fire and mortar, thinking
to herself, "This is *it*." That evening, when she understood that it
was not, she reflected on that, too, what it would mean in her
life, and when she went to church that Sunday, the pastor would
say to her, "Young lady, God has a mission for you," and when he
asked her what she thought it might be, she would say to tell, for
all her life, "of God's love."

For the Hannis family that night, the complexity of God's love
was hard to bear. W.T. was at the hospital when Ronny died, he had
seen the condition his boy was in, and he would never forget. He
would wish to himself for years that he had had the money to buy
the boy a better car, and his other children would tell him that
Ronny had loved the Oldsmobile and that he should not feel that
way, but still he did. Mae Hannis put away the shirt that Ronny had
been wearing that morning, the blue one with the sleeves rolled
under. Over the years she would take it out when she was alone,
making sure the cuffs were still tucked beneath. From that day on
Ronny's sister Sharon would always think of her brother when she
saw a grocery checker or a bag boy, and when one would bring her
groceries to the car, she would tip him well and smile. And from
that day on the number 66 would always make her pause, no matter how it was used. The next week in school, when her class was
asked to write a poem, Sharon would write one about Ronny.
About his smile. That night the family talked about Ronny's funeral; that morning they had talked about his college plans.

Fred Hudgins cried that night. It was the first time his daughter, Gloria, had seen her father weep, and as the Hudgins family
waited for word on Doris Freeney's condition, Mary Hudgins
trembled and sobbed without control the more she heard about
the afternoon that had passed. It would be a response that would

rise up in her for the next thirty years whenever the storm was mentioned. Mary Hudgins had watched the roof shingles of a house raise straight up and then fall back down, and she had heard the nearly indefinable sound of the tornado that she would describe as "the world rolling over." Young Tony Hudgins, Fred and Mary's son, asked where Juland Jones was. Her car still sat in the dark driveway of the Hudginses' home.

Homer Lee Howie thought that night of how the Lord didn't want his shopping center there anymore, of how a wind so strong was surely a sign from God. And he thought of the people who had died and was overcome with sorrow. But in time he would say that God had come to him through the people of South Jackson and that they had asked him to rebuild, and he would speak of that: "I said, 'Well, if you want it back, I'll build it back,' and all the people down there wanted it, so I said, 'Well, I'll try to get some tenants, but didn't nobody show up with any tenants.' I called 'em all. Nobody came, so I prayed to the Lord and the Lord did it. He brought them on. I give all the credit to the Lord. He is the instigator. He does everything, and in time the Lord provided thirteen tenants when I built it back." But Homer Lee Howie's dream did not have wings to rise from the ashes. They had been torn clean that afternoon, and in time the specter of the old Candlestick undid the new, and no one went there anymore.

At the hospital Larry Swale's head had been swaddled in gauze to cover the gash behind his ear, and his hands were bloodied still from digging with the others through the night. His mother had found him at Candlestick after the storm and had run to him screaming, grateful he was alive, and she had tried to make him come with her, to get help, but he had stayed on, working quickly, without thinking, because if there was time to be regained from the time that had been lost, that was the only way to do it. And at the hospital the news reporters had stopped him and asked him to talk, but he had walked past them and had gone to sit with the families who were waiting for news, and he had tried to comfort them.

Charles Parker, the husband of Sarah, the woman who had worked at the Laundromat, would find his wife in the wreckage, dead, and soon after would move away with his son and daughter, and no one would be able to say, though they would try to remember, where the boy I had once liked had gone.

Meland Smith went home from work alone that day, never to share a ride with her sister again. For eight years depression would haunt her. "And I didn't write no more songs after she died," she would say later. "I couldn't. There was nothing in me then." When it was suggested to her, years later, that she could perhaps write the song about Juland that would somehow make it better, a voice out there for all her loss, she would say, "No, I done that when she was alive. I cain't do that no more. What would be the sense?" Meland would begin that night to help care for Juland's children, and would do so through the years to come. "No child could wants for a better mother," she would say. "Juland was a good mother, the very best mother. When her littlest boy was growing up, he'd come over here to stay with me and he'd get sad and start crying and say he wished he had a mama, and he'd ask how good she was and what she was like, 'cause, see, he was no more 'n a year when she died, and he'd cry some more for wanting to see her, and how does a child know why his mama is gone? Ain't no good answer to that for a baby boy. And all of 'em, all her children, have asked me to tell how she was, what she looked like, her ways, 'cause they was young and they may have a little memory, but it's not strong, you know, not strong enough for them to bring it up, so I fills in those parts they don't know, and once a year or so we go to the grave site and puts flowers on her grave."

Meland's brother-in-law Eddie Jones, born in the Mississippi Delta, would go home that night to take a bath after work at the fertilizer factory so he would be clean when Juland came home. And when she did not come, he called out to Candlestick, he says, "but the phone was dead. And I got my brother-in-law to take me out there, but they wouldn't let me in. They say the car that hit her mashed her head in. That's how she died, from a mashed head. The Lord knows this, you can never know what's comin' to you. But it all comes with life."

IN THE DAYS TO COME the funeral processions would roll slowly along the old roads of South Jackson where the honey-suckle lay tangled in the ditches, the headlights of the cars dimmed by the bright sun that came with the clear weather that belied the skies of the Thursday before. On days like these it was hard to believe how death, without mercy and in such numbers, had come. On days like these, when the spring bloomed early in the raw heat and the land turned wild again and green, spring was a cruelty to witness, a mocking brightness that only burned the memory deeper.

PART II

GOING BACK

CHAPTER FOURTEEN

WINTER CHANGES A PLACE. So does the passing of thirty years. Going home, the more it's done, the more it can't be undone.

When I was a kid, winter in Mississippi was the time to hope for, not for others but for me. In winter things were peeled off, the leaves were gone, and there was no hiding how stark the landscape could be without them. The creek ran at a normal level, turned cold and clear, and sometimes there was a thin skin of ice along the edges. The humidity dropped, and the skies widened to an unthreatening blue. There were no tornadoes in winter. That is what I remember of winter, but I hear now that I am wrong, that tornadoes now come in any season. In a December tornado in 1992, six people died. There have been more since.

I saw the aftermath of the '92 tornado, driving up from the Florida panhandle, coming in on the southern route. I stopped for boiled peanuts at a country market. Up the road, along one side, a grove of pecan trees stood leaning at odd angles, their roots exposed, their trunks cracked, split and bowed like green wood. Back from an open field the foundation of a house still stood with lumber heaped around it. On the other side, nothing had been disturbed. I asked the woman who worked the counter what had happened.

"Tornado," she said. "It came in the middle of the night. I was asleep, thank God." She was quiet for a minute, thoughtful-looking, and then said, "Well, maybe not. Next time, if I need to, I hope I wake up."

"Why's that?" I asked, eyeing the quality of the peanuts as she dipped them from the boiling pot with a slotted spoon.

"Because a woman's baby was carried out into a field by that tornado. They haven't found it yet. They heard it once out there, but they don't know if it's still alive. You want to be awake when something like that happens. You want to be able to do something."

It had become almost a macabre cliché, the baby in the field, taken by the wind. I had heard it nearly a dozen times. For each tornado there seemed to be a baby in the field or a baby pulled into the sky from its mother's arms. Sometimes the baby survived; sometimes it did not. Sometimes the father found it, sometimes the mother or a stranger. One time the baby had a broken leg, another time just a scratch, or no scratch at all but its clothes were gone. And there were times the baby was gone forever. Often, though, the child lived because, the reasoning goes, babies are resilient, they bounce, they don't tense and brace for the worst the way adults do, and when they are taken for a ride, they trust. Or at the very least they do not mistrust. They have not been watching the skies, waiting. The stories are true, most of them. But there is an archetype at work here, too, the image of motherhood desanctified and at peril. And it is a disturbingly punishing nightmare, the child taken back from God himself.

And there are the ghost stories of those children taken, how in the field at night where the body was found you can hear a child crying, and the mothers keen to this sound, set up their own wailing as they stumble into the field, searching, and the cry comes from one direction and then the next. It fades out and then grows sharper, but it never becomes embodied, it does not show its face. Sometimes, they say, instead of the crying, there is a light in the field, a light nearly as bright as a clear-day noon reflecting off snow, a light that blinds if you stare too long. And sometimes there is just a faint green or blue light, loping along the horizon of the field. And at daybreak there is nothing.

"I hope they find the baby," I say to the woman as I balance the damp bag of hot peanuts on my palm. She nods at me quickly, her eyes lowering. Good words from a stranger are taken well, but better when I add the words, "I'll say a prayer." She smiles at me outright, then says, "God bless." I know the password here.

I drive on deep into a world populated by Job's children, who are, by brave acquiescence, God's also. They will tell me this time and again when I go to talk to them, to force the magnitude of my obsession into their lives that have grown quiet to some degree, changed in the thirty-year aftermath of war and loss. They will tell me that without faith they could not have held up and that even with faith their ranks have been cut.

JESUS SAVES. I pass a sign along the road, a white cross, the word "Jesus" written along the cross bar, the first "s" in "Jesus" the first "s" in the word "saves" that runs the length of the vertical beam. I wonder, idly, about false advertising. I think about people taking God to court. It is a silly thought, but it is something that occupies me in place of the fear of what I will come upon. Ghosts. Everyone from the old neighborhood grown up now. Some dead. Some missing. Some dissolute, unsavable. The glitter dream of Candlestick gone. I don't want to see any of it. The part of me that fears says this. The part of me that does not believes that there will be some beating heart of it left somewhere in all the tarnish and that I'll be able to recognize it, move toward it the way I would toward a maternal heartbeat, and then I understand that the two are the same, indistinguishable, and that I am going home to Mama. It's in the creek, I tell myself, back in the wild tangle of Caney Creek where we took our baptism in the flood those summers long ago. I make an agenda in my head: where to go, what to do, whom to see.

But now there is the drive through territory remembered in flashes, recognizable, it seems to me, on a genetic level, on the level of the red clay and the black dirt. "It's the dirt, girl," I hear Linda Flowers's slow, round melody of an accent defining what I have known, will always know, about this place: that it is the dirt that bore us up.

FOR THE FIRST PART of my trip, back in the winter of 2000, I had taken the train, moving away from the Iceland of New Hampshire, a place where birds scratch hieroglyphics in the snow, a place where the snow lingers when the yellow squash is already coming ripe in Mississippi, a place it is always good to leave because it can never be home. I was heading home.

It is good to take the train when the journey is important. Distance is a thing not to be obliterated then, but to be understood. The world and what defines it becomes mutable by degrees, by the miles that extend behind you like a contrail. On the way I could think of what it would be like to breathe the warm, low-lying air again, because even in winter it is distinguishable from ordinary air. Ronny Hannis's sister Sharon would say to me that even in winter you can smell the dirt and the grass that still wants to grow. In New Hampshire wood smoke is comforting only because you know it is salvation. In Mississippi things do not freeze and stay that way. They burn and twist and bind to familiar elements—to the iron in the dirt, to the metal in your blood.

One morning after the train had left the dark and crowded depot in Washington, D.C., I sat in the dining car across from a middle-aged man, black, dressed in a saffron-colored business shirt, a sweater vest and tie. The dining car was empty, but still the car attendant had put us together. I remember not wanting to talk, not wanting to wade through the usual train chat, not wanting to know or care where people were going, where they had come from, where they lived, if they had kids, what they thought of riding on the train. It got old after a while, just like the drunks in the smoking car.

But there was something about this man, an almost studied dignity. I say this not in retrospect, but knowing it as I knew it then, with peculiar certainty. There are people like that, those who do not give themselves away, who own the exclusive rights to a self-containment that is an order unto itself and that does not need to be fed and charged and preened by unnecessary contact.

I ate my eggs and bacon and grits. I looked out the window. The man did the same. I noticed his meticulous manners, the way he laid his knife carefully on the bread-and-butter plate, the way he slowly folded the napkin, creasing it to a point, before wiping his mouth, his posture erect and graceful. I worried that maybe I'd licked my plate without thinking.

I began to like sitting with this fellow. It was calming. And I began to think that I wanted to know about him. It is the reserve that does that, the self-composure that draws you toward a gravitational center, a place that flighty people understand, instinctively, is home base. You want to make that connection because it means something. You want to be on this guy's team.

So I asked, Where are you going? I added "Sir," because he commanded that.

"Home," he answered. The smile he gave was not impolite.

Fair enough. We were heading south. It could be one of three dozen places on the route. It could be none of them. He gazed out the window, implacable.

"Sir," I persisted, "and where is that?"

Maybe he liked me, maybe he decided I was worth his time and that I'd shown some respect for letting him eat in peace. He told me the Sea Islands, off Georgia, land that had belonged to his family for generations, land that had rightfully belonged to the Gullahs for years. He was trying to save his heritage, he said. I said something about that being a noble thing and told him of my interest in his homeland, how what had happened there was a crime.

The train rolled and jolted. He was quiet for a long time, and when he spoke it was really as if he were speaking to himself.

"It is very hard now to do things peacefully," he said. "I try, but it is still hard. It is passé now, you know? A joke. Martin always said, Do not resist. Do not let them get you angry because when you are angry you have no power."

I remember the sensation of my eyes opening wide as I watched him stare out the train window as he spoke, the Virginia countryside blurring beyond us. I remember trying to shift quietly in my seat so he would not notice, would not quit talking, but he did.

I waited a moment, watching him carefully, thinking, Does he mean *the* Martin, *the* doctor, *the* hero?

"Martin?" I asked, almost choking.

"Dr. King," he said, turning from the window and meeting my eyes evenly. "I was young. I went down to Mississippi for the protests. He came to talk to us. We worked with him. He taught us how to comport ourselves. I was beaten when they pulled us off the buses. I went to jail. But I didn't resist. I didn't get angry. If I had we wouldn't be having this conversation."

I watched the flesh rise up on my forearms in dark points, and it all came slamming back: those summers we had watched roll by from a distance great and incalculable, those bloody summers that seemed to have so little to do with us in white-bread South Jackson. In other parts of town, in other parts of the state, people had been murdered, and we had looked on feebly, dumbly. Still, I had come away with heroes.

Here was history, bound still to that time I had known in Mississippi, a man whose mentor had known better than all of us how to stare down danger and had taught this man when he was a boy how to move forward wearing this skin that was so dark now against the bright yellow shirt, yellow straight to black, like a tornado sky, and had taught him how to survive with it, how to get by, and the ways in which self-respect could be owned. The man had learned well, I could tell.

Shameless now, I asked his name, and as he told me, I drew in a breath. The recognition was immediate. I told myself I should have known. I told myself that when you go looking for ghosts, ghosts rise up.

He asked then what my business was, and I told him about Jackson, about the tornado, the people who had died that day, the place I'd used to live and why I was going back, so I would know, finally, what had healed and what had not.

"You know," he said, rising and extending his hand, "you have to remember, you have to talk about it. Those people who are gone now, they have a right to be remembered."

He took my hand then and held it for a long moment, and it mattered then that his hand had touched Dr. King's all those years ago and was now touching mine. I like to think that history burned on his palm. I like to think that it was scored deep, like a scar.

CHAPTER FIFTEEN

UP FROM GULFPORT, PAST WIGGINS, I take Highway 49.
When I was a child it was a coast untamed, dirty-looking gray
sand along the shore, the smell of salt and fish buoyed up by air
light as hydrogen, air that rose from the burning waters of the
gulf and rolled toward Jackson, air that looked innocent enough
and smelled like life, like the whole world being born over again
in a ripening rush of smells. There were no casinos on the Mississippi coast then. Shrimp boats plowed the waters, their nets
creaking at portside as they were lifted by men whose arms were
the color of boiled lobster claws. Along the pilings of the pier at
night, illuminated by flashlights held to draw the shrimp in
schools, seahorses would float, their prehistoric forms in rictus,
fossilized while still alive, their absurd snouts pointed like a
needlefish. This is the place from which the warm riot of air
blows across the baking land, seeking fearlessly a way to stabilize
itself, searching for the balancing act of the atmospheres, hot and
cold, Heaven and Hell.

When I was a kid I didn't think about it, how dangerous this air could be. But it made me uneasy the way it clung to my skin, settled heavy in my lungs, and the way the skies, purple going to black, out across the gulf, just made the air feel closer.

I remember the aftermath of Hurricane Audrey as we crossed the coastal line, moving from Louisiana, then up to Jackson. There had been tornadoes spawned on the whipping edges of the hurricane, but there had been, too, the unerring blast of the wind itself, and I had seen the dimensions of the word "aftermath," a word that says that what comes later is the real horror, a word that says that the calm after the storm is a negligible thing when what the wind has speared on trees begins to rot.

It is the smell I remember most clearly, salt and fish overlaid with the sick, sweet green of cattle flesh rotting in the heat. I could see them in the fields, their skins bloated to the point of rupture, legs tilted up at forty-five degrees where their blown-up bellies had put them at a cant. The sight might have been silly if it had not been what it was and if it had not carried that undeniable smell. Trees were denuded, and those that were not had caught everything from the pathetic cattle to laundry baskets to a lost wardrobe of clothes. One tree was hung with flannel plaids, prints, whites gone gray, and a shoe, a man's workboot, its steel toe pointing at the sky.

I think of the miles falling away as we traveled further north, how the busted ropes of barbed-wire fences and flattened clapboard shacks gave way to a place untouched outside Jackson, and I thought then that here was the safe place, the point at which the winds that scoured the coast had given up, retreated, spent themselves on a shore far from where we would live. And I think that if I had known the lie it was, what a hope misplaced, I might have run.

Past Hattiesburg and Prentiss, the rough edges of Mississippi unconcealed here in winter, the rusted roofs of barns red like the clay. Prentiss, where Juland and Meland had been born, where the family of sixteen children had learned what it was like to be born black in Mississippi. It might have seemed strange to someone else, given everything, that this is where they had wanted to be. They had tried Chicago but had moved back home. Often Juland had returned to this country dirt town. She and Meland had family here, friends, and Meland says that her sister loved the smell of the dirt. Through the open car window the smell rushes in, and I know there is a creek nearby because even in winter you can smell the catfish.

What had taken me away had been not fear but circumstance. I had been a kid, bound by the dictates of parents, and when I was grown I had left the parents far behind, but still I did not go back to what had been home. But I had dreamt about it, thought a thousand times of that day in March when I had not been there, removed from death by a matter of days. It ate at me sometimes. It left me wondering at the oracle of fate, when it shows itself and for whom. I was afraid now of what I would see, the fear that never bound itself to this place full in me now.

Sure, it had changed. Equations of time and space allow for variables, for damage done, for points relocated or removed entirely. But there are constants that, even though they may erode, still retain the ghost.

Highway 80, the dividing line between north and south Jackson, is still the same run of restaurants and car dealerships and broken-down hotels. A place called the Brown Derby in the shape of a hat. A place called Creschel's that made the original kumbach salad dressing, a good old Mississippi steak joint where the welcoming grin of the owner is a thing you step back from instinctively.

There's a restaurant in Jackson now that wouldn't have had a chance in the '60s, Miss Perry's Soul Food Restaurant, owned by the flamboyant—and black—Miss Perry, a woman with three-inch fingernails painted gold and an ambition with its sights on Hollywood. She can cook. Chitlins, fried okra, pork rinds, greens, ham hocks, sausage, catfish, corn bread, sweet tea, all the food laid out in stainless-steel bins under heat lamps. A big open room filled with tables, and a partitioned-off area for special events.

I stopped at Miss Perry's on the way into town, dazzled by the strobe of the neon sign and the promise of the food. I could smell it even from a distance, the dark, rich aromas from the wide-open windows of a too-hot kitchen seeding the already ripe air.

It was a Sunday and the place was filled with the after-church crowd, every single one of them black but me. They looked at me when I walked in, just once, a glance, in turn, mild curiosity, nothing hostile. Miss Perry beamed from the region of the cash register, waved her castanet claws. She has a good reputation in Jackson. Her reputation had preceded her, so I knew she was the one and only.

The mild scrutiny rattled me because it was a vague hint of what it might have been like to have been a minority in Jackson, way back when. For people to stare at you, such an inconsequential thing. But to see a sign outside that states NO COLOREDS ALLOWED is different. I remembered the signs. WHITES ONLY. The segregated drinking fountains, movie theaters, restaurants, churches, ad infinitum. The fact that we as children in Jackson were often taught that the mouth of a black person was a dirty thing. But apparently their hands were clean, because they cooked for us. And now Miss Perry cooked for her own kind, but she didn't keep you out because you were white. There's the rub.

I ate my food alone in the big room, picking up the fried okra like popcorn, remembering the distinct smell of it cooking, and how you could tell in South Jackson when you stood at the back door of a friend's house if the family was having okra for supper. It is an almost sweet smell, not quite ripe, with a little dirt thrown in. I looked at the dark faces around me, at the bright spray of Sunday clothes, prints and yellows and reds and purples, at the big hats the women wore, the jewelry gleaming at their throats, their wrists, their ankles. They were a wash of color and reflected light, and sometimes when they laughed you could catch a flash of gold. Their talk was loud and familiar, and I remembered an old wish of mine, one absurd in its naïveté, its blindness to fact and treachery. I had wanted to be a black girl. It had seemed the most rooted, tethered thing to be, a black girl in a big family that laughed all the time, the assurance of comfort and identity in a clan so huge that you would never be lonely. It was foolishness, a child's unknowing, but here, once again, I felt that inexplicable pull. I wished I were friends with these people, that I could sit at their table, understand what it was like to have formed your own legion so impermeable that no white-skinned girl could ever get in.

In the restroom three elderly black women stood waiting for an open stall. One held a gold-tipped cane carved in the shape of a snake. It was an impressive carving, twisted, but still holding a vertical plane from point to point. I caught her eye and smiled at her. She returned the smile, hers nearly toothless, the bright pink of her tongue filling her mouth. I must have smiled too eagerly, looked a little too needy. The woman looked back at me, studied my dark (for a white girl) arms that paled next to hers. I could tell from listening to the women that they had just come from a funeral.

"Lord bless us today!" the woman with the cane called out. She fairly shouted it, and then again, "Lord bless us today," this directed at the whole of the tiny restroom, but she smiled at me again as she said it and openly looked me up and down before she spoke.

"And what is troublin' you, child?" The question struck me dumb for a moment. I had forgotten the straightforward way here that could blindside you. "Say? What on you mind?" She said it in that open, no-nonsense, "tell Mama" way that older black women sometimes have, with a vast eagerness to get to the point and not waste time on small talk. I thought about what she had asked, what *was* troubling me. Meeting up with haints, getting in too deep where I no longer belonged. Leveraging the past from someone who had laid it over in mortar, asking the wrong question that would bring the pain on fresh again. I felt out of place and out of time and out of luck. And I was homesick.

"I'm homesick," I told her when the list that ran through my head had stopped at the one that was true. "Homesick."

"Well, then, you better get on back home." She said it kindly.

"No," I said. "I'm homesick for *here*. I moved away. *Here* was home."

She was quiet now and nodded her head, looking from my eyes to my mouth, back to my eyes. I supposed they told her something, some tattoo on my soul showing in them.

"Ahhh, then," she finally said, "I sees now. You done ripped your roots up right at the root hairs, has you? Well then, come on back. Come on back home, baby child."

And I had forgotten, too, how they will call you "baby" here, and how you feel younger and vaguely adored just for hearing it. And I had forgotten how they could drive right to what was cutting your heart, hold it out there so you could see it and quit denying that it could be dressed up and called anything else but what it was, and then offer up a solution you could not refute. "Well, then, come on back." Why not?

"Maybe I should," I said, still trying to be polite, to act as if I were talking to someone else in some other place, and not here toe-on-toe with a black snake charmer who suddenly knew my heart.

"No maybes when you knows, child. You knows, don't you?" She looked me dead-on now, and when I looked down she raised up the tip of her cane and pushed my chin up. "Say? You knows."

She had got me beat. I thought about backing out the door and running, but if I did I might as well run all the way back to New Hampshire. The thought sickened me.

"I will then." I said it so forcefully that I think she half believed me.

Suddenly, for no good reason, I wanted to go to church. With this woman.

"Can I ask you something?" I said, the question urgent in me.

She gave up her turn at the bathroom to hear me out.

"How would people feel, I mean honestly, if I came to your church? I mean, a black church. How would they feel?"

She laughed out loud now, the cavern of her mouth making a whistling sound where the teeth used to be. And then she caught herself, realizing I was serious, that it meant something to me.

"Well, I ain't sayin' you could *pass*, child, but that ain't the point now, is it? What do *you* think? You tell me. You think we'd slam the door in your face, or do you think we'd shout out 'Praise the Lord, here come the white sheep, make way for the Lamb'? Hmmm?" She had me smiling. "Now, you *knows* it'd be all right. All God's children is perzactly that, God's children, ain't no difference in my eyes. We welcome you, you knows it. Didn't even need to ask, but it fine all right you did."

I asked for the name of her church, and she gave it to me. I said I'd come by for the Wednesday prayer meeting.

"What brought you back, baby?" she asked. "Family? You got family here still?"

I told her what had brought me back, why it had brought me back. I told her about the dead and Juland being the only black person killed in Jackson. The woman's friends were waiting outside for her now. We had the restroom to ourselves.

She remembered the tornado, although she hadn't been living in Jackson then but further south in a smaller town, but she knew of it just as everyone in Jackson did.

"Just remember this," she told me, rubbing her palm on the worn head of the cane and tapping it several times, more forcefully each time. "If you never remember nothin', just remember this. God had his reasons. Ain't always apparent to us 'cause, see, we's feeble-minded when it comes to the mind and the will of the Lord. We can't claim to know, now can we, what his aim is. But know this, baby, they was a reason. Nothin' happen by God's hand they ain't a reason. Praise the Lord!" She held the cane up like a scepter.

She hugged me then, and I could smell the talcum powder on

her neck. She told me I must be a willful child to be digging up the past, but that *God would forgive me* because he forgave youth their trespasses. I told her how old I was, expecting to shock her. She just laughed and lifted her heavy hips, leaning down hard on the cane, and took her turn in the stall. I called out "God bless you" to her and slipped through the door. It was getting to be a habit.

CHAPTER SIXTEEN

JACKSON IS A DIXIE TOWN but laid out along Thomas Jefferson's city plan, the line of public buildings broken by wide, shaded parks, a grid of greenery and brick, the sense one of toil flanked by respite. Some would say it is the scab left when the wound healed over and that in a sense it is still the Chimneyville of old, never having fully recovered from the ravages of Sherman's troops. And in a way, it is still the ancient Choctaw village of the 1500s, rough along the riverbank before the Spaniards came.

I remember it only from childhood, a field trip destination to the Old Capitol Building, which had been completed in 1840, only to be burned twenty years later. There we would peer through the plate-glass display windows at the arrowheads and jewelry made of rock and bone, and the woodland scenes of stuffed deer and Indian maidens bent low over a cook fire. No matter how many times, no matter in what year we rode the yellow school bus to the old building, the deer still stood transfixed, the squaw still seared a rabbit haunch.

And there were the Saturday trips with family to downtown, where you could still shop for clothes at the Emporium and have lunch at the old Mayflower diner. The shops are gone now, a small business district having risen in their place. Malls gird the outskirts of the city. No one dresses up now to be seen on a Saturday down here.

For a state capital it is not much to brag on, but in its very decay history still hangs tenuously. There is the governor's mansion, a place of columned splendor we as kids gazed upon wide-eyed, imagining the opulence beyond the iron gates. There are the Old Capitol Building and the New Capitol Building, several marginal hotels, the Farish Street District, the historic black part of town in the tedious process of restoration. From the top floor of the tallest buildings there is a cow-town view of a rusting grain silo on the edge of the city where the railroad tracks rise over the still rutted streets, and beyond the silo the deep woods and tributaries of South Jackson.

The train depot is a gutted, dark place where elderly women pull heavy suitcases up steep flights of stairs to the platform. Across the road from the depot a turn-of-the-twentieth-century building falls closer to rubble each day, a sagging structure that with the Midas touch of restoration would be a thing of beauty. But there are priorities here, and things do not move quickly in Jackson, but at the slow-drumbeat pace of the heat. The windows are busted, the doors are boarded up, and transients crawl into and out of the razor-edged windows. On Terry Road, which leads from the center of the small city toward South Jackson, prostitutes walk bedraggled and sullen along this strip where the houses are still clapboard, shotgun runs with narrow front porches and cinder-block foundations. It is a messy, dirty, forgotten-looking place not far from where the few nice office buildings end.

The Walthall Hotel is the best there is in Jackson, at the strangled heart of town, two blocks from the Old Capitol, and it is a place that pretends to the gentility of the past. Out front a fancy awning with the hotel's name in gold script shades a small patch of sidewalk, but there is no doorman. There is a porter, an unctuously drawling, badly aging former fireman who quotes the Bible while trying awkwardly to fondle the rare female guest who appears alone and unguarded. In the lobby portraits of hunting dogs hang. There is a piano, an open dining area, a bar, all in a sweep of mahogany and pale chandeliered light.

I am staying at the Walthall for a reason. Those I had talked to had told me not to stay in South Jackson, they said it wasn't safe anymore. They said not to stay at an isolated looking hotel on Terry Road, that there was too much crime there now. For a time I heeded the warning, imagining myself stranded in occupied territory, a place I had once known intimately that had now become a place of incalculable risk. I thought of the irony of this and of the risk, disguised, that had grown beyond volume as that hour in March had neared.

I WOKE THE NEXT MORNING in the Walthall to the tornado siren that is tested the first of every month. At the sound of the siren I ran to the window, yanked back the drapes, and stared hard at the sky. It was clear. On that side. I ran from the room and found the outdoor walkway that connects to the other side of the building and stood leaning over the eighth-floor balcony, scanning the skies to the southwest. They, too, were clear, a robin's-egg blue Mississippi winter sky that paled to white along the horizon. For a long time the siren sounded, an air-raid screech, I imagine, although I am not old enough to make that connection. I make the tornado connection and, instead of diving beneath the bed, run instead to the window. It seemed a foolish thing to do, but you have to know.

There were no sirens when I was a girl. There were no sirens for Candlestick except for those that came after. Still, I know why this one wailed, either a test or the real thing. The real thing could come again someday, hit downtown Jackson the way it did before. I wondered about Linda Flowers across town, what she was thinking, the Hannis family, Mary Hudgins, and if they had even heard it. I wondered if Larry Swales, on his way to meet me now, had checked the sky, too.

I REMEMBER LARRY SWALES. He does not remember me. I was younger than he, just a minion then in the barely pubescent Dog 'n' Suds brat squad, the little girls who didn't know they were still little girls, who squawked and hyperventilated over pictures of Fabian and did pretty much the same in the presence of Larry Swales. By simple virtue of the fact that he was an older boy, a high school senior, he had been, without having to do anything to prove it, possessed of a godlike mystique that kept us up late on weekends at slumber parties while we mooned over Larry's picture in the annual, talking idiotically about marrying him, what it would be like, we who were intimate strangers to intimacy and romance, the scorned of the scorning older crowd, boppers with no marketable bop yet to our walk, no tits, no curves, no luck with boys who made us keen, save for here in these sleeping bag–heaped bedrooms, in our fantasies.

Marrying Larry Swales was a thing to strive for, the one thing that might possibly be attainable in our chubby little lives if we were to cut back on Twinkies, exercise, and get a whole hell of a lot older. Then, maybe. We wanted a good Christian boy with a little bad in him. That is what we imagined Larry Swales to be.

Then the tornado came, and even I, far away in the hollows of Tennessee, heard the news of heroism, who among us had died and who had summoned courage from the strength of youth. You could never look at people the same way again once you knew what they had seen that day, once you knew in what capacity he or she had acted and on whose behalf. Tragedy, we perceived, made men of boys overnight, scored deep the hearts of young girls and prepared them for each tragedy that would follow. Larry Swales had been the object of our childish desire. Now he was the object of our respect. But more than that, having been there, having been wounded in war and living on, trying to save the others, staring at the gore, moving to entrap it, cut it off, staunch it, he now knew things that we did not. He knew about death. Would it have marked his eyes? Would it show?

It is what I thought about as I waited in an upstairs lobby for Larry Swales, who was taking time away from work to come see me, to talk about that day, because it had been his eyes that had drawn us all first, long-lashed and wide, startling green eyes with a little wickedness in them, or so we imagined.

His eyes were the same. I looked at them directly as he walked toward me, extending his hand, a tall, lanky, Dennis Weaver sort of man, dressed in good jeans and a good plaid shirt with an easy confidence about him, the sort that people have when they are tall and have the eyes of a cat.

And I stared on at our pajama-party dreamboat, feeling silly the way you feel silly when you see the kids grown up who were thirteen the last time you saw them and you expect them to be kids still and find instead the outsized bodies of the child ghosts, expecting the voices to match the voices of decades past, and when they speak with deepness and maturity, it scares you. But Larry Swales's voice had not changed. There was still the boy in him.

When he speaks it is with a voice young and eager and fast-talking, the soft, steel-guitar twang of Mississippi in it, a voice that never trips over words but races ahead of them, taking a blind curve at full tilt, rarely putting on the brakes. It is the sort of quick talk that makes you wonder how people think that fast, until you understand how familiar the territory is that they describe.

I ask Larry Swales to please tell it as it was, to go anyplace he wants to go. We sit in the upstairs lobby on round-backed chairs that flank a floor-standing ashtray with fresh sand in it. The hallways are empty and it is quiet except for the neon-bright Coke machine that hums and shudders.

"I was there," he says, looking at me intensely, his gaze, it seems, already half in the present, half in the past. "It was Friday the thirteenth at four thirty-three in the afternoon."

History rewritten, undone, re-formed. Friday the thirteenth. The day all bad things happen. The day you should never walk under ladders, spill salt, take someone's name in vain. A day of curses and witchcraft and evil. What other day could it have been?

I correct Larry gently, tell him that a lot of people remember the day as Friday the thirteenth, that it is understandable why they do. I tell him it was the third, a Thursday, and he looks at me quizzically, as if something small has been punctured in him. "Positive," I tell him, watching those eyes. I can see the mark in them now. It is beginning to show, that place carved out that holds that one day separate from all the rest.

"Okay," he says somewhat reluctantly. I show him a newspaper clipping with the right date. He looks at it as if it were counterfeit.

"But the time," I tell him. "You're dead-on about the time."

I regret the description immediately, the word "dead." He winces almost imperceptibly.

"It was four thirty-three in the afternoon," he says. "No one misses that."

I ask how he knows the exact time, and he says he does not remember, but that he has always known that was the time just as he has always known the date.

I smile, and he smiles back. I ask him again just to start where he remembers and go from there, that no detail is too small, nothing that comes to mind too ridiculous.

"Okay, then," he says, his upper body agile-looking and long-muscled, tensing now as if he is standing on a mark, ready to sprint. For a moment I see the boy in him, the yearbook photo taken before he had to pull a dead man's body from the wreckage. He is still full of life, hopeful. Even before he begins to talk for two hours straight, I like him naturally without having to work at it.

"I was there. I was a senior in high school, so I was about seventeen. I remember the day it happened. I had taken my mom's car to school, 'cause back then, you remember, the only time you ever got to take the car to school was if you were a senior and you took your mom's car, you know?"

He smiles at this recollection, at being so young he would have to ask permission to drive his mother's car.

"And, see, on that Friday, I mean Thursday, like you said, I had taken her car to school that day, and you know, it was a privilege to do that, a real privilege, and my buddy who was in the tornado with me, who lives in Austin, Texas now—Larry Temple—yeah, Larry and I were good friends and still are, and he and I went down—he worked in a little convenience store there, Polk's grocery, in front as a car hop, you know, the person who takes the little ol' bag of groceries out to the car, and I worked at the grocery store, at Liberty. So what we did, I went down there and was going to pick up my sister a Coke. When I got there, Larry found out he had to work, and I went on home to take her her Coke. I was goin' back to pick him up—he was just goin' to work a little while till the other guy showed up—and lo and behold, when I was leaving my house and walking out the front door my boss called and said he needed me to come to work. And I bagged groceries there at the Liberty. That was Mr. Webb Jones."

Larry Swales stops his rush of words momentarily and looks up at me and asks, "Is he still livin'? Mr. Webb Jones?"

I wonder quickly at the sudden power Larry Swales has bestowed on me, that I might know what has become of all the bygone people of South Jackson. But it just so happens that I do. I tell him that the last I heard Mr. Jones was still alive, still listed in the phone book.

"Anyway, when Mr. Webb Jones called and said for me to come to work, I took my mom's car down there, parked it, went to work, and I hadn't bagged but one bag of groceries, and I went to take them out to the car, and there happened to be a lady sittin' in the parkin' lot out there that was my next-door neighbor, and she said to me, kindly agitated, 'If you see my children, will you tell them to come on? I'm waiting on 'em.' Well, her two daughters were in the grocery store shopping, and then this guy come runnin' down the sidewalk, little guy, a kid, and I know his name, too, and I'll tell you when I think of it. This boy come runnin', and he was hollerin' a tornado was comin', course, crazy me, I'd always read about 'em, and saw them, you know, on the TV, and all this kind of thing, but I never pictured it in real life. I never imagined seeing it like that. You never do. So I ran down to the end of the grocery store—well, you started at the grocery store, by the field, and went all the way up to Cooper Road, the stores in a line all the way up to Cooper Road—and I looked, and sure enough there was one great big ol' tornado, I mean *big*, and a little bitty one, there might have been two little ones, I can't remember, but I saw the tornado so I ran back inside and started to hollerin' and screamin' and tellin' everybody a tornado was comin'."

He stops for a minute to think, the look in his eyes faraway and focused.

"There *were* two," he says, "two little tornadoes besides the big one, and they were, like, followin' it, and it was like they were behind it, then beside it. I mean, I just ran down and I saw it—them—and it wadn't far, wadn't far, not far at all, right on us almost, I mean at that point just behind us, comin' our way, smack dab our way, on a line for us, just behind the grocery store, comin' out of the west, southwest, yeah, like they all do, from Forest Hill, 'cause I had just left school and came home and that was where it was comin' from. So I ran inside and I just started screamin' and tellin' everybody it was comin'. Well, nobody knew what to do. How would we know? So we just started . . ."

Larry trails off here and does not pick up the thread right away. His eyes begin to tear up, and he looks away for a minute toward the Coke machine in the lobby.

"Ronny Hannis," he says slowly, and I sit up straight because every time I hear the name it is as if someone is speaking a benediction.

He tries again, the words choked. "Ronny Hannis . . . Ronny Hannis and I were real good friends, real good, and Ronny was over at the Dog 'n' Suds. He got killed over there. You knew that? He got killed, and he was supposed to come to work, too. He worked as a cashier and everybody was crazy about him, and we all knew each other. We were buddies."

I hear the last words as an understatement. I suspect the boys could have been friends for life.

"So we just—Ronnie Clark and I—just started pushin' people down up under the counters and everything, and people just scattered and screamed. All that screaming. And if you remember then, your advertisements on your windows in the stores were about as big as that wall right there."

He indicates an expanse of beige wall beside the Coke machine, about eight by seven feet.

"You had big ol' plate-glass windows, you remember them? You put all your advertisements on the windows, and as we were doin' that, shovin' people down, Ronnie Clark turned around and hollered at me, and in that instant I turned around and looked at him, and he screamed, "Help me!" I could not believe what I saw. I just could not believe it. It was like out of a movie. He was holdin' on to a door handle with both hands, holdin' on for life, and the wind was just whippin' him in the air like this."

Larry Swales holds a hand up, lets it go limp at the wrist, and snaps it back and forth frantically.

"It was at that time," he says, "when Ronnie was holdin' on to the door, that the tornado hit the buildin'. And it of course pulled a vacuum on the building, and the door that Ronnie was holding on to slammed shut like you wouldn't believe, and that's when everything came falling in and flying off, and that big ol' plate-glass window with the advertisements is what got me. It came, sucked right out of its frame, and hit me square in the back and drove me ta all the way to the back of the meat counter, which was *all* the way in the back, in other words straight down the aisle on my hands, and I slammed into the meat counter and stopped.

"I got back up, I don't know how, and I crawled as fast as I could back up front, got up under the counter, knowin' it was screwed down, hopin' it was, and I just sat there dazed and watched it take out parts of the roof and then all the cars in the parking lot, I mean, *all* the cars. You could see them being picked up through where the window had been, and I heard people screamin', they just kept on screamin' the whole time. It seemed like it lasted a long, long time, and it probably lasted only a matter of seconds, and then once it was over those of us who *could*, got up, and the first person I saw was the kids of the lady who asked me to tell her children to come on, and it was Carol and her little sister—I can't remember her name—and her thumb was just barely, just *barely*, hangin' on there, this little kid, so I took my apron off—we wore white aprons then, like a butcher's apron— and I just wrapped her hand up real, real good, and I said, "You go out there, and you find your mama." And we took a bunch of 'em, whoever seemed hurt worse, and we ran 'em all up to the front, to Cooper Road, and we flagged a guy down that had a pickup truck with a camper top, and we just started piling people up in it, and we sent him on his way, wadn't nothin' else we could do but find help wherever help was, you know? After a time the emergency personnel started showin' up, and we had one lady who was workin' the grocery store, she was pregnant, and she was just hurt real bad. I mean, she was, I think, real real close, and we got her out of there, Ronnie Clark and I did, and got her up to the street."

Swales is crying softly now. He stops for a minute to brush the water from his eyes, takes a deep breath, and looks at his long fingers locked together in his lap. He is no longer sitting ramrod straight, looking eager and hopeful. The weight of what he is remembering has slumped him in his chair, taken some of the color from his face. I tell him to take his time, that there is no hurry, and he looks at me as if perhaps I am insane, not in an unkind way, but as if by my suggestion to slow down there might be some vague hope that none of it is true, and that by letting the words come less quickly some other reality will be revealed, and he knows there won't be, and I figure that is why he is looking at me this way.

"Okay," he says. "Take my time?" I nod. "It just comes in this big rush." He takes a breath again and starts out more slowly, but only for a sentence or two, and then he is off again, and I imagine that this is the sound of the locomotive they talk about, what it does to the words that come in a fury when the time comes to tell the memory.

"And then I spent the rest of my time lookin' for people, pullin' up debris and tryin' to find everybody—anybody. I was hurt, but I wasn't hurt that I was physically impaired too bad. I just had a lot of cuts in my—"

He reaches for the back of his head, behind his ear, draws his hand down along his shoulder.

"I realized that night," he continues, "after I finally got to the hospital—I probably was the last one to go to the hospital, 'cause I was just more interested in tryin' to help those than I was . . ."

Larry Swales trails off again, forgetting to tell about himself, his injuries, what they did to him at the hospital. He seems almost embarrassed to have mentioned that he was hurt.

"Like I say, we made sure everybody in the grocery store was taken care of, got the ones that were hurt, got them out. We got 'em all up to the sidewalks and up to Cooper and had 'em stationed there for people comin' by, and ambulances and everything else, whoever with a car or a truck came by who could take somebody to a hospital, they did. And then we started goin' through the barbershop, and then we went through that little race car track, and then we started pullin' people out of those places. I mean, the debris was just actually like you picked it up and broke it all up like a cracker and just crumbled it back down. Just like a cracker busted up, except it was concrete and wood and glass and steel, all piled on top of people, pinnin' 'em down. And you could hear people moanin' and groanin', and we dug a guy out of one of those debris piles, we dug him out and several other people, and we just kept doin' that, over and over, and workin' until a lot of the personnel started showin' up, a lot of the emergency folks."

For a moment Larry's eyes smile a little, and he begins to shake his head.

"I will never forget," he continues. "My daddy had gone to pick my mama up 'cause I had her car, and she worked downtown in the Standard Life Building."

The Standard Life Building was the tallest building in Jackson in 1966. From the top floor that afternoon people could see the dark cloud over South Jackson, and then the power went out, the elevators stopped, and they hurried down the stairs to find out the news.

"See," Larry says, "my daddy didn't tell her. He didn't tell her I was down there workin', so he drove all the way back down home, and she said to him, 'Well, wadn't that terrible, the tornado that hit Candlestick,' and then she said to my daddy, 'I'm sure glad Larry didn't have to go to work.' And so here they come drivin' home, my mama and daddy, and he didn't take the exit for home then, and she said to him, 'Where you goin'?' and he said to her, 'I'm goin' down there to Candlestick 'cause that's where your son is.' I remember turnin' around and seein' her runnin' toward me and screamin' and hollerin', and I said, 'Good gracious, Mom, I'm all right. Back up, now.'"

He smiles at this image, his mother hysterical that he is alive and how he tells her to "back up."

"But anyway, she came, and it was a horrible sight for her to see, but I convinced her that I was okay and that I wanted to stay and help. She knew it was important. I was wearing brand-new white Levi's—remember those?—a brand-new madras parka— you remember madras?—and it just tore all those up, I mean, just tore 'em up."

I tell Larry that everyone I have talked to remembers what he or she was wearing that day, and when he says, 'Wonder why that is?' I tell him my theory, just a blind guess, that you remember because that's all there was between you and the wind and the missiles it carried. And he says, no, he thinks it might be something else, at least for him, that it is because he was a teenager and "clothes were your badge then, especially brand-new clothes that you felt good in, and to see them all ripped up and torn and blood on 'em, well, it makes you wonder how important they were to begin with."

He looks at his clean new jeans, presses his palms along the crease in them, and smiles at me.

"Sometime that night," he says, "I know that it was *dark* dark by then, after we felt like we got everybody out—we'd form lines, you know, pullin' stuff out, handing it along to the next fella, just pickin' through people and everything—yeah, it was way dark by then, and then I'd heard a lot of my friends were . . ."

He falters again as the tears come on more quickly now, the memory pricking him, showing him through the little capillary-sized holes it makes that the fear that some of his friends were dead was real, and the hurt from that is a slow draw. It is not gone now. It won't ever be gone.

"I'd heard some of my friends had, you know, gotten hurt seriously, just odds and ends I'd heard from people who'd been at the shoppin' center, so it was hard to know then, but it was at the back of your mind, while you worked gettin' people out. And we found that woman over there at the Dog 'n' Suds, I guess she'd gotten decapitated, if I remember correctly. I didn't know her. I just knew she worked there, 'cause we all went over there to eat, a lot of times, when we worked the grocery store and everything."

It is Juland Jones that Larry Swales remembers, and as the memory comes on strong he begins to shake his head slowly. The sad and tragic decapitation of Juland has become a thing of mythic proportions now, and even those who were not there speak of it with reverence and dark fascination.

"There was so much confusion," Larry says of the desperate digging through the ruins. "I finally made it to the hospital that night. They, the people I was workin' alongside, said you got to go, you need to get checked out, so I went on to the hospital.

Somebody took me up there. They got me in the emergency room and one of the doctors finally came in, and he started findin' there were cuts all over. There were cuts in my ears, and there were cuts in my back where the glass hit me and where I slid, and I was bloody all over from these cuts. I may have had some stitches in my ear or somewhere back there, and then I walked out of there and I went upstairs to visit people who'd been hurt. My friend Larry Temple got a Coke bottle through his leg. I thought he was dead. I'd gotten word that he was dead, and he'd gotten word that I was dead, and then I found out that he had a bottle in his leg and that he was alive."

But for a while at least they did not think Larry Temple was alive, the irrepressible boy I remember from fourth grade, blond, skinny, silly. He was on a gurney in the hospital corridor, and he'd been covered with a sheet. When he came to, he understood what had happened, that they believed he was dead, and he started screaming, "Let me out of here. I'm not dead. Let me out of here!"

"I went on up there to visit all of them," Larry says, leaning back in the chair now, his forearms balanced on the armrests, "the people waiting to hear, and the people they'd let you see. I mean, the hospital rooms were literally full of people—it was Hinds General Hospital—so I stayed up there for a little while, you know, to give moral support, and when I hit the stairs downstairs, when I was comin' up the elevator there was a bunch of news cameras and folks there, and they came at me to talk, and I told them no, I didn't want to talk to them at that time, and I left and went upstairs, and then when I came back down, they were still waiting on me, so I did an interview with somebody. I know the next morning my girlfriend, who is now my wife, her mother and everyone, they lived down the street, and they were watchin' TV and she come in there and she said, 'Idn't that Larry right there?' I had a big bandage on my ear, and I guess that made it a little difficult to recognize me, but she was sure and she said, 'Yeah, that's him, I'm sure that's him!'"

There were a lot of kids I had known in South Jackson who had married their sweethearts, some of them together since they were in junior high. Larry Swales smiles when he mentions the girlfriend who became his wife.

"Then I started to get mail. I got mail from people all over the world, just sacks of mail, sacks and sacks of mail, just, you know, a lot of 'we're glad you made it,' and people from New York and all these other places. I remember just sacks and sacks of mail. Anyway, I saved all of it, but my mother, she had a big cleanin' up one day and threw all of it away."

The silence, abrupt, comes on him again, and Larry Swales is not thinking about the sacks of mail anymore, about his brief celebrityhood in the wake of a tragedy.

"The bodies, the people," he begins again, "most of them, you know, they were piled . . . they were up under all this rubble. We found [a man] . . . he was just . . . he had a lot of abrasions all over, like someone had beat him up, probably his back was broken. He was just kinda doubled over. And he just . . . well, that was the kinda things we found. A lot of people were hit with flying debris, like that guy that was in the beauty salon there, Mr. Dorwin. I remember he had a huge gash down his back, from glass cutting him open, but people in the grocery store, some of them walked out, but a lot of 'em were just trapped up under there and probably never had a chance, because, you know, it took—well, it left two buildings on the end, parts of them, and took each one in the middle, and the Dog 'n' Suds. It just picked that up and just crushed it all up and piled it back down, and that's where most of your deaths occurred, right through there. Most of Liberty was still standing, the roof gone, the glass out."

Larry Swales uses the standing ashtray that sits between us as a drawing board now. He moves aside a cigarette butt and begins to rake the sand with his fingers, showing me the way the stores were lined up and where the tornado came through. It is the clearest picture anyone has given me of where it hit.

"This is the shopping center," he says, and draws a straight line in the sand. "And here's the Shell station on the corner, and here's Cooper Road, and all this right here is the shopping center. It's just a little ol' strip shopping center, what we had then, you know. We thought it was such a fine thing. Now there are malls, huge malls, and little ol' Candlestick would seem like nothin', wouldn't it?"

I tell him I know what he means. I tell him about the excitement we all felt when the stores went in, how modern and well heeled it seemed to make us.

He shows in the sand where the Dog 'n' Suds stood, right out from the middle of Candlestick, across the parking lot.

"And it came right through here just like that."

With the palm of his hand Larry erases the lines in the sand with a deliberate shove, and Candlestick is gone but for two partial lines left on the periphery.

"Just like that," he says again. I watch a sheen of perspiration bloom on his forehead. We both stare foolishly at the now-smooth sand with two small furrows left on either end.

"It just wiped right between both of 'em and took parts of Liberty here on the corner, 'cause we were all right here in the front, but everything between here and here," he says, pointing to the small indentations left in the sand, "was just picked up in a mighty way, wadded up and thrown back to the ground. Course all the cars, and my mom's car was one of 'em, was just totally destroyed, and then of course that little Dog 'n' Suds was here where Ronny was, and it killed him there."

We are back again to Ronny Hannis, and I understand for the first time that the story of this tornado revolves, in the ghostly image of its afterspin, around the memory of the hero in this boy, and that his distinction came early and unbidden.

Larry Swales, too, says that Ronny rose from the crush of rubble, wounds gaping, and walked forth. His voice is choked, and he casts his eyes down when he talks of his friend.

"I never saw Ronny after that—after the storm hit—I never saw him prior to the storm that very day, but they say he walked.

They say that he helped. I'm sure he did. Ronny was a very caring person, a good guy, real, real, real good guy, God didn't make 'em any better, and I'm *sure* he helped, even though he was hurt, I'm sure of it. I don't really know what happened. I'd be scared to say how he died. But I know he helped. That was just like Ronny, to put himself aside for someone else."

We are both quiet for a minute, thinking of Ronny, of the grin on his face that is in almost every picture of him that survives. It is an engaging smile. A real smile. Larry Swales looks up at me and smiles in a similar way, tears in his eyes, and for a moment we are both haunted, but in a good way.

The noise is something he remembers now, the enormity of it. The noise and the time it hit, and how it is an anniversary for both him and Larry Temple, survivors of that day, friends for more than thirty years.

"Larry Temple and I always call each other, no matter where we are, on that day, at four thirty-three, and we say, 'Happy anniversary,' but we don't mean it that way, like it's happy. We can't forget. And I can't forget the noise. That you remember. It was tremendous, the noise was tremendous. I think I told them that night on one of the news channels that it sounded like a thousand freight trains, like a grinder grinding everything up. It was so noisy that when the thing hit and the vacuum was so heavy and the noise was so loud, I just grabbed my ears because it made them hurt. I covered them up, and when that plate glass hit me in the back it was just like I was a piece of paper. Your emotions are so high at that point, and you're scared slap to death, and you don't have time to say a whole lot. I said a few things, 'Oh, my God,' and when it was over with it was so quiet. When you walked out of there, it was so quiet it was like you could hear a pin drop real quick, and then all of a sudden you could hear the moaning. It was real quiet and calm before it hit. I know now what I need to be lookin' for if it happens again. If it gets real quiet, just kinda calm and balmy-feeling. I just kinda feel like that was the whole setting of the day, right before it hit, you almost knew something bad was gonna happen, it was like, *This is what it's gonna be.*"

The sun is coming in through the lobby window at a slant now, and a maid appears and begins to vacuum the hall. We try to ignore the noise, but it is somehow appropriate. Larry slaps his knee hard, remembering something.

"That red-haired boy? Charles! That was his name. Charles. I've called his name a hundred times. He lived right across the street over there, that was him, yeah, yeah, yeah, little redheaded boy, that's him. He was the one come runnin' down the sidewalk, a-hollerin', 'There's a tornado comin', there's a tornado comin'!' and I remember looking at him and saying, 'Yeah, right.' And he screamed it was comin' from that direction over there, and I looked, and the boy was right."

We talk for a minute about what a know-it-all the little red-haired boy was, how if there were one person who would be the one to scream "Tornado!" it would be him. I tell Larry Swales that I once hit the kid in the face with a toy truck and bloodied his eye, and he laughs and says the boy probably deserved it.

The sunlight has spilled out onto the lobby carpet now, long sodium-lit afternoon rays that make me think of Linda Flowers, of the light that day, the same light she saw the day her father died.

I think that maybe there is a cue in this light for Larry Swales, perhaps something unconscious is prompted. Whatever it is, God looms large now, enters the room on that wash of sunlight and touches his tongue.

"At the age I was then, I'm thinkin' I'm invincible anyway," he says, the words coming slowly now, reflective. "I was just fortunate to make it through like everybody who made it through was, but I never really thought about it, how I coulda been killed, even though people I knew died. I felt like I had a long life ahead of me. I just never thought about those things. My parents were very, very religious. We were churchgoers, and my parents did some missionary work. I'd always grown up in a household where you believed in God, and you believed in the Bible as the greatest book ever. So I had the faith, I guess you would say, at an early age. I knew right from wrong, and I knew that the Lord would take care of me, because the Bible promised that he would, you know, never burden me with things that I couldn't handle. I guess I had actually more maturity than I thought I had as far as that goes, I guess the upbringing, too. My instinct wasn't to run. My instinct was to dig in and help, and that's what I did. I mean, we just jumped in there shoulder to shoulder, and just started diggin', you know, helpin' get people out of there, and I think that speaks a whole lot to my upbringin' and my parents. And the community we lived in—you lived there, you know what I mean. It is, for lack of a better word, a blue-collar community that had a lot of respect for people and bidnesses and everything else. Course it was a different society back then in a sense. We were real close-knit, the Forest Hill community, you remember that as well as I do. There wadn't many problems then that needed help figurin' out. And once a problem was gone, once it was figured out, well, we just said let's move it off to the side and start another chapter. You got to believe that that tornado changed a lot of people's lives, old and young. You got to believe that that tornado had a bearing on people. Even today we never forget it. We *never* forget it."

His eyes are bright with tears again, and it is easy to see the brave boy that Larry Swales was in the man he has become. He wants that old way back, where the community was a place of sustenance in a time when the world was rounder than it is now, because once the edge is there you are at risk of falling over it. But he has another community now, one he has helped build over in Rankin County. Larry is a county supervisor, "the man," he says, "who helps get things done.

"They would say that the supervisor's probably on the lower rim of politics, and I've had opportunities to run for office, but I feel like God has given me the gifts to be able to talk to people and to help people, and I'll listen to you. I might not be able to help you, but I'm gon' listen, and if I can hep you, I'm gon' hep you, but if I can't, I'll tell you right up front. I use a lot of biblical messages and stories when I relate to kids. I had to get 'em inspired to go out and build handicapped ramps, replace windowpanes, paint, cut grass—for people in the community who can't do it for themselves. And I have to let them know why they should do this and what benefit they'll get out of it, what reward they'll get from Heaven, when your master sees you doin' these things that you're told to do to be a servant. It's what we are. We're servants. That day at Candlestick, that's what we were. We were the Lord's servants."

The talk of that day has brought us to focus on a point in time we would both be inclined to return to if we could. I feel it as I sit in the comfortable lobby chair, smelling the supper frying downstairs, watching the outside light begin to fade, the glow of the nearby Coke machine taking its place. Larry has lost the manic, tumbling word pace, given it up to an easy posture brought on by the calm of nostalgia. He sighs deeply, looks at me with those eyes that drove us wild, and says, "Oh, Lordy, we had some good times then. I ran all those woods down there. I knew everybody down there. Those woods was fulla all those kids. Larry Temple, Wayne Bowlen, Mickey Mobley. All the girls loved that boy."

And I want to say, no, you got it wrong, Larry Swales, it's you we all loved.

"Do you remember the MacAnallys?" he asks. They were two high school boys born to be greasers, rough and tall and handsome and too dangerous for our slumber-party dreams. I tell him I do, that the older boy was injured in the tornado but survived. I tell him how the younger one drove me off my bike into a gravel skid and how I was cut up. I show him the deep scar on my arm.

He smiles at my recollection, winces at the scar.

"Yeah," he says, "they were some wild boys, the MacAnallys. I swam many a time in that creek down there with them, with others. We had some big times in that creek, and that big, big creek ran all the way up and back through Oak Forest. I can remember doin' stupid things in there, me and my brother. We would jump in off one of them sewer pipes, and we would float it to the next one, and we would hang on—oooooooooooooooh . . . crazy! It's a wonder we didn't get killed."

I ask him if he remembers the girl who drowned and floated so fast along the chute of the ravine when it was heavy with spring rain. I ask because I remember her face, transparent as oiled paper, and I want someone else to remember, too.

"I remember the girl who drowned," he says, his eyes bright with the light of recognition in them. "Yeah, I sure do remember that. That was a tough, tough creek to play in, the water would just pour into that creek. But it was fun, it was sure enough fun. We'd cross that thing with that water flowin' under us. We'd cross that big ol' black sewer pipe like there was nothin' to it. Couldn't do it today if you had to. See, when I moved in on Woody Drive none of them houses existed. I remember that was nothin' but woods. We hunted all up in there. I remember when they built that school—Oak Forest School—the elementary school down there, and there must have been hundreds and hundreds of rabbits running out of there because of the fire. Somebody set the field afire, and out come all those rabbits."

He is gone now from the origins of our talk, gone way past Candlestick and into the green dimension of childhood we both shared in a place we both held to with something even fiercer than loyalty and remembrance. Larry Swales would not describe it exactly as I would, but he would feel it the same way in his chest, a tight longing, an ache to have the past reborn. I look at him, and he smiles that smile of youth, that yearbook smile, and I want to kiss him on the top of his head, he is such a good boy, such a good man.

"Oh, man," he says, drawing in his breath, "we had us some good times back then."

I say "Amen to that," a phrase I haven't used in years, and as he walks toward the elevator I want to ask him if he will go look at the creek with me, but instead I thank him for his time and watch his eyes turn away as he steps into the elevator, our history trailing him like a shadow flecked with light.

CHAPTER SEVENTEEN

I BORE MYSELF AWAY TO SOUTH JACKSON that night after meeting Larry Swales, leaving the safe confines of the catfish-scented corridors, the bathrooms with magnolia-scented guest soap, the porter who would not let me be until I reported him. In the two days I had been in Jackson, I had traded in my rental car three times for a laundry list of safety hazards, and I now was driving my third free upgrade, a Cadillac convertible. It was, I had been told, perhaps just the right sort of car to take to South Jackson. I would immediately be recognized as a drug dealer. The windows were even tinted.

The roads were as I remembered them, potholed, pitted, with sharp rises and gullies that set the car bouncing even at slow speeds. At my new residence on the bad side of Highway 80, a seedy motel where the walls of the office had been torn out to reveal shims and support beams, a handwritten note card was taped to the makeshift front desk: "Pardon our mess," it read, "we're remodlin." I vaguely appreciated the sincerity of the note when I saw the middle-aged woman who managed the desk. She had a decent sort of smile, the kind that said you must have some powerful burdens only God can fix if you're staying in this dump. She told me about a few places to eat. She told me they were having some problems with the plumbing. She told me to keep my door locked.

Armed with these rudimentary yet vital words of caution, I retreated to my dimly lit corner of the small complex, to my room that had never seen a better—or a worse—day. In fact, it was the sort of room that would have appeared to exist timelessly in a very bad movie about very bad people. It smelled of cheap air freshener and cigarette smoke and a sort of contemporary antiquity that takes hold in places built thirty years ago and rarely opened to natural light. The bedspread was a bright, disturbing shade of orange seen only in certain chemical spills. The mirror above the cigarette-burn-pocked vanity bore two hairline fractures, one horizontal, one vertical, in the shape of a cross. I pondered for a moment the logistics of such a break, how it could have happened, and concluded that the mirror had been the stopping point for someone's head. I searched for blood in the fissures and, finding none, went to the telephone to call a few restaurants. A suicide hot line sticker was stuck to the handle of the receiver.

IT WAS BIRTHDAY NIGHT at Shoney's, which meant that parents with adrenaline-wired children could allow their kids to unleash their mania on perfect strangers. All was chaos in the beribboned, balloon-festooned cave of Shoney's where the gnawed nubs of fried chicken parts and fresh pink globs of bubble gum littered the floor. I assaulted my way to a table far in the rear, was handed a raffle ticket by a young, kind-eyed black waitress, and promptly won a kid-sized football, which a toddler two tables away immediately coveted, yelling, "Gimme foo-bah, gimme foo-bah." I chucked the rubber ball at the child a little harder than was necessary, bouncing it off his head, and when his parents frowned back at me, I told them to just keep it.

What would turn out to be a very bad meal was brought to my corner by the waitress, a chain-restaurant bastardization of southern fare shakily suspended by limp pools of grease. I gave the waitress a peremptory thank-you, and she looked at me concerned, probably wondering why a woman had come here alone on birthday night. Her gaze turned to pointed alarm when she noticed what I had spread before me on the table, the obituaries of Candlestick. They were photocopies, more urgent-looking for this simple fact, the dark ink with the grim news, four or five obituaries crammed to a page. She pointed to the headline on one: "Mosley Rites Conducted Today." It was the obituary of the Reverend Mosley, the teacher at Oak Forest Elementary School whose body had been thrown into the field where the rabbits used to run, the field Larry Swales had talked about that had been cleared for the school where Mosley taught.

"You lose somebody?" she asked, her tone gentle, concerned. I kicked myself for not having turned the pages over.

"You want some coffee?" she asked when I didn't answer right away. "On the house. On me, my treat. You want some coffee?"

I told her no, thank you, and that I hadn't lost anyone, that these obituaries were from a long time ago.

"I see," she said, lowering her gold-sparkled eyelids in a look of deeper concern, as if she were trying to make out my particular affliction and decide what action was needed next. She seemed like a nice woman, and I felt badly for confusing her, so I told her something about the death notices, who the people were and how they had died, and why on this night in particular I was studying them. I told her I was going to talk to some of the families of the people who had died in the tornado, and to some of those who had lived.

"You know," she said, sitting down in the chair opposite me for a moment, looking back quickly toward the kitchen to see if she'd been spotted, "I heard tell about that tornado. Now, I don't think I was even born yet, but I heard about it, yes, I did. The Candlestick Tornado, yes, ma'am. Bad. Very bad."

I told her yes, it was.

As she rose from the chair, she reached across and put a warm hand on my shoulder, and I had a flashback to when I was a girl, of Gussie Mae's hands and how hot they always seemed, how the palms slid across my face like heated oil.

"Now, you just do the best you can," she said as she moved away. "God'll see to that."

There he was again. God. The name came rolling off the tongue of every other person I met. I could go an entire year in New Hampshire without ever hearing the word "God." But here, where the Bible Belt was its broadest, God had elbowed His way into Shoney's, taken a backseat, and watched in horror. There were the beginnings of comfort in it, hearing from people what God would and would not do, what He thought, what He had planned, what I needed to do in order for Him to listen up. And the comfort was somehow greater when it came from a black person. I figured they knew, had to know.

In their short, unerring style, the obituaries tell the news of who died, who was left behind, where the dead would be mourned, and where buried. If the family did not want flowers sent, the notice says so. It is an act of respect in its terse, ungiving way, and a way to spread the news so we are able to count one, five, twenty, one hundred fewer among us, depending on the day, the hour, the year. There were fourteen dead at Candlestick, and I wonder if there was solace for the bereaved, knowing that those they loved did not die alone.

There are few pictures with the notices, only two: Joe Bullock, the would-be congressman, and young Ronny Hannis. It is his senior yearbook picture. In other pictures I had seen of him, he was smiling big, as if he and a friend had been laughing together just moments before. It is a grin of immense affability and an uncommon emotional readiness. In the solemn yearbook photo there is the trace of a smile at the corners of his mouth, but it is his eyes that look beyond the immediate into the time beyond graduation. There is a seriousness here, a determination, and the words "young man" come to mind because Ronny is not a boy in this picture but someone who, you suspect, when presented with the consequences of an action, would act according to an internal standard. I caution myself against reading something that may not be there, but I know better. I see the strength in the boy who has become a young man. A handsome young man. A good young man. They want you to be serious on yearbook photo day because, presumably, you are looking to the future. If they could have known what would happen to Ronny in the days to come, they might have told him not only to smile as openly as he could but to shed the dark graduation suit and retrieve what was left of boyhood.

The Shoney's celebration rages on behind me as I keep to my corner with the sheaf of death notices. The waitress has come once again, to ask me about that coffee she has offered and, I sense, to check on my mental condition. When I tell her thank you, that I do not drink coffee, she looks at me with outright pity.

"Well, all right then," she tells me as she picks her way between the children and back to the front counter.

I have lemon pie for dessert as I study the bespectacled head shot of Joe Bullock. Joe Bullock was not at Candlestick, but since there is a picture of him I am curious. More telling is the other photocopy I have of the field in Scott County where he died. It is the field where, as the caption states, "Joe Bullock met death." In the picture there is a pile of splintered posts and boards in the foreground, and a barely discernible circular pattern in the dirt at the periphery of the heap of wood. In the distance a dark tree line rises up, a few trees taller than the others so that their opaque silhouette and what they are is unmistakable. Being from the South, I know instantly that this tree line marks a river. It is a natural demarcation of the land, the broad plain of fields, sown and unsown, fanning out to meet the ribbon of water that defines them.

Staring at the busted-up pile of lumber, the field, the trees beyond, and the river imagined beyond that, I wonder where, exactly, Joe Bullock's car landed when he was picked up by the tornado and then smashed down. Death on these rutted roads when I was a girl was always news. A tractor might block a lane and someone might pass in a moment of impatience and hit another car head-on. The driver might be drunk and spin off one of the low-lying bridges that spanned the river. Sometimes a car would be found in a field, flipped over onto its top, the driver dead. They had a mystery to them, those deaths, and when they happened the victim did not meet with a guardrail or a concrete median, but often with the dirt, the water, the buckled macadam that smelled like dirt, a tornado.

It is a stark, ungiving photo, black and white, and without the caption it means nothing. Given the words "Roadside field in Scott County where Joe Bullock met death," it becomes a grave site, the splayed boards a grim headstone, and now there is purpose in studying the picture and it becomes natural to imagine the photographer standing on the strip of macadam that is Highway 13, the road Joe Bullock drove along not knowing what would meet him. Looking at the scarred, oddly marked ground around the pile of rubble, you wonder where the bloodstains are, if the ground took them up or if they remain like oil stains in the dirt, deeper than a white cross placed in remembrance.

The lemon pie is bad, too. I have ordered it out of a driving sentiment for times past. It looks just like the pie that used to sit on a shelf behind a plastic shield in any number of cafés in Jackson and just like the pie that was served after the revival meetings, the meringue deep and toasted on the top, sweating drops of sugar onto the picnic table, sliding off the cut slices in the liquefying heat. It was never very good then either, but it looks like the past, smells like the past, and that is what I am about now, pulling everything to me that makes up the sphere of memory taken from this place.

Next to the half-eaten pie, the slick, sugary oil of the meringue pooled on the plate, lies the obituary of Sarah Parker, née Sarah Nelson, born in Lawrence, Mississippi, a member of the Forest Hills Methodist Church. I try to remember the distinction between Methodists and Baptists in the South. My family—those who went to church—was Methodist, with one stray Catholic. My sense, unfounded, is that the Methodists were a little more refined. Baptists baptized and Methodists sprinkled. It is a silly thought but one taken from some archive of obscure teachings. I think about Sarah Parker's boy, the one I had the crush on, the one who in my fantasies walked with me in the moonlight and who danced the twist with me before I went away—to safety, to higher ground, to a place unnamed that day on the list of fate. I wonder, once again, what happened to him. I have been unable to track him down, have been unsure of what I would say if I did, how I would dare to ask him about his dead mother. Those I have asked, those from our school days whose home was and always will be Jackson, say that the boy left long before graduation, moved away maybe in the eighth grade, maybe a little later. It intensifies the mystery of the boy for me, his having disappeared from this place where everyone has seemed so beyond uprooting. I think of Mrs. Parker with her nails painted as she lay in the casket, how, I've been told, her nails were never painted, and I wonder if her son stared at them, thought them out of place.

There is the notice for J. C. Callaway, who lived on Rainey Road. I did not know him, had never heard his name, but I did know Rainey Road, right off Cooper, a rural stretch with slow hills and farmland, the road where a friend had lived. She and her father had outrun the tornado and traversed the churned-up field where a body lay. I know Mr. Callaway only by where he lived and by the barred lines of his obituary. He was a housepainter. A blue-collar neighborhood, Larry Swales said, people who respected other people; painters, mechanics, farmers turned to the trade of small "bidness." Callaway was forty-six when he died.

I push all the plates and utensils to the back of the table and pull another sheet of paper to the center. It is the notice for the Carpenter woman and her son, a seven-year-old boy named David.

I remember that Karei McDonald was the one who found them. Some say she was in her car at the filling station, some say she was parked in front of Dog 'n' Suds. It is hard to imagine in the wreckage that followed the blast of the tornado that much could be decided as to where, exactly, someone had been. Mrs. Carpenter, a Methodist from Pennsylvania, had lived in Jackson only six years. Her body and her son's would be sent back to Pennsylvania, and I think again about what it is like to be a stranger in a strange land and meet up with catastrophe on alien ground. The thought of the bodies being shipped back is natural and at the same time disturbing. Who wants to bury someone in the very place that has killed them, a place that is not home? Yet there is something, too, that seems almost to demand that they be buried where they fell, that in this community of quick death all those who were taken should remain together.

I see the obituary of the kindly pharmacist, the old man, a Canadian by birth, Theodore Gaetz, whose body was sent back to Fitchburg, Massachusetts. To my mind, all of Massachusetts, and all of New England for that matter, is an ugly, forbidding frozen place, and I wonder at the burial so far north in March, if the ground had been thawed enough to let Mr. Gaetz in. It is a thing that happens there in winter, a surprise to me when I learned it.

I take the sheaf of papers and shuffle them like a giant deck of cards, closing my eyes while I do, then opening them to see who rests on top, who, in my hunt for the memories of these people, I should search for next. And I know before I open my eyes. Ronny Hannis, the photocopy before me faded like a tintype. I slip the clutch of papers into a notebook and tell myself I will put the Hannis boy off for a couple of days. I am not ready to think about what I will ask of his family.

The waitress gives me a curious little salute at the door as I leave, and I head across the road into the warm, weightless night, watching headlight beams the color of sulfur, the color of a storm sky.

CHAPTER EIGHTEEN

IT IS A SOUTH JACKSON LANDMARK NOW, Hudgie's Restaurant, part of Fred Hudgins's brave new empire built on the heels of Candlestick. The low, sixties-looking building sits at the intersection of Daniel Lake Road and Cooper, near the old Cook Center Donna Durr left the afternoon of March 3, on her way home. Cook Center is the place we drove to, my family and I, the day John F. Kennedy died. I had stayed home from school that day and had watched Walter Cronkite on the TV screen as he interrupted *As the World Turns* to tell the news. I had called to my mother and Gussie Mae then, told them the president had been shot, and my mother said, "You're wrong. It was his brother Bobby." It was an odd thing for her to say and I never asked why, but I can still see her standing in the doorway between the living room and the kitchen in the house on Cherrywood Drive, looking at me reprovingly, saying I was mistaken. She learned soon enough that I was not. As we drove to Cook Center that evening for groceries, my mother and stepfather were silent, and when I asked what was wrong, my mother turned to me in the backseat, gave me the same look she had earlier in the day, and said in the most solemn voice that ever owned her, "Our president has died." It is what I associate with Cook Center, Kennedy's death, that and Donna Durr riding high in the sky. As I pull into the parking lot at Hudgie's, I am thinking of the two of them, Donna Durr and JFK, and what a golden pair they would have made.

It was a Sunday, and a brightly clothed after-church crowd filled the restaurant. The Hudgins family—Fred, Mary, and their daughters, Gloria and Fredna, and son, Tony—had agreed to meet me here to talk about the day the tornado took away Dog 'n' Suds, Fred Hudgins's first business.

Hudgie's is the classic cafeteria of the southern working class, with an open floor plan, a steel-binned buffet in the center with plastic hoods that catch the steam from the hot food, Formica tables scattered at angles, and a big room in back for meetings. The sense of the place is well worn and familiar, the smell of fried catfish and chicken, boiled greens and black-eyed peas, and the inevitable banana pudding ripe in the close air.

As I walk in, past the front counter, I hear a woman, one of the help, say, "There's a woman coming for Mr. Hudgins, to talk about the tornado. We're supposed to send her back."

And her coworker's response: "What does she look like?"

The woman laughs and says, "From out of town, I guess."

They barely glance my way as I pass them and head for the back room. So after all these years away, I think, I still don't look like a Yankee.

Several tables have been shoved end to end so we can all sit together in the back room that is dark and cool with fans spinning overhead. Fred Hudgins is waiting at the center of the line of tables and immediately rises to shake my hand, a grip that is firm for an old guy and one that drains the color from my knuckles. He is a tiny man, a sawed-off version of Colonel Sanders, his features more delicate, his eyes wickedly bright and alert, like a hamster's. He wears a suit and a bow tie and is a man, I am guessing, who likes to talk.

His daughter Gloria says so right away, affectionately, telling how "Daddy" likes to hold court with his "cronies." She says I can find him here all the time if I need to. They are accommodating people, the Hudginses.

The women are dressed in a cascade of flowered rayon, bright dresses that put a glare in my peripheral vision. Gloria seems the most at ease, a roundly pretty, dark-haired woman in her forties who smiles a lot in a caretaking sort of way. Mrs. Hudgins is nervous and excitable-looking, already on the verge of tears. The son, Tony, is handsome, steady, calmer than all of the others. I assume without asking that the quiet Fredna, oldest of the three children, being the firstborn, was named for her father, Fred.

When I place the tape recorder in the center of the table, Mrs. Hudgins, her hair immaculately done, her eyes red-rimmed, recoils from it as if it were a weapon. She looks at me as if asking for sympathy, to ask that I not ask too much, go too deep, but at the same time I see that she is willing, that talking might be a purgative. We have all met on the phone and know something of each other, although I remember Fred from thirty years before, how we idolized him as the king of Dog 'n' Suds.

"Just remember this," Fred Hudgins begins as he leans forward on the table, his small, strong-looking hands clasped before him, "say that you got a telephone call that says that a tornado just hit Candlestick, and you're right here, and think just what all's going through your mind and what you can expect when you get there."

Fred Hudgins pauses, and the noises of the restaurant come up around us as we do what he asks, imagining the call that comes. Mrs. Hudgins begins to weep quietly, a pathetic, broken sound that will punctuate her husband's words at odd times.

"It's something to remember, that call," he continues, "and that's what was going through my mind when it happened. What went through my mind is, I'm lookin' for the worst, really, and I did find the worst, really. I found an employee killed. I found one in critical condition, buried. And they's not a whole lot you can do immediately, but just be patient, and it's hard, you know. They ain't a whole lot you can do. You got to be patient in a situation like this, because that's the way it is. Let me tell you this, I've gone through World War II. I've gone through some tragedies in the world war. I've had lots of close calls. I've come home and I got married and raised a family, and this happened to me, and I've had other things happen to me since then. I fell off a building. I had a bad accident from that, but Candlestick was the worst. I just recently had a bypass back in May. I've survived, and the Lord has used me for some reason. He's got something for me to do."

"We're afraid of weather now." Mrs. Hudgins's breaking voice comes from down the table. It is an understatement and a non sequitur at the same time, and we all look quickly back to the aging Fred to tell the story, but it is Gloria who speaks first.

"It was March the third and I was seventeen, it was right at my eighteenth birthday, and my mother is exactly twenty years older than me, so, Mother," she says as she looks down the table at Mary Hudgins, "that would have made you thirty-eight." Mrs. Hudgins nods and smiles and wipes her eyes. "It was very unusual that day that no member of my family—my immediate family—was in the restaurant because we all spent so much time down there. I don't know if you remember a boy, he was eighteen, I believe, a senior at Forest Hill, Ronny Hannis, who worked at the grocery store across the parking lot?"

At the mention of Ronny something jumps inside me as it always does. I tell Gloria, yes, I do remember Ronny.

"Well, Ronny was at Dog 'n' Suds that afternoon. And I had been in the afternoon before, on March second, and we drank a Coke together then and talked. And you know, he was killed at the restaurant, and the afternoon that it happened, Mother, didn't we decide the time was four thirty-three?"

It is the time of Armageddon, recorded in stone. Those in this town who would misquote it by a minute might never be forgiven. Mary Hudgins nods to Gloria, a frantic jerking of her head that is alarming. Fred is ready to talk again, you can tell by the way he is edging back and forth in his chair, his fingers locked together tightly.

"I had just left Candlestick," he says, "and had gone to the other place on Raymond Road to get an adding machine, and while I was there at Raymond Road, I got a phone call from my wife and she said that we've had a tornado out here, and I tried to call the store at Candlestick and I cain't get an answer, so I jumped in my car immediately, and I had—I believe it was a '57 Ford—it was a nice car, I'd bought it new, and anyway, I proceeded to get back down to Candlestick, and when I got down into the vicinity of, like, Meadowlane and all in there, all the trees and other things were across the road. I had to go in north of Candlestick and come back in, through that area, and I got in there at the site and I had three flats on my car. I had run over different debris. And my building, which I saw immediately, was demolished. They was cars piled up in my building."

Fred Hudgins's voice sounds like the voice of a little boy when he mentions the cars piled in his building, the disbelief still strong that his tiny place in the parking lot had been so insulted, so assaulted. I have a quick picture then of Dog 'n' Suds, a crowd of us packed in tight, listening to the jukebox, eating hot dogs, when suddenly cars begin to fall from the sky.

"I got out of my car and walked over there, across all the debris and through all that dust, and the first thing I saw was Doris Freeney's hand stickin' out. Doris was an employee of mine. I knew it was her hand because she had a watch and rings on, and I said, 'Oh, Doris, oh, Doris, now listen, we'll get you out in just a minute, just hang in there.' But that's all I could see, just her hand, and I couldn't know if she could hear me. 'Oh, Doris,' I said, 'now we'll get you out, don't you worry.'"

The little-boy voice comes up again, cracks, and almost breaks when Hudgins imitates the way he spoke to Doris that day, pretty Doris Freeney.

"Course I was the first one to get in there." Fred Hudgins says this as if it is fact, and it may well be, but it seems as if everyone

I have talked to was the first one in, the first to begin helping. I think that this perception is perhaps normal, that faced with what they saw all those who say they were first may have believed it all these years because not until they beheld another living person did they know that they were not the only ones alive.

"I remember the weather that day." It is Gloria now, sitting next to me, her voice low, eyes unfixed on any point. She is speaking as if she hopes her mother will not hear her. "I remember it was so peaceful. Right before it hit it was so peaceful. I had just had my car serviced. I was coming from the Buick place.

"Mother, you all right?" she asks, watching Mary Hudgins as she wipes her eyes roughly with a tissue, trying to keep herself from breaking down. I can see the wish for control that she hopes might bind her up and stop the rush of tears, but it is not even a battle. When Mary Hudgins speaks it is as if she wants to wail instead, just start wailing and never stop. It is hard to watch.

"I could see this black, black cloud," she says, her voice a lurching turn of sounds that never hit a cadence, "and as I went down Cooper Road it seemed eerie, so eerie, so black. Oh, it was black. Fredna and I were going to work, and when we started out I heard the roar. It rained real, real hard right after the tornado. Oh, it was an eerie feeling."

Mary Hudgins clasps her hands to her shoulders as if she is hugging herself, trying to keep the memory away.

"Oh, the clouds were *so* dark. We had started out to the car to go to Candlestick, and I hear this roaring sound. I ran back inside and told the kids it was a tornado."

Mrs. Hudgins breaks down completely now, and Gloria gets up and walks slowly to her side, pats her on the shoulder, and tells her to go ahead, that it is all right now. We wait with our eyes averted as Mary Hudgins collects herself.

"And I was at one door," she begins again, "and my two daughters were at the other doors, which was the wrong thing to do, but at that time we didn't know you were supposed to go somewhere and lay down."

The image startles me. I imagine Mary and her children lying in their beds with quilts pulled up around them, waiting. Waiting like the boy years ago whose mother tried to wake him.

Gloria rubs her mother's shoulders gently, sighs, and smiles at me.

"But anyway," Mary says, "I was standin' at the front door, and the debris came all in the yard, and I looked across the street and the house over there, the shingles stood straight up, just straight up in the air, and then instantly fell back down. It was so fast. How could something like that happen? How could it?"

The question is a plea for understanding, for mercy almost, as if one of us here could tell Mary Hudgins why, and that by telling her, at least a part of that day will be borne away, cease to haunt her, but as she looks to each of us in turn no answer comes and she begins to cry again.

"Well now." It is Fred again. "As I was saying. I was the first one to get in there, and then several people gathered with me. I summoned help. I yelled for help, and they started coming out just like from under leaves. They were just submerged, and they started pulling themselves out. I guess they was all in shock, but some came to and we moved hard and we moved fast and we got Doris out. She was hurt so bad, I didn't think she'd live. We kept movin' people out, just dragging people out, had a little boy. The first thing I thought it was my son, Tony."

I look down the table to Tony. He has lowered his head, and I see the first big tear fall between his elbows, splash on the table as if it has come from a leak in the ceiling.

"And I said, 'Oh, Tony, oh, Tony,'" and there again is the young, stricken voice that Fred Hudgins can summon so effectively.

"I thought it was my son, Tony, but it was a little boy that had had all his clothes blew off, right there by the building. He was three years old, he was the Carpenter kid, the name was Carpenter, and they had stopped at the gas station to get out of the storm, but they didn't make it. When it blew it blew 'em out of the car and killed Mrs. Carpenter and one of the sons. This child, this little boy, was the only one that survived out of the car. I'm so glad it wadn't you, Tony."

Fred Hudgins looks down the long table at his son, who raises his head and meets his father's eyes. "Yeah, I'm glad, too, Daddy."

I am reminded at this moment of these southern endearments for parents, Mama and Daddy, and how, no matter how old a child becomes, there is still this endearment from childhood, and how odd it seems that it never sounds foolish or unmanly when a grown man speaks it. I think this of Tony now, how he says the word forcefully and with a vague pride, and of how it carries both respect and affection.

"We started movin' people out to the road then that were survived," Hudgins says, "and the dead, too, we moved them, and it was a horrible thing."

"But, Daddy," Gloria says, her tone urgent now, "I didn't know that you were okay, and Danny had come by to see about me and I was getting him to take me down to Candlestick, and we couldn't get down Cooper Road for all the wreckage and the power lines, and we went down the other end of Meadowlane and up McCluer Road, and then up Rainey Road, you know, to the back side. And I was runnin' around lookin' for you and cryin'. I thought you were down there. And everybody I saw was in shock. You could just look into people's eyes and see it. You couldn't believe it had happened, and I thought my daddy was dead. And I remember finding him there and him crying, and I had never seen my daddy cry before."

Fred Hudgins looks to his daughter Gloria, a remembered compassion in his eyes from that afternoon for his daughter who found him alive but so vulnerable that he cried in front of her. It is a thing often withheld from children, the mask of tragedy worn only when there is no other mask.

Fred looks smaller now and waves away the waitress who comes to fill our water glasses. She looks at me, the stranger here, and then protectively at Fred. I am intruding, and I know it.

I am the fool obsessed with all this death. I meet Fred Hudgins's eyes on the level and believe there is something there that says, "Sure, I'll tell you more. How bad do you want it to get?"

"We dug Juland, our cook, out," he says. "She had ahold of her purse, tight. She had gone to the restroom, I guess."

Or, I think, she was just hoping to run with the one thing that belonged to her.

"And she was a twin girl," Fred says, "that worked for us, and she was dead. And we had Doris Freeney there workin', she was tending the store and managing it, and when we got her out, I hadn't heard anything since they took her away, all the radios and things was out at the time, and we didn't know whether she was dead or not, but we got in late that night and we got the message that she had survived, but she was in critical shape, Doris Ann, and she was in a body cast. I mean, they just had to sew her up with rocks, gravel, everything in her, and for years and years she went through them goin' in and openin' her up."

"But Juland was dead," Gloria says, remembering the girl she used to dance with in back. "Daddy found her, and she was dead and that was terrible. She and her sister, they both worked for us in different stores."

From down the table I hear Tony's voice again, a low cry, and he looks at me when he speaks, his voice breaking, the tears unstoppable now.

"For days and days and weeks," he says, "her car just sat in our yard. It just sat there and I kept waiting to see Juland, but I never did again. She never came back, and I didn't understand why."

I remember Gussie Mae when Tony talks, how it was when we left and I stood holding on to her, refusing to let go until my mother pulled my whitening fingers loose from Gussie's starched uniform, saying, "You'll see her again, I promise, you'll see her again," and I had, and the promise had been true, but there was no promise given Tony, and I imagine how he felt, how perhaps Juland had been like a second mama, and I remember what Meland said about her sister and her ways with children, how there was nobody better with a child.

"But I do know"—it is Fred again, trying to deflect attention from his son's weeping, perhaps trying to spare him—"yes, I do know that we got down there and we worked, got all the boys we could and scratched through my building, thinking we could find some employees or somebody, but we never found nobody else, but this is what we went through to try to recognize that they wadn't anybody else in there."

Mary Hudgins's voice comes up again, spooky, disembodied. "You know what it was like?" she asks, trying to gather up everyone at once with her haunted stare. "It was like the world rolled over. Just like the world rolled over that day. It's what it sounded like."

The image comes up, and the bizarre horror of it is mirrored in Mary Hudgins's eyes, and I realize that she lives alone in her perception of that day, of the sounds, the smells, the darkness, the fractured, paralyzing sense of it that has become one thing in her consciousness, a fear that fairly owns her.

Gloria smiles at her mother in a sad way and then says, "But Ronny Hannis, the boy I was tellin' you about that I had drank a Coke with the day before, he was a senior at Forest Hill, and worked at the grocery store, you know, right across from the Dog 'n' Suds, he was in the restaurant. Now correct me, Daddy, but they—Ronny, Juland, Ms. Freeney, the little girl—looked up and they saw the tornado comin', and Ronny said, 'Let's get out of here,' and Ms. Freeney said, 'We don't have time, hit the floor,' and then it hit, and Ronny, afterward, even though he was badly hurt, Ronny helped put some people in ambulances, didn't he?"

"He did," Fred says, "and what happened was he had injuries he didn't know about, but he didn't make it. I guess he had blood clots. But he helped others who needed help, that boy did." Fred stops for a long moment and looks at his family, each in turn, and it seems that he is gauging what he is about to say, whether it might be misconstrued.

"I'll tell you," he starts out, sounding a little defensive, and I wonder what is coming now, lean forward in my chair to hear him better. "I will tell you," he says again, "what happened to me is this. I got criticized for being on television. I was on television on the anniversary of the tornado, and I made the statement that some people was unfortunate enough that they lost everything they had, but I was able to take a tragedy and improve on my bidness. In other words, I had several bidness locations after the tragedy. I was able to move forward, and I wadn't boasting, but I was telling the truth, that sometimes a tragedy can put you in the right direction if you let it. And I also said I'd rather not have been successful and have the lives back. Some lady wrote me a letter about it, but you got to tell it like it is, and some people they take things different."

"On my eighteenth birthday, I went to his funeral," Gloria says. "We sent flowers."

My family is whole and Christian," Fred begins, "and I mean, I'm talking about my family and my children and their spouses—*all* are Christian—and I think a lot of this comes through tragedy sometimes, and it can change a person's life and work miracles for them."

Fred looks off across the big room, a vacant stare, and when he speaks again it is as if he is speaking only to himself.

"We didn't want the boy dead. We didn't want nobody dead."

Everyone is quiet now, staring ahead or down at the table splotched with water rings. Through the door of the back room I hear the sound of plastic cups being filled with crushed ice, a soft winter sound, the sound of plates set sharply on tables, a baby crying, and then here, where we sit, Tony crying, Mary Hudgins crying. It is a long, long time before anyone speaks, and it is almost as if we are praying together, and then I am convinced that we are.

CHAPTER NINETEEN

"What I like about the outdoors is freedom. I like the elements as
they are. I like the things that are outside. You are free to move,
you are not boxed in. There is so much beauty. . . . The oak
leaves this year are the most amazing that I have ever seen
them. . . . Outside everything is beautiful—inside everything is
artificial. The stove is there, and the dishwasher there, and the
sink is there, and it looks the same every time. The seasons don't
change indoors. Outside things are alive and active. Not only is it
beautiful, but it smells good. The sounds outside are soothing.
People think that the woods are quiet, but it is anything but
quiet deep in the woods. The sounds inside are irritating, and the
sounds outside are soothing. I guess that's the difference."

—Karei McDonald

KAREI MCDONALD IS THE THOREAU of Byram, Mississippi,
a small town south of Jackson on the Pearl River. I think this
about him before we meet, from our talks, that there is a poetic
streak in him wide as the gully I used to play in as a kid. But I
know, too, that he is like a lot of Mississippians, held tight by this
world of dirt and smells and woods. It comes up again and again,
what holds people here, and through seeing it and remembering
it and hearing it, I understand what keeps pulling me back on
this loose leash that has stretched thousands of miles. Karei Mc-
Donald doesn't mention that what is always the same inside—
the sink, the dishwasher, the stove—can be changed, too, by
what is outside, and that everything that once seemed fixed and
immovable can be pulled like a missile into the vortex of March
winds. But he doesn't have to say it. It is something he knows

155

firsthand, and he would say, perhaps, that you would be a fool to let that keep you from the world.

Karei McDonald is not a man of great physical stature, but he is strongly built, his body low to the ground and compact, his movements purposeful and confident. He is the sort of man, seen from a distance, who catches your eye simply because he is familiar with his own body, with what it is capable of. He is not a man in whom fear has made an inroad. He is instead one you would be inclined to turn to when your own fears became unbearable.

He is the man the folks at Jackson Fire Department said was "my man," the department's unofficial spokesman for the Candlestick Tornado. When I call to ask him when we can get together, he apologizes that it cannot be that very day because his brother has just died. I find the apology startling, that he would even think to give it. He says the next day then, and when I ask if he is sure, he tells me that his favorite thing to do is to get together to eat and talk.

There are half a dozen reasons right off that I find the man compelling. His accent is one of them, a strong, melodic, born-in-Mississippi tilt that puts unexpected, hard-vowel stresses on certain words—*si-reens, free-yunds, hay-yure*—and another is his direct and interested look—at anything, everything. Karei McDonald has eyes that assess, not in a critical or uncompassionate way but in a way that bears the mark of his lack of fear. He is not afraid to look hard at something in order to know it, and he does not pay as much attention to the possible meaning of words as he does to what he sees. After less than half an hour, he strikes me as a man entirely unpossessed by ego.

We have supper together at a chain restaurant where '50s and '60s music is blaring overhead. Karei does not seem to notice.

"Mrs. Baker," he says to me from across the small table next to a window that catches the fading Mississippi afternoon, the light that same light again that Linda Flowers has described and that I am beginning to believe is a haunting. "Mrs. Baker," he repeats, using my married name. "Tell me what has brought you to me."

So I tell him, mixing obsession with other things that merely hide obsession. I tell him that somehow I know he will talk to me straight. He will tell me how bad it was, what the injuries were like. I tell him I want to know.

"How old are you?" he asks, as if checking to see if I am old enough to hear what he has to say. I tell him I'm forty-five, and he doesn't say that I look young for my age or that he doesn't believe me, things I inevitably wait to hear when I give my age. What he says instead is that he had guessed that was about my age, and I give him some vague credit for knowing this and being straight about it. I come to the conclusion that it is his way of telling me he will not coddle me, that if I am here to discuss the anatomy of death, the number of years I have spent on the planet will suffice for passage to his memory of that day.

As much as I have liked the other people I have met, as good as they have been to talk to me, it is Karei McDonald with whom I feel completely at ease because he is a man at ease with himself.

"It was a Thursday," he begins, and I immediately think of Joe Friday on *Dragnet*, how "just the facts" of an event finally bore in and create a reality separate from the visceral. The word "Thursday" is becoming for me more than a day of the week, more like Sunday, set aside, exalted.

"I remember that," he says. "I had worked that day, came in, hadn't eaten lunch, and it was about four o'clock. My wife told me to go clean up and she'd put lunch on the table. I was in there taking my clothes off, and the window faces right out to the west. Course they had tornado warnings all day, and I saw that there was a funny-looking cloud and it had two tails coming down out of the one cloud, and everything came together and made one big tail. Later on I went scouting, because I'm curious about these things, and I saw the two different distinct destruction paths on the ground. I lived on Charlton Drive, two blocks above Cooper Road. I told my wife—I had two kids then, one was a little over eighteen months old, the other three years old—I said wrap the kids up because there is a storm about to go on the ground, right there at our back door. I said I'll go out front and watch the thing and if it comes straight to us we'll dart in that storm sewer. There was a big storm sewer, and it hadn't rained enough that it would have been a problem. So she wrapped 'em up and I went out and saw all the debris in the air, way up in the air, tin and all of that stuff. We had friends that lived right on Cooper Road, and it looked like it went right down Cooper, so we jumped in the car and got down to Cooper and saw that the thing was really really bad. I told my wife to go on back to the house and I'd go see if I could help somebody."

McDonald says that on the east side of Caney Creek the tornado tore the bridge out.

"They was a sewage pipe, a pipe about eight inches," he says, "and I walked across that thing and got over to Candlestick." For those who made it over, the pipe became sacred in the way that kids sanctify the inanimate, but never on those hot days when it had burned beneath our bare feet did we imagine that it would become South Jackson's version of the bridge over the River Kwai, that by its narrow conduit a stream of people would crawl and list and pull themselves along because there was no other way in to the place that no longer resembled the place they had known, and I imagine small, compact Karei McDonald in his relative youth, running across the tarred pipe, giving no thought to the finesse of his actions, no thought to which foot went where, and then what he beheld at its terminus where the ravine lip fanned out into the broken neighborhood.

Karei McDonald does not say that he was the first person on the scene. It is my guess that he was.

"'Bout the first person I met over there," he says, "—you know, people were just walkin' 'round in a daze, with just all kinds of injuries imaginable—I met a doctor named McMillan. He had been off on a house call and had gotten back to Candlestick Park. He had an office there at that time, and he had gotten back right after it happened and he told me, he said, 'Well, you can gather them up and lay 'em right here, and I'll triage 'em.' So once we get the ambulances comin' in, when they find a way in, 'cause everything was pretty much blocked, I toted up, eight or ten, eight, nine or ten, I don't know the exact number, and I don't know how many of those were dead, but they *all* looked dead."

The waitress arrives with our food as Karei speaks this last sentence. She is a high school girl, maybe, or early college, working evenings, and she has the look certain kids have nowadays, sort of blank, colorless, unfazed, and her eyes merely widen at the word "dead," the nonexpression on her face unchanged. "Y'all need condiments?" she asks, speaking the last word as if it is foreign, a proper word that has been taught her.

"The miracle about the thing," Karei continues, "was they had a little ol' slot car track in the shopping center at the time, and they had a race at four o'clock, and there were probably forty people in that thing, but it had gotten over at four-twenty, maybe four-ten, maybe with just ten minutes to spare, and most of the people had gotten out, but that place was just obliterated, it was just obliterated, so it would probably have killed eighty percent of those people, but it didn't, it killed one or two that worked in there. There's a Dog 'n' Suds that was there, and they was a lady and a child in a car pulled up to the Dog 'n' Suds, and I got most of those people out, the ones that had been in there."

For a while Karei McDonald talks about how the tornado picked up after it hit the power station by Caney Creek, and that once it touched back down at the Knox Glass Company in Rankin County, it stayed on the ground all the way to Philadelphia, Mississippi. Later on he and his wife followed the path of the tornado, discovering that it was a mile wide at certain points.

"I made friends later on," Karei says, "with a guy who lived close to Philadelphia, Sebastopol to be exact, and it hit his house and killed his mama and daddy and one more member of the family. The thing that was striking about it was that it picked up a twenty-one-cubic-foot freezer completely full and carried it ten miles and set it down still unopened."

He stares at me hard, his eyes narrowing. "Now," he says,

balling his hand into a fist and striking the table for emphasis so that his plate of barbecue jumps, "my little ol' simple brain won't comprehend that kind of power. That thing probably weighed four hundred to five hundred pounds. I don't comprehend the kind of power it would take to do that. Down before it got to Candlestick, I started walking and looking for other people hurt, and it was amazing to me. Pine trees a foot across, that big, that sturdy, would be twisted off, just like a matchstick, but twisted, and a foot away from it there wouldn't be a shingle missing on the roof of a house. That amazed me."

It is clear that Karei McDonald, despite the urgency of that afternoon, studied the scene carefully on his way to help and then later, not satisfied to let it pass away, scrutinized it the way a cop would a murder scene and followed its widening trail because, he said, it was necessary, within the possible scope of his understanding, to at least try to comprehend.

He says that that night, long into the night, his children, safe at home, were kept awake by the ambulances.

"Because of the *si-reens*," he says, speaking the word with that drawn-out hard vowel run, so that it sounds like what it is. "It was just ambulances, ambulances, si-reens in and si-reens out, and the po-leece, and the ambulances, and the fire personnel. People there hadn't been exposed to that sort of thing for that long a period. Usually it was just a si-reen in the distance. Now it was all night long."

I ask him about the trauma because I know that he is the person who will tell me, but still I am not prepared for it, still it is unbelievable because I have not seen, as McDonald has, the wounded core of such tragedy.

He takes a sip of his sweet tea, the ice nearly melted in it now, and begins to speak again in the same level, unself-conscious way.

"There are the gory details," he says. "There are always the gory details, because that is all they are, and that is part of life, horrible as it is, and that's something that I learned to live with. I don't say like, but it is definitely something that I learned to live with in my life. I worked the ambulance with the fire department in Jackson six years, and you know, I've seen a lot of death, but that time at Candlestick was the worst. I think the most astonishing thing was that people would walk around with part of their head tore off."

The image slips in like a ghost, like a voodoo haint.

"Or their ear tore off, or a arm tore off. And they walked around like this, just in a daze like they wadn't hurt."

And then the haints gather and grow in number, and I look for faces I recognize, for what is left of a face.

"They was a good bit of that," Karei says. "Course if they were massacred up too bad, they were dyin'."

"Massacred up too bad," the southern twist to the description so abrupt that I raise my chin sharply at the words because for the first time I see what happened that day. A massacre, pure and simple.

"But it was amazing to me how many people were walkin' around with bad bad injuries," Karei says, "serious injuries, and not even acknowledging it, and I don't know the reason for that. Certainly they were in some form of shock, but to what degree I don't know. They were addled. They were just walkin' around, kindly addled or kindly in a daze, or just kindly out of it. They were just wandering around, and it didn't seem that those people seemed to want to congregate up, like you normally would think. They were just straggling over the parking lot."

I can't help it, horror movies begin to play beyond the window where the sun pales now. I see the zombie walk, the glazed eyes, and I wonder, as Karei does, what happens to the brain, to perception, when one moment you are putting a coin in a Laundromat slot and the next moment part of your head is missing. If there is consciousness you keep on moving. Neurons cannot transmit this fast. They must refuse. There must be a stampede in the electrical system of the brain that blocks all roads in. And perhaps, I think, they did not "congregate up" because then there would be the dawning of recognition, and something in someone's eyes would say, reach up, touch your head, part of it is gone, and then what would you do?

The restaurant's music speakers, concealed somewhere within a foot of our table, are playing a Buddy Holly song, and when Holly sings the refrain, "That'll be the day when I die," Karei McDonald does not miss the irony. His eyebrows raise sharply, and he looks at me in a precise way that estimates, perhaps, my capacity for subtlety, and I think then that Buddy Holly was the spokesman for our days at Dog 'n' Suds.

"I went over to the Dog 'n' Suds and found this car," Karei continues, pounding the heel of his hand on the table for a moment to the rhythm of the song. "It had a kid and a mama in it. Best of my knowledge, they were both dead. Yes, they were dead. I got both of 'em out. The car was smashed. I believe the little boy was hurt worse than his mother was, but she was smashed bad, too. She didn't live any time after the tornado, so she didn't suffer long. The cars were smashed up in ever' form of imagination. There were many flattened, some of 'em rolled over. They were indescribable as to how . . . well . . . they were just tore up. Whole cars. The bodies were just about in every form of mutilation, decapitation, some of 'em were cut half in two, then they was people that the debris had just hit 'em and taken part of their head off, not all of they head, but just taken part of it, and they were people with broken backs that died, and broken necks, they were a lot of people that had fingers and hands cut off, some of them had legs cut off."

I think as Karei is talking, his tone deliberate and factual but not clinical, how helpless and fragile affection seems in the face of this roll call of the mutilated, how none of this is a thing that ordinary medicine, or kind words, or even emergency surgery on the spot, could ever heal. It is an absurd thought and a defense mechanism, because what I am now, as I sit across from this old-bird firefighter, is just some dumb American kid grown up who has been raised on the sap and syrup of the naive. I am naive. I don't believe people die this way. Or do I?

Karei's voice comes up now within the place where I have been wallowing, a place where you do not want to hear or acknowledge, and he has seen this, perhaps, in my face and been told, perhaps, by the fact that I have twisted my napkin to shreds.

"I know all of this sounds really bizarre and gruesome, but you are in this atmosphere and you kind of forget just how traumatic some of these injuries are because you see so many and it becomes commonplace in this atmosphere. I've never been in battle in the military—I been in the military, but not in battle—but it's something that must be similar. If they dropped a bomb on a city and everybody's kinda walkin' around dazed, this is what the atmosphere was like at Candlestick, people walkin' wounded, people walkin' with they leg broken and maybe the bone stickin' out and they don't even know it. It is gruesome, but it is still part of life, and a lot of people just don't like to talk about it. If you hang around long enough, you're going to have to talk about it. I guess it was the first time that I had ever seen mass deaths. I thought that death was amazing, it impressed me immensely, but what do you do? You do the best you can. If people are dead, what do you do? I think Daddy helped me a lot on that. Daddy was not a worrier. He said if there's something you can do something about, get your butt up and go do it, and if there was something you couldn't do something about, then don't worry about it. I guess that day was one of the first times I had ever become acquainted with the triage-type thing. You try to figure out the ones that's gonna make it, and you try to help them, you try to help the most critical of the ones that's gonna make it. If they're still alive and a trained doctor can say that they're not going to make it, then you put them to the side and let them die. And this is hard. It was hard for the doctor there that day to do, 'cause he was agonizin' over this little ol' girl. I've been in the same situation myself since then, but it's a real real big responsibility to say, 'Okay, Mrs. Baker, I'm not going to do anything for you because you're gonna die.' That bothered me, that bothered me because some of these people were still alive, and I always thought, you help the worst ones, I thought, yes, that's a pretty good rule of thumb, but I found out it's not always true. You help the ones that you can help, and eventually it makes sense. But at the point that all this is going on, it doesn't. Course Dr. McMillan was trained, I trusted him, so I didn't have a big problem with that, but I thought about it later on and I did have some problems with it, and this has been on my mind many years."

I think now of how people mark the passage of their lives, by these milestones of dark discovery, by initiation into the deliberate and unholy knowledge of the mortal. Death to a child is not the same as death to a thirty-year-old man, I think as I watch Karei slip somewhere back to a time before Candlestick, before he understood that you might have to choose who would live and who would die. I can almost sense him weighing this, testing it psychologically, fitting it to his mind as he remembers it, asking which is better, to know or not to know that life can pull this sort of sucker punch, and I know without thinking too hard that he will decide that knowing all of it is the better bet. I know that there are more people who are not like Karei McDonald than are, and that some try to hold at a distance even the intimations of mortality, and for a time it must seem as if the world is not jagged because there is no pockmark in the glass that separates us from it, no threadlike fracture, no blood on the ground. And I think then that the day does come when the only shield against the stone that moves at a speed incalculable is that dressed and polished window front, behind which we stand unwitting, fools even, and that once the break is made and the pieces fall like ice onto concrete, there gapes, for whatever time allowed is left, an aperture to the mortal that will never seal itself again.

Karei McDonald sits with his eyes wide open now, the pupils uncommonly dark and empty, and speaks entirely to himself: "I would like to know if those who survived ever came back to normal. I would like to know if they ever did come back at all."

Before we part, Karei talks about how he likes to sit with his daughter, talk to her over breakfast. He says she makes good biscuits. He says that God has taken care of him and that his parents were his heroes. He says that the woods are full of mysteries and that the fox is an amazing creature. I walk him out to his pickup truck in the parking lot that edges the woods. Everything is close to the woods here, to the fields, the river, the farmland, because if all these got too far away then it wouldn't be important anymore and this wouldn't be Mississippi. I smell the night air coming on in that slow burn of pine resin and water moving up out of the ground into the air. I smell the red clay cast in a mold the shape of Mississippi, and I feel a great sense of calm standing in the twilight next to Karei McDonald because I know he smells it, too, and he feels these same things, even if to himself, at this moment, he does not articulate them. We shake hands warmly, and he asks that my husband and I come see him on his land, that we walk the woods with him, have some supper, and I tell him yes, meaning it.

That night I go to sleep in the bad motel in the bad part of town, listening to Karei McDonald's voice on tape. I love the sound of it, how it matches the feel of this place, precise and unformed at the same time. I think to myself that I wish I had a father with a voice like that because it would never matter if what he said was good or bad, but only that he spoke at all. "He was a *free-yund* of mine," I hear Karei say right as I am falling to sleep, and I dream the old dream again, of the bodies laid out head to toe in the parking lot, but this time there is no wind, no grocery store, no house nearby, just a circle of woods grown in close to where I stand, and all the trees are red.

CHAPTER TWENTY

I DO NOT KNOW WHERE THEY ARE BURIED, and I have not asked, nor will I. It is not my place. A clear demarcation line is scored between my need to know and the resting places of the dead. Those who have earned the right by birth or friendship can go and trace the names on the markers, lie in the grass beside a headstone, lay flowers against the hot ground. I have no business gawking. I would not be welcome because I have not left well enough alone.

Still, the urge is strong in me after talking with Karei to go to a cemetery, any cemetery, if only to be able to imagine that this is the sort of place where they ended up, covered in grass, girded by stone, in the deepening shade of hardwoods, so I can shake the picture of where they went down, so I can understand that their families carried them far away from that ruined place.

I wonder at my reasons for any of this, wonder as I have wondered for years *why* this one place, this one time, this one tragedy. As I run headlong once again into the simple, clarifying notion that this is home and nothing less, nothing more, and that that is why I come back, I am caught up in the brief but disturbing delusion that it is 1966. Staring at the wide rutted macadam before me does it, as I search for a graveyard. The very texture of the road takes me back, the jagged tar patches like blackened scars. I remember the rough look of these streets, how crabgrass would follow the fault line of fissures in the seedier parts of town and then disappear entirely out where the smooth, unmarked tar roads had been poured. Cherrywood Drive, where I had lived, had been a wide river of tar with the soft sheen of obsidian in the first cool days after it had been poured. But in summer the tar would bubble up and at night the air pockets would harden like a shell, and come morning, when the dew and the heat began to soften everything again, there would be scores of tiny bugs concretized on the dome of each bubble, glazed and held suspended like ants in amber. When the air pockets multiplied we would ride our bikes over them and listen to the muted popping sound, or barefoot we would crush them beneath our heels as we walked listless in the heat, later leaving blackened footprints on the kitchen floor. I think as I pass the wrought-iron gate of Greenwood Cemetery and then turn around that the roads then were as tactile as the dirt.

Greenwood Cemetery is Jackson's oldest landmark. In 1821, there were six acres called simply "the graveyard." Now there is nearly five times the original expanse. Seven governors are buried here, clergymen, whites, blacks, slaves, masters, the dead from the insane asylum, paupers, prison inmates, Confederate generals and soldiers, and children in a vault known as "Babyland." The belief in Jackson is that every inch of ground here holds the dead, with bodies stacked one on top of the other. There are those here who died when Jackson was burned during the Civil War, when the women and children went to hide in the swamps and came back to nothing.

I go in through the Wright and Ferguson Funeral Home on the west side of the cemetery. It is a shortcut, and within the cool vault of the funeral home that smells of gardenia oil there is a very old, very brittle-looking, pale-as-chalk man, one of the directors, I can tell by his somber suit, his graciousness that borders on the unctuous. He tells me I can make my way to the cemetery through a downstairs door. He escorts me, smiling in a peculiar and compassionate way, and I realize that it is a smile that he has given the bereaved hundreds of times and that there is probably no other way he can smile. A minimalist smile. A smile that says something about how God understands when grief makes fools of us. Still, in my rare experience of funeral directors, this man has some class. So much that I think he will not be taken aback if I ask if the caskets were closed in March 1966. I know that Wright-Ferguson handled most of the bodies, and it is just by accident that this is where I find myself.

As he opens the door to the even cooler basement of the funeral home, the atomic brightness of noon streams in on a tide of humidity. The old man turns to me, straight as he can hold himself at his advanced age, his white hair combed back with lemon-scented pomade—I smell it as he turns—and says, "Now if there's anything at all that I can do for you . . ." in a voice as rich as the air in this close place is sterile. I think so loudly in my head that I believe I have spoken it: "Were the caskets closed? Were they all closed?" I know that Sarah Parker's was not, so I must have a look then on my face so addled that the old gentleman is spurred on to even further graciousness and concern. He asks if I would like to sit down. He asks if I would like a cold glass of water. I tell him no as politely as I can, sweating now, wanting to get out the door and into the bright air so badly that I fairly push past him, upsetting his balance. He continues to smile the benevolent smile, the all-patient smile, and suddenly I want to scream, if for no other reason than to confirm that I am real. Instead I hear myself saying one word to him through the haze of heat that separates me from the entrance to the cool interior where he stands, the place that has to be cool all the time.

"Candlestick," I say. The word sounds idiotic, like a command, and then, in case he thinks I am madder than I know myself to be, I follow up quick with the word "tornado," the two together an open sesame to the memory of anyone who has lived here long enough, and the old guy nods sagely. I see the cataracts on the lenses of his eyes for the first time, how they look like milk glass in the light. He says just this: "Nine funerals in one day." And I run then toward the broadening green of the cemetery, deep into the low-voltage hum of cicadas that hangs like static in the trees, past the wrought-iron gate and down into the heat mirage of headstones and crosses and tombs.

It is a place of vandals, Greenwood Cemetery, heads of angels broken off, a stone Bible lying cracked on the ground, a portion of the iron fence twisted like barbed wire. There are low, twisted trees, too, like the myrtle trees along the South Carolina coast, and hardwoods that grow in stands and spill out shade like water. Deep in the interior of the cemetery is the grave of a young girl with a stone dog lying beside it. The story goes that when the girl died, the dog, bereft, came to sleep on her grave.

Yellow fever epidemics once plagued the town in summer, and at the center of the carriage road a monument stands to the doctor who succumbed to the disease while tending the sick. There is a monument with a broken stone heart. Headstones are down everywhere. Some lie split in half, others on their sides, some facedown so that when they are lifted free the names on the markers are pressed, written backward, in the dirt. The cicadas are nearly deafening.

Though it is the edge of winter, the heat is as potent as late spring's. I study the markers as I walk along, uncomfortable with the thought of so many graves, how I cannot avoid stepping on them. I think that I have never been taught not to do this. It is not the sort of instruction given in childhood. I am looking not for names but for dates. I am not even looking for the year 1966 but for beginnings and ends, for the significance of life spans in a place where everyone is dead. The shorter the life, the greater the pull, and from that comes the hollow, yet familiar, wondering about someone you have never known and why that person died

at the age of four or twenty or six months or lived for no more
than a day, and whether or not grief is proportionate to these
days accrued alive, in proximity to another. Lives cut short somehow always seem cruel, and it is natural to wonder what, in the
face of cruelty, you would do. I move quickly past the graves of
the ancients, those who lived into their eighties and nineties, and
search for the young ones, the unformed, and find instead the
plot of an entire family, all dead on the same day, five of them, the
children all younger than ten years, the parents still youthful. No
matter how hard I stare at the stones, placed here at the turn of
the twentieth century, and no matter for how long, I cannot
know what caused all of them to stop breathing at, perhaps, 4:33
in the afternoon, on a single February day in the year 1899. It de-
pends on how they died whether or not it is good that they lie
here together. If the father killed them all and then himself, well.
But fire, yellow fever, smallpox, I cannot guess. The Civil War
had ended. The town had stopped burning. So I decree by nothing more than the force of my own ignorance, and because I am
alone here, that they died by tornado one hundred years before
and that I will remember their surname if I ever hear it again.

But I am not alone here. The riffling, high-pitched sound of
children's voices spills out, and now I can see them, gathered in a
semicircle in front of the grotto of a tomb. They are black children, perhaps fifty or more of them, and I notice what I always
notice about black skin in the South, how the colors these children wear stand out, the reds and yellows and blues more distinct than the dark faces. I edge nearer them, down into the
shallow valley where they stand with a few adults, two black
women and one white. The white woman is talking to the children about the ghosts of Greenwood Cemetery, how in the old
caretaker's cabin a child's bottle often went missing and would
reappear when the father demanded it. It is a harmless ghost
story for kids, I think to myself as I watch them, wiggling, trying
to stand still as their teacher has bade them, but they are, all of
them, struggling with boredom, with the determined pull of the

heat of the day, and when they spot me in the shade of the tomb their focus is gone completely.

The white woman calls to me, tells me that they are doing a play about the cemetery, and since they do not have enough readers, will I join them? It is an odd request because I am, after all, a stranger, but the kids are jumping up and down now, shouting, "Do it! Do it!" and the worst I could do would be to show cowardice in front of them. The woman tells me that the next part in the ghost play is mine. She hands me a sheaf of papers with a star mark by my lines.

I walk down the low steps into the grotto, in front of the tomb of a family whose name I do not remember, and watch the children tumble down the steps and then surround me. I sit in the middle of them, on the cool stone, study the lines that I am handed, a poem about the Civil War dead, and I am reminded of the battlefield in Vicksburg when I was a kid, of the ghosts in the kudzu vines lying, like fog in the trenches, and I think that if these kids have been taught Mississippi history specific to their race, specific to their struggle, then that loyalty has already been driven deep into them, but from a different angle. I begin to read the poem that tells of how it would be if we forgot the dead, how there would be nothing for those who came after, and the kids get restless right away. The sun is shining straight at their backs, and I see them lit up like a miniature choir as I search their faces. Then I stop and try to tell them what the words mean, in kid language, and they nod their heads when I tell them what it means to honor someone, drawing a parallel to the gang loyalty of children, and then I tell them what it would be like if one day they forgot that loyalty, and they seem to understand, but I am not betting on it. The white woman is nodding approvingly. She thinks I am doing a good job.

And then I come to the stanza that stops me cold, the one that without the overadornment of the other passages, makes some hard sense: "Nor ever considered their battle cries, / or tears their families shed, / and no longer stood in silent respect, / close by

the graves of our dead. . . ." And it strikes me suddenly, the bro-
kenness of the South and how all who live here move and live and
breed with that ache in them from another time, and that in some
ways it is little different for the families who have lost people in
tornado season. The place where they live suffers violence, and
people die because of it. The war dead. The weather dead. The
world each time upheaved and missiles flying through the air.
And if there is a next time, then maybe that next time will have
the word "victory" scored above it, but it will always be impossible to tell.

The kids are satisfied that I have not read too long. They are
all sweating now in the heat, as am I, and their movements remind me of a bee colony, bodies rubbing together and turning
one way, turning back. A young girl, perhaps seven years old, has
come to sit on my lap. She pulls gently at my ponytail, takes the
silver chains and pendants around my neck into her small hand,
and I think how pretty the silver looks against her dark skin. She
says nothing, and I wonder what has made her this trusting.

After we stand and move out onto the grass that is browning
like a leaf held to the fire, a boy runs toward me and pulls hard at
my sleeve. He is maybe eight years old, his skin blue black from
the sun, his eyes the soft shine color of the freshly poured tar
roads when I was a kid. He talks to me in a rush, agitated, insis-
tent.

"Hey, hey," he says, "I want you to take me in your car to
Memphis. Right now. You gonna take me in your car to Memphis
so I see Elvis?"

And when I stand dumbfounded, unsure how to answer, he
says again, "I gotta see Elvis. In Memphis. Okay? Okay?"

I stall, ask him how he knows I have a car, and he tells me all
grown-ups have cars. He says again that he wants to see Elvis, and
I am reminded of the pull of Elvis here in the South, in Mississippi, more than anywhere else, not just because of who he became but because he was a country boy who made good. I think of
Big Mama, the weather witch, who instilled her Elvis worship in

me, driving me by the gates of Graceland in her old car back before the place became a shrine, back when Elvis actually lived there. And of how she told me Elvis's mother had leapt from one of the upper windows and died, a suicide. It was a lie, like most things Big Mama told, but it stayed with me, the image of round Mrs. Presley, busted up in the front yard, one of the flowered dresses she always wore stained green with grass from the impact.

I tell the boy that I hate to disappoint him but that Elvis has gone and died on us all. He looks at me as if I am a fool and says as much.

"Well, dummy, I *know* that. I *know* he dead. But he still *here*," and for the first time I see what the kid is getting at, that after all this talk of ghosts and sitting by graves to remember how those who have died live on, Elvis is sitting just as big in Memphis as he ever did, and this boy wants us to blaze a glory path all the way there in my car, him and me. I tell the boy to give me his address and I will think about it, and he walks off dutifully to his teacher to ask for a scrap of paper and a pen.

The surrealness of the afternoon has sneaked up on me, and I look blankly at the white woman, hoping I'll be dismissed now. She asks what my business is here, not harshly, just curious, and I tell her about Candlestick, something she already knows well, and she says offhand, because the boy has brought Elvis to mind and it is as if he were standing there with all of us, saying, *"Aw-huh,"* because once you bring Elvis up he just doesn't go away, she says, "You know, Elvis did a benefit for the victims of the Meridian tornado. You know, he and his mama were in that Tu-pelo tornado when he was a baby, in that little bitty house."

I knew about the Tupelo tornado, but I did not know about the benefit Elvis did. I stare stupidly at the woman, nodding. I am dizzy now in the heat, swamped by it the way I remember, every-thing on me wet and close. I feel as if I am steaming.

"You know," she says again as some of the children fan out behind her and begin to run in all directions, happy to have her distracted for a moment, "you just have to think about that, about Elvis and that tornado. What would have happened if he had died in that tornado? His little ol' twin brother had already died. Elvis was all that was left, and suppose he had died. Well, we wouldn't've had ourselves an Elvis, would we?"

She says it in that declarative sort of way that I hear often here, a "by golly" slap-on-the-knee kind of tone that always seems to carry something deeper, like gratefulness and the urgency that you should share in it, too.

"Well," I say, "the world would not be the same."

"Amen," she says, thanks me, and walks into the moving, brightly colored wave of kids who have run amok.

And I am left standing in the heat, by the low stairs to the tomb of God knows who, in this place where the tombstones are cleaved by vandals, to think on what it means when the wrong person dies, what is lacking, what never comes to pass, and how the adage that what we don't know won't hurt us does not apply when good people die young. And because I am thinking this, I think again of Ronny Hannis, the last picture taken of him, and I wonder what he was thinking and how great were his plans.

CHAPTER TWENTY-ONE

THERE ARE FORMS OF TRESPASS that reach beyond the ordinary, that have nothing to do with fences and stakes and signs posted at the border between the known and the unknown. Emotional trespass has its own sanctified fields and each heart its hallowed ground sown deep in the name of remembrance. Each family has its heroes and its saints, its liars and its thieves. The outsider may speak of none of them with presumption. The outsider is an outsider for a reason. Blood runs wide and deep and wider still. Among your own kind it can be an ocean.

I wrote to the Hannis family. I told them why I wanted to talk to them and that I wanted Ronny to be remembered. I said that I would not contact them again if I did not hear from them. Mae Hannis, Ronny's mother, left a message on my answering machine not long after. She said that it would be all right to call, and after the family talked, they might agree to see me. I liked her voice on the machine. It was kind, small, almost girlish, her accent pronounced, up and down, like dimes bouncing together in a pocket.

The night after I had left the cemetery, I sat on the orange bedspread in the no-tell motel, studying Ronny's yearbook photo, trying to get up the nerve to call his family. I wanted to run, jump into the bad-ass, bad-news Cadillac, drive it back out to the airport, take a cab to the train station, and be gone. This was not my forte, slipping a knife along the spine of people's lives and expecting them not to wince. I was the kid in school too shy to ask for dessert in the lunch line. But I was a grown woman now, poking in deep where I didn't belong, and I knew that if I turned my back on all the memories I had set into motion, they would rise up and slam my face down in the grit hard enough to scar me. Maybe tomorrow. Maybe it would happen that quick.

I called. Mae Hannis answered, her voice such a lovely scale of sounds it made me smile to hear it. For an instant I didn't care if she told me to go away and never bother them again, it would have been worth it just to hear her voice. It is the kind of voice that takes you in and holds you up high above everything else. She told me that she had talked to her three surviving children and her husband, W.T., and that I could come to their home the next evening. I told her I would take a cab to Bobby Grant's barbershop at Candlestick, talk to him, and then walk on over to their home on Ridgeland.

"Oh, goodness, no, please don't do that," she said, immediately distraught. "Now, that wouldn't be safe. You don't want to be walking alone out here by yourself. Now, I don't say necessarily that anything would happen, but it just wouldn't be safe."

I remember how it felt when she had said that, as if my claim to childhood in the old neighborhood had fled so fast that the world turned colder than it had ever been. I had imagined walking around Candlestick in the warm dusk, catching Bobby Grant in the old barbershop before he closed up, then moving along the maze of streets, beneath the oak and sweet gum, along the rough edge of the ravine, stopping to look at the house where I had once lived, checking to see if the maple tree I had planted in back when I was ten years old was still there, maybe running like I used to along the tarred streets or borrowing some kid's bike for half an hour. It would still be deep and dark and green in there where we all used to live, the trees grown to monsters now, and I wanted to smell it again, take the pulse of it, be far inside it until everything grew still in me. Not safe to walk there anymore. To conceive of fear, beyond the fear of wind, in this place where I had been an orphan brought to awareness by the Mississippi dirt, was a thing I could not at first comprehend. Who would get me here? Who could take my rightful claim to the past and scare it into running? I thought for a moment of doing it anyway and not telling Mae Hannis, but I could not turn the voice down. I could not disobey. I told Mrs. Hannis I would take a cab straight to their house.

"Well then," she said, "we'll be waiting for you."

I TOOK A CAB BECAUSE THE CADILLAC was running rough. I hadn't even bothered calling the rental place. I figured when it choked for good I would just leave it on a backstreet like some steaming monument to my return home.

The cab driver was steady and calming. I asked him to take the old way to South Jackson, out Terry to MacDowell to Cooper. He said he understood taking the slow way, that people were in too much of a hurry anymore. I told him of my need to see these streets again and again, so I could burn them back into memory where they belonged. He asked how long I'd been away, and I told him more than thirty years. When he asked why I had come back I told him, and that now I was going to talk to a family who had lost their son.

He was quiet for a long time, and I watched out the window as we rode along. Everything looked old, even the commercial buildings, the sad-looking Hi-Lo supermarket, the oaks that grew wide and whose browning leaves were covered with dust from the passing cars, the residential roads that disappeared into the trees, the sky that was heavy with clouds. It all looked old. There was a comfort to it, in the same way that wrecking yards are comforting. Buildings get jammed together and the road and the dirt start to take them over and they have a certain smell then, of rust and water and heat. They smell as though they belong.

We rolled up the first long hill of Cooper Road where it still looks calm and untouched, where it seems as if the houses grow straight out of the ground, where the green holds everything in tight and still, and where my heart charged into another rhythm because I knew that a mile or two around the bend we would come out of the trees at the bridge across Caney Creek that had been stormed to dust, long since replaced, and I would know instantly where I was. Candlestick would be to my left, the creek to my right, and the entire world as I had known it in between.

"That's a hard thing to do." It was the cab driver. I thought maybe he could hear my heart beating clear up in the front seat, and I told him, yes, that I thought at that very moment I had no right whatsoever to intrude on these people and maybe he should just take me back to the motel.

"Hold on," he said, and turned in the seat to look back at me. "Now, you don't *do* that." It was a friendly, vaguely concerned directive.

I like talking to cab drivers, the ones who are willing. They can't help but have a philosophy. They can't help but give advice or act paternal or brotherly, like your best friend. It's a cheap way to get counseling. It seems as though they see every person they pick up in a sort of bas-relief, and they can pin you fast, know your fears, know if they should fear you. They go on dog instinct, on some sort of psychological scent mechanism sharpened by the smell of gasoline and oil and wadded-up currency.

As we took the short hill up Cooper, Candlestick was behind me before I could look, then the sharp right onto Ridgeland, where the Hannis family lived. I began to panic.

"No, come on," I said to the cab driver. "Just take me back. Really. Let's just go on back." My palms were beginning to sweat.

"Hey," he said, stopping the cab abruptly a few houses down from the Hannises', turning full in the seat now to face me. "Listen here. I know this. If you don't go in, you won't like yourself for a long, long time."

He had a point. I imagined waking to that sick feeling of disappointment, like a hangover, and of the excuses I'd have to make. I imagined the Hannis family, all waiting for me in their living room. I imagined Ronny, not the smile on his face but him shaking his head and turning his back to me. It was an image I couldn't bear.

I took a breath, looked at the protective cover the trees made above this simple street. I remembered waking to them one day bare and then the next day, it seemed, their leaves so full and broad that light came through in dusty spines, the sky no longer blue but the deep chlorophyll green of summer.

"Sure," I said to the driver as he began inching the car nearer the Hannis driveway. "You're right. I bet you're always right."

As the cabbie pulled away, I noticed that it was almost dark and that even though I had expected to feel otherwise, I felt safe here, at home.

IT IS RONNY'S SISTER SHARON whom I see first, getting out of her car on the short, steep driveway in front of the low, brick house, her feet clad in cowboy boots, her face pleasant and intelligent, slightly guarded. She is a few years older than I, wiser-looking. When she smiles and greets me, I look for her brother in the smile.

They wait in the living room that catches the last light of the day: Mae and W. T. Hannis; Ronny's other sister, Darlene, my age; and his brother, Donny, the oldest of the four children. Sharon shows me to a chair opposite the bright print couch where Mae and W.T. and Darlene sit, Darlene's arm draped casually across the back of the couch, Mae and W.T. sitting with their hands folded in their laps.

As I walk across the living room that is homier than most, clean and settled-looking, I see the yearbook picture of Ronny in a handsome frame, propped up on a sideboard, and beside it a framed copy of the poem Sharon wrote after he died. I know without having to think about it that the picture and the poem are here day in and day out, that they have not been placed here because I have come to visit, and, knowing this, the sense of intrusion is even stronger in me now, as if Ronny is watching over his family, making sure I treat them right.

In the history of awkward silences, the quiet that falls upon the Hannis living room as we all face one another is not the deepest nor the longest, but it seems to have at its core an insistence that things be said right, that no mistakes be made. I have the tape recorder clutched against my belly, hoping maybe to hide it, feeling my palms turn slick against the molded plastic. I think what a stupid thing it is.

Donny, slender and quiet, his face open and honest-looking, not unlike his brother's, sits at the dining table. Darlene, with her sandy hair and pretty face, her wide eyes that watch me, says nothing. Mae and W.T. sit small on the couch. They are tiny, white-haired now, Mae's face as lovely as her voice, a gardenia belle with smooth, pale skin; W.T.'s face sharp-featured, reddening and muted by a vague confusion. The children will tell me later that W.T. no longer has the rein on sadness he once did since he was shot by a robber while working at a store. It is not a picture that fits itself to the small man on the couch.

I have made myself a promise, and I consider it as I sit forward in the low chair, the tape recorder still held tight against me, my legs beginning to tremble, and it is that I will not pretend that we are not all uncomfortable. I will not smile a lot and try to chat and make comments about how I like their house, although I do, and wish against some broken hope that I had once lived here, too. I will not say anything but what is straight. I will not dishonor these people.

Already it is hurting them all. I can see it in each face, in each pair of eyes, in the way Mae looks at her lap frequently and then up at me. She smiles when she does.

It is Darlene who speaks first. She asks if I have seen the poem that Sharon wrote that was in the Forest Hill yearbook, and then a remembrance a friend wrote about Ronny in the church paper. She hands me copies of both, and I study them for a while. It is quiet again, so very quiet, but for the papers rustling in my damp hands, and I say what I am thinking, that I am intruding and that if they would like for me to leave, I will, right now. I tell them I would understand if they wanted me to go. And I do, but now I am hoping they will want me to stay. It is not just imagination, not just a wish told in the dark because I will think of this later, but suddenly I want and need to be near these people. The words "When two or more are gathered in my name" flash into my consciousness, and I get the feeling of what is at the heart of it. This is Memorial Day. Right here. Right now.

In fits and starts the talk comes as they begin to walk the periphery of memory. Sharon says that they have checked me out and they want me to stay. She says why she wrote the poem for Ronny.

"I was in the eleventh grade, and Ronny was in the twelfth." Her voice is even, easy to listen to. "And in the eleventh grade we had to write a poem, which was due just a few days after the tornado, so that was my poem, to turn in for class."

It is a poem about her brother's smile, his goodness.

"He worked afternoons and Saturdays down at the supermarket." It is Mae now, still looking at her lap, then at Sharon, who is sitting across the room. "He worked at Liberty. We had known the manager, Mr. Webb Jones, for years when we lived out off Bailey Avenue, so he went down there and got a job. Ronny told Mr. Webb Jones that he could work in the afternoons and Saturday, but that he had to go to church on Sundays." Mae smiles at the memory. "And he, Webb Jones, said, 'Oh, I understand.' Ronny went to Cooper Road Christian Church, he was in the band at school, he tried to play football and he didn't because he was too little. He decided he'd stick with the band. He loved everything, and he was always smilin', jolly, good Christian child—*young man.*"

Mae makes the distinction for her son, the one I have made when studying his picture, that at some point before he died Ronny Hannis had become a young man with conscience and foresight.

The living room is comfortable, a welcoming nest of deep chairs and sofas, the maple-colored dining table off to one side where Donny Hannis sits, listening closely. I imagine the family at the table at Sunday dinner, covered dishes being brought through the door from the kitchen and laid out on hot pads, and the nervousness I have felt begins to dissolve, replaced by a growing knowledge that I will not be judged here for what I want to know. I am among decent people.

Sharon laughs now, leans forward and clasps her arms around her knees, and rocks back and forth. "He *always* had pennies everywhere in his room," she says. "Pennies all over, and he loaded 'em up in a sock one day and took his sock to school—that thing was *heavy*—so he could buy a surfer shirt like everybody else."

I smile at the memory of the surfer shirt craze and recall a picture taken of the school principal, S. M. Bailey, wearing one of the striped shirts with a group of kids. I am reminded of the sense of community in the school and of how we respected the elderly principal because he wore the shirt. It was daring then, the Beach Boys California surfer style, and represented some vague, freedom-loving bohemian lifestyle foreign to Mississippi.

W. T. Hannis has not smiled. In fact, he has been on the verge of tears since I arrived. He sits on the couch close to Mae, deep in the cushions, and then leans forward to speak. He leans politely toward the tape recorder that I have finally had the nerve to place on the coffee table between us. Suddenly I want to tell him that he doesn't have to do this, that I will just turn the thing off and throw it in the yard, but I do not because he is making such an effort and there is immense dignity in the way he holds himself up as he leans toward the table. There is no need. His voice carries well and is as distinct as Mae's.

"I had a old car," he says, "set up out there three or four

months, wadn't it, Donny? And one day I told him, I said, Ronny, I says, now you can have that old car. I'll give it to you 'cause they won't give me nothin' for it in trade-in, and he didn't ask me to borry money or nothin', till one day he got that job down there and he said, 'Well, Pop, I'll take that ol' car off your hands now,' and I said, 'Okay.' I said, 'Now, you have to pay for the insurance on it, but anything else I'll help you put it together.' Well, I got some brake shoes, and I think Ronny and his cousin—cousin had his leg in a cast—they come up here one day and that cast was hangin' out from under the car and he never put them brake shoes on, and he said, 'Daddy says you can take these ol' shoes back, they wadn't no good,' he says. 'I couldn't put 'em on there,' but he'd already replaced 'em, see?"

I nod at Mr. Hannis as he looks to see if I have gotten the point of the story, that his son had fixed the brakes on his own, that he had some pride in it.

"Now, every Saturday he'd get paid," W.T. continues. "He'd come in and lay 'bout three or four dollars on that dresser there for the insurance. I said when you get it paid for—it was about thirty-five dollars, somethin' like that, a year, you know, this liability insurance—I said don't get no collision or nothin' like that 'cause the ol' car ain't worth nothin' nohow. But he would lay the money right there."

W.T. points to the small sideboard by the front door where Ronny's picture sits.

"And every once in a while," W.T. says, "he said, 'Pops,' says, 'I can't leave you no money this time. I had to buy me some clothes,' or somethin' like that. He bought his own clothes, everything, he had certain . . ."

W.T. trails off, begins to shake his head, and pulls back into the couch. Mae pats his leg and says, "There, there, it's all right now." The old man has started to cry but sits forward quickly again, urgently, and speaks directly at the recorder.

I am touched again by his politeness, of how, by this small gesture, he offers his respect.

"Last thing, though, that we heard, I'd already gone to work, and then Mae, she was gettin' ready to go to work, and Ronny grabbed that ol' garbage can and throwed it up on his shoulder and put it out to the street, and she says, Mae says, 'Ronny, don't get that dirt all over your shirt,' and he had some papers to mail off, for him to go to college, and he laughs and he says, 'Don't worry about this ol' shirt, you just mail them papers off.'"

Sharon says now how Ronny would turn the shirtsleeves under, not back, like most boys, and that Mae saved the blue shirt he wore that day and kept the sleeves turned under. I imagine her holding the shirt that smelled like her son, pressing it against her face, and of how insubstantial, yet vital, what is left behind can be. I imagine Ronny's shirt in a drawer somewhere in this house, separate from other things, the sleeves still turned under, and I wonder if when she is alone Mae takes the shirt from its special drawer and sits quietly with it folded in her lap. I think of how Ronny called it "this ol' shirt," never realizing how valuable it would become.

"Now, that was a funny thing," Sharon says. "You know, we asked him what he was gonna do. He was just determined to go to college. And we asked him what he was gonna do or be. He was gonna go to school for somethin', he didn't know what, but he was gonna be good at whatever it was. He made the highest that you can make on a college test." She says it proudly.

W.T. sits forward again. His hands are shaking, and his eyes and face are red. Each time a memory strikes him, his eyes begin to tear up and he rubs his knees hard with the palms of his hands.

"He'd be workin' down there in that store," W.T. says. "Webb Jones'd tell him, says, 'Ronny, come on up here, we need ya up here on the cash register,' and he'd drop whatever he's doin', he'd run up there and he'd work on it, and all them little girls what come in—two, three, four years old—every one of em'd come through the line and he'd give 'em a sucker, and they, after the store reopened, they was wonderin' where Ronny was, and after they didn't get no suckers, their mother'd have to tell 'em."

I think of the little girls and the candy Ronny gave them and wonder if they have carried the memory into adulthood, hoping they have.

Mae's smile is almost beatific as she starts to speak, and I am moved once again by the voice that runs and jumps with its own frequency. It is a voice that if it ever turned stern would make you want to beg for forgiveness, tell any number of lies just to have it turn soft again.

"But all the little older ladies," she says, "our age, I guess, now, that lived out in this area, he touched all their lives. Some of 'em I'd never seen before. But I didn't know any of 'em hardly, 'cause I worked, but I never seen so many, and they went and asked—Mr. Jones had stuck a picture like that one—some kind of picture in the window at the store, of Ronny, and they come and asked him to take it down, because they just couldn't stand it. And one little lady told me, she said, 'You had a wonderful child.' She said, 'I stood in line Christmas Eve for about thirty-five minutes just to see that smile.' She said he always had that smile, and he did, don't you know."

Mae Hannis charms me into beaming outright, and I think that perhaps it is not proper that I am smiling so, but I can't help it. When she says, "He always had that smile, and he did, don't you know," the last three words are spoken as she tilts her head to one side and looks up shyly, like a girl. It is an affirmation of her son and a benediction at the same time. I want to say, yes, yes, I do know, because always in his pictures it is the smile that holds you.

The room is darker now. The sun has set. Sharon turns on a light and sits back down.

"We don't know," she says, her voice heavy, almost pleading. "We weren't there, so we don't know. We just know what we've been told. Ms. Freeney, she worked at Dog 'n' Suds. She wrote to us."

"But what I don't understand is"—it is W.T. now, urgent again, seeming confused—"they say that he fell on top of a little girl, that he pulled a little girl inside and fell on top of her. But I never heard who the little girl was. Now she, Ms. Freeney, did tell us that."

I tell them the little girl's name, that it was Pamela Pace.

"Well," Sharon says, "her mother was sittin' in the car, waitin' for her to pick up somethin', and Ms. Freeney told Ronny to get the little girl and come back behind the counter. They went back there and he lay on top of her, that's what she told us. He was that type person, to do somethin' like that, certainly to try to take care of a child, or anybody for that matter."

I say that Pamela Pace lived because of Ronny and they all nod their heads slowly, eyes unfocused, imagining. I hear Ronny say, "Let's get out of here," the way I've heard it in my head a dozen times, and then Doris Freeney yelling, "There's not time. Hit the floor." Then Ronny throwing his body on top of the girl. Juland grabbing her purse. The bomb dropping.

"He was on his way to work," Mae says. "He went in there to play pinball before he went to work."

"Excuse me." It is W.T., carefully polite again but needing to be heard. "He said there was one colored woman in there and this Ms. Freeney, and he said he never would go in there and get a hamburger unless they was in there to fix it for him."

I think of Juland fixing a hamburger for Ronny in the tiny kitchen, listening to the jukebox, singing along. I think of how it was supposed to be her sister Meland working there that afternoon, and I wonder if Ronny would have stayed as long if Juland hadn't been there. It is a dangerous way to think, and I imagine the thousand "what if's" that have fallen hard on W.T. and Mae all these years.

I hear now what I have been told by many others, of how Ronny pulled himself out and began to help.

"Dan Smith, Ronny's cousin, said Ronny was tryin' to help everybody, but he didn't realize he was in shock," Mae says.

Then W.T.: "Somebody said to him, says, 'Boy, you need to go to the hospital yourself.'"

And Mae: "That was Dan. Dan got hold of him. Ronny was walkin' toward work. He told Dan he had to go to work."

The image of Ronny comes up, the good boy, mortally injured, his head battered, his legs cut deep, stumbling through the wasteland, through the heaped-up cars, remembering an obligation.

"He got out of that mess one way or another," W.T. says, twisting his hands as he leans forward. "I don't know how he . . . he had a big hickey over . . ."

He breaks down now, and Mae pats her husband on the leg and says "Shush" quietly. Coming from Mae, it is a sound infinite in its gentleness. W.T. pulls in his breath sharply at the comfort of Mae's voice. The tears have made his old skin shiny in the lamplight, and he looks like a boy who has stood with his face to the rain. He takes another long breath and speaks again.

"He had a big hickey over his head and one behind his head. When I come home, we were lookin' for him. Donny was workin' for the post office up there, and he got here some way or another. We were all right up on the corner. They wouldn't let us go down in there where all that trash was, and I started goin' to one hospital to the other to try to find him. At Hinds General, the lady on the switchboard—we used to live next to her on Idlewild Street, off a Bailey Avenue—she says, 'W.T.,' says, 'I think he's up in ta the operatin' room right now,' and I went up there, and he was layin' on this couch, this stretcher, with his leg up like that." W.T. holds his leg up and bends it at the knee. "And they were sewin' these flaps, these cut-up places under his leg, and Dr. Hodges—I picked up laundry for him—when he saw me, I think he . . ." W.T.'s sobs break free now, as if something is being pulled loose in him, and Mae tells him firmly but kindly that he doesn't have to talk anymore, that maybe Donny can talk for a while.

"Don, can you talk?" she asks her son, and the silent Donny, whose face has been a mask of pain as his father speaks, says, "Y'all are tellin' me stuff that I never knew."

"Donny," Sharon says, wanting to pull everyone back from where they have begun to fall, "Donny, now we want to know the good things about him that you knew, as a brother."

But Donny remains transfixed by what his father has said, things he has never heard about that day, about how his brother died.

"But, Sharon," he says forcefully, "we've never talked about it. We never, as a family, have talked about it."

Everyone falls silent, and Donny looks down at his hands twisting together in his lap. What Donny has just said is not a thing I would have guessed.

W.T. has heard none of the exchange. He has been with his son in the emergency room, fallen back through the years as if they had never been, and he sees as he saw that day, the unbelievable and the irrefutable.

"Dr. Hodges come out two or three times," he says, his voice as far away as the day where he now stands, "and the third time he come out, that's when he said, 'He's gone.' Of course I wouldn't believe it. I couldn't."

Sharon is watching her father, at the way he has gotten smaller on the couch, his body folded in on itself, his head bent now as if he is praying, and there has washed over her face a compassion that cannot be measured. When she speaks it is forcefully and in a rush of words such that she does not take a breath until she is done.

"I can tell you this," she says. "I cannot tell you everything in the world, but I can tell you this. I thought all these years that Mother and Daddy hurt like the three of us did, because I couldn't think of any worse hurt than losing my brother, and I thought Mama and Daddy hurt like we did, that we all hurt just the same, until my son was in a car accident." A picture of Sharon's son hangs on the wall of the living room, and W.T. catches my eye and points to it.

"And when they called me they said, 'He may not be alive when you get here,' and my mother rode with me, and goin' down Highway 49 I looked at her and told her I was sorry, and she said, 'What for? You haven't done anything.' Mama has never smoked in her life, but she lit cigarettes for me all the way so I could watch the road. Almost thirty years later, then, I see there is one big difference in losing a child and losing a brother, and as much as I hurt for my brother, there is a difference that is indescribable, and I don't want to know it. My son lived, thank God, but I came as close as I ever want to, to what it's like to lose a child, and I came close enough to know now that my mother and daddy hurt a lot different than the three of us did, and we hurt, we hurt bad, 'cause we loved him. We were just always together. We had the big brother and the little brother that wasn't littler than us, but we had to call him the little brother because we had two that were older." She laughs now and breathes in long and hard.

"'S' for Sherry." It is Darlene, almost as quiet as Donny, pretty Darlene who has a languid, relaxed way about her and eyes that have not missed a moment this night. I do not know what she is talking about, but everyone else smiles.

"Ronny's girlfriend," she explains. "Sherry. He had a big 'S' on the gearshift of his car, like on the old cars, you know? I think it really meant 'Super,' but Ronny said it meant 'S' for Sherry, so I remember him doin' that, putting it in the 'S' gear for Sherry."

"His favorite song was 'Sherry,'" Sharon says. "They were going steady. Ronny was buried with her class ring on his little finger. They were in love. They wanted to go to college together."

I had thought of him that way before, in love, but now I saw him in the Elvis days we had once owned, the Formica countertop and stick-on linoleum days, the jukebox, saddle-oxford, leather-jacket days, the days when we pulled the world to us from our small corner at Dog 'n' Suds, the ones my gawky friends and I witnessed from the fringes of puberty, envious of boys like Ronny and girls like Sherry who traded class rings and rode to school together in old jalopies. I imagined the two of them at Fred Hudgins's tiny little café, the jukebox playing "Sherry," and then the two of them riding together in Ronny's '56, at night in the summer when the Mississippi moon was full and the frogs sang along the edges of the muddy ponds and the strobe flash of lightning bugs stuttered across the fields, the tires of the car making wide tracks in the red dirt along the road that smelled like rust in the damp heat of the evening, Ronny with the shift in the "S" gear because it made Sherry laugh, his cigarettes hidden up under the dash where Sherry could not see them because she didn't want him to smoke, and then the cigarettes spilling down one by one, hitting the boy's foot, a thing his sister Darlene would remember.

And I think of the jokes about Mississippi, about how all there is to do is ride around and drink beer, and I think about the true reason for riding long into the night here, because to be in it and to smell it and know it the way you do when you've been born here is not a thing you do because there is nothing else, but because it is communion. What pulls can never be denied, and night is when it sings the loudest and blows its breath out hard so you swear you can feel the ground move and hear the trees shudder at their roots and see the cotton grow in the platinum light of the moon. The air then is a potion stronger than any pale, watery vial of nothing that sits in a dust ring on a bathroom shelf, and it is the air I imagine carrying Sherry and Ronny along on those nights, moving slow through the open windows of the car like cotton soaked in honeysuckle. I had never known just how in love the boy had been.

For a time they talk of Sherry, and it is clear that she has reached middle age still bearing their respect. Sharon shows me a picture in the yearbook of a pretty brunette with a smile to match Ronny's. Mae says how Sherry wrapped up Ronny's class ring and gave it to her as a gift for Mother's Day because she knew Mae would not take it otherwise. I imagine Mae opening the box with her son's ring inside, the one he had given to Sherry in commitment, and thinking this I find that I am not immune to fairy tales, to the need for happy endings, and then I find myself wishing long past a hope that lies buried with Candlestick that what was in that box was not Ronny's ring but some small, personal gift for Mae, from her daughter-in-law-to-be, and that Ronny and Sherry married and would grow old together. With no claim or right to this at all, I get the deep-down feeling it would have worked. Not because the world is a fair place or even a lucky one, but because they were good kids from good families who cared, and their lives mattered to more than a bunch of sad punks on a street corner.

"On Class Day," Sharon is saying now, "the girls all wore red corsages, and after the Class Day ceremonies they all went to the cemetery and took off their corsages, and on Ronny's grave they made them in the shape of FH for Forest Hill."

I remember the red corsages, how the halls on the way to class were bright with them.

"I went down there looking for Ronny that afternoon of the tornado," Sharon says, and it seems that she is back where her father has been all evening. "I don't even know how I got in. I don't know if we walked, rode bikes, I don't know, but I remember when we got there I went to a lady that worked at the grocery store and asked if she'd seen my brother, and she said no, and she started crying because she knew he had to be somewhere in all that rubble. But I didn't find him. His car had been parked in front of Dog 'n' Suds, and that wind just rolled it over and over down to the creek. I got down in the mud and crawled up under there and got the keys. So I could have something of him. I'm glad God saw fit to take that old car. None of us could have kept it without him."

A blue shirt with the sleeves rolled under. A key chain. A class ring. Pictures. Poems. But not the boy.

W.T.'s eyes are still bright with tears. The night is settling in outside. Even in winter, as the evening air cools, I think I hear the cicadas. I hear the clipped cry in W.T.'s voice again.

"That school bus driver," he says, each word a note that vibrates and then breaks, "that school bus driver, don't you know, when he would be behind her, that, that school bus . . . he would wave at her as she looked in the mirror and he would never try to pass."

Mae pats W.T.'s leg again, his shoulders. She says, "No, no, he wouldn't pass. That's right. He wouldn't pass, would he?"

Scores of kindnesses, I think, ten dozen reasons this boy should not have died.

I grab the cross around my neck, filigreed silver with a garnet in the center, and feel it sharp against my thumb. I do it to hold my concentration. It is not my place to cry.

"Faith," Mae says, almost in a whisper. "Well, you got to have a whole lot of faith to endure. There's still a whole lot of people that believe in the one up above. If we'd been outlaws, I guess, if our lives had been that way, nobody woulda cared, nothing to remember, nothing that mattered. We know where Ronny is."

She looks up and smiles at me, and I think how many times that smile could break your heart in one day, never mind a lifetime.

Sharon says, "I don't know what people do that don't have faith." It is an honest speculation. Concern shows on her face for those whose lives are damaged and never regained. "Or a belief in God," she continues. "I don't see how they can accept any tragedy or any death. We grew up thinkin' that everybody did what we did, that everybody's daddy polished four little pairs of shoes every Saturday night, because that's what my daddy did, polished four pairs of shoes every Saturday night for Sunday school, and he tied our sashes on our dresses because he did it better than Mama. Well, I was grown up before I found out that not everybody did that. I found out people had alcoholic fathers or mothers. I mean, very close friends of mine. I didn't find out until I was grown. The girl down the street—I had no idea, all through school, that her father was an alcoholic. I just assumed they did the same thing the rest of us did. Daddy polished shoes and tied sashes, and we all got dressed up and we all went to church together whether we wanted to or not."

And those of us, I think, as I watch Sharon, who had alcoholic mothers and fathers thought we were the only ones, and we borrowed our faith from families in the neighborhood, like a cup of sugar, going to church with them on Sundays, to vacation Bible school in the summer, and patched ourselves up halfway so we could at least spot faith when we saw it. But it never quite took with our kind, because it never grew from a seed but was grafted on, and I remember praying, imitating the devout, but not until I was long gone from Jackson and far from childhood did faith match itself to me, scar for scar.

Mae is studying her lap again, about to speak.

"I'll have to admit," she says, "for three or four years I wouldn't go down there, by that shopping center. I'd go the way around to go to my mama's and daddy's, and finally my daddy said, 'Do you still go all the way around to get down here, honey?' and I said, 'Yes, sir,' and he said, 'Now, Ronny wouldn't want you to do that.' But it was a long time before I could drive down that road at all. I didn't ever quit believing, you know, it's not that. I just wouldn't do it. I just didn't think I could."

The Hannises' home sits not three blocks from Candlestick. From the rise on Cooper Road where Cooper meets Ridgeland you can stand and look down on the tiny shopping center and onto the drugstore parking lot that in 1966 was a horse pasture. For four years, I think, Mae Hannis never turned left onto Cooper Road, and I imagine her closing her eyes so she would not see it, so she would not have to think about what had happened there, and I understand that it is not denial that kept her away but wanting to keep the memory of her boy separate from that place.

W.T. startles us with the force and pitch of his voice. It is a booming plea made with his fist held in the air, defiant, and we all sit suddenly at attention.

"Well, I tell you!" he shouts toward the ceiling. "Sometimes it makes you feel there's not a God in Heaven don't answer prayers or anything like that. Course we won't hardly understand why He don't answer prayers, when on my way home nobody knows how we prayed that he wasn't in that tornado. From where I was I could see debris flyin' in the air, all over there, and I said something has really tore something up somewhere, and about that time I tried to call Mae. She was working at the bank up there, and the lights and everything was out, and you couldn't come out this way, every road was blocked, but I knew a lot of those streets on the side, and I finally made it through. I got right over here on this corner, and this policeman, I worked with him at Colonial Bakery, Alfred Graves, he was directing traffic and they didn't want to let me through here, and I pulled right up in the middle of there, and I said I'm gonna stop this car right here and leave it right here until you let me through. I said you know I live right over here on this next hill, and he said to the others, 'Y'all let him on through,' and I got to this corner right down at the end of the street and another fella stopped me, and oh, it made me so mad, I tell you. Things like that never happened like that before around here, and nobody knew how to do it. I was tryin' to get all the kids together, see where they were. I've asked a lot of preachers about how God will see you through everything all right, but I don't know. I have tried and asked preachers, and some preachers say it's weather like that when somebody gets killed, that it's not God's work, but I believe it is God's work. I believe God had that thing to happen, to cause maybe a lot of people to join the church, after they knew him and what He could do. A minister came out to the school, and they said a lot of people went down and a lot of those kids accepted God. A lot of those kids went out to the grave and they had a sermon theirselves, had a picture and the flowers and everything, and they placed their flowers around the grave, and they had a picture of Ronny . . ."

W.T.'s voice softens as he mentions the picture of Ronny, and I think of all the years he has spent talking to the preachers, weighing different answers and finally finding one that holds redemption so the mark against his son's life will not be so final, so without cause. I think, perhaps, that it is a merciless quest to seek answers to such questions, but that anyone would have to ask, I would have to ask, and that trusting someone to give the answer is like trusting your own unconscious. I think that it is exactly as W.T. has said, that God did it, not the God of pale-skied Easter Sundays and front-porch picnics, but the God undone, exposed and vengeful, the wild that meets the calm in Mississippi, the Devil Wind. The God Carl Jung said was two-faced, not from deceit but from the very nature of all things. Opposites, he said, you find them everywhere.

DONNY AND W.T. sit awhile longer in the living room, talking. The women move to the kitchen. On the way we stop to look at the pictures that line the small hallway. Graduating class pictures from Forest Hill, senior class pictures of the four Hannis children, all in black and white. We pick the kids out in the group photos, surrounded by girls with rhinestone flare glasses and hair bows, boys with bow ties and Brylcreemed hair. They all look older than their age, the conservative sixties hairstyles and dress pinching in their youth, blurring it so they look on the verge of thirty. Wanting to look older when we are young and younger when we are old. I say something to this effect, and Sharon smiles. I think, though, that we were all older then, despite our naïveté. It had to do with belonging and knowing your place, with calling adults "sir" and "ma'am," with showing respect and then getting it back when your turn came, when you had earned it. It had to do with progression and with watching a life unfold. I feel a great affection for the faces in the pictures. Even though I recognize only a few, I know that we were all formed by this place, this school, this climate, these values, even if some of us had been outsiders to it. The point was, someone would always let us in.

Mae and W.T. and the kids would let Ronny back in if they could, throw open the door wide and let him float in on the deep, abiding air.

We are sitting at the kitchen table. Darlene and Sharon have opened a beer each when Sharon says, "I can remember going out to the cemetery and sitting and talking to God and saying, 'God, just let him get up. We won't tell anybody this happened. It won't matter,' I'd say, 'This'll be the only time, nobody'll know. Just let him come on up with me, and we'll go on.'"

And we'll go on. It is the way Sharon has said the last words that strike me. I can see Sharon and Ronny moving out of the cemetery quietly together, careful not to talk, careful not to cause God to change his mind, careful not to fracture any portal to the world through which they have just walked. I think of Sharon sitting there and asking for this and of how it is a thing that comes not so much from grief as from faith, and how that faith blooms, childlike, in the shadow of pain.

A wall phone with a stretched-out cord hangs near the kitchen table. Sharon points to it and tells me, "This is the same phone we had when Ronny was alive, and we'd stretch it around to the living room so nobody could hear us. It is a long time, but it seems like sometimes yesterday to me, it is like it just happened and it's just a part of your life and it never goes away. Mama believes me. But I know after he died, I know he sat on the bed and talked with me. Now, it was years before I ever told Mama that, and I didn't think she'd believe me, and she said, 'I believe you,' because he stood at her bed and talked to her, and she didn't tell me that until—I mean—this must have been twenty-five years later, and I know he and I sat on the bed together and we talked, and I couldn't tell anybody 'cause they're gonna think I'm crazy, and she said, 'I believe you,' and then it was several more years passed and she said, 'I'll tell you why I believe you.' She said that Ronny was dressed in white, standing at the end of her bed, and he told her it was all right."

As I look around the bright family kitchen, I think of the comfort of darkness in bedrooms, how sleep can pull you clean and unaching from consciousness, and that this is how I have heard that people come to say good-bye, by the bed when the room is dark and still and when the realm of the unconscious swings open wide enough to trammel the stronghold of the rational, and that in this dusk between waking and dreaming what is real, truly real, takes form.

Mae is sitting at the table across from me. She looks tiny and shy but made of whipcord, too.

"I go to bed thinking about him every night," she says.

"It doesn't go away," Sharon says. "It gets better, but it never goes away. You and Daddy made our lives matter."

"You know that policeman," Mae says, her hands pressed against the table with the fingers splayed so you can see the tendons tight beneath the skin, "the one who escorted us to the funeral. Well, you know, he was a friend of mine, went to school with him, well, he come to the bank three or four weeks after the funeral, sat down on the desk and he said, 'I just gotta tell you somethin', somethin' burning in me,' he said. 'I just *gotta* tell you something,' and I said, 'Well then, what is it?' and he said, 'Well, this is not gonna make you feel any better, but I have to tell you a secret. Ronny had more cars at his funeral than Governor White had.' I know he was telling the truth. And I know that there wasn't a lady in our church, or a man either, that didn't come to this house and pray with us."

I imagine the scores of cars at Ronny's funeral, the rival band from another school with its wreath in the shape of a cornet, the little ladies who had once stood in line to see his smile, and I imagine, too, the church people at the Hannis home, praying together with Mae and W.T., and of how rectifying a thing prayer can be when it is not done alone.

"I went back to work," Mae is saying now, "and everybody was so sweet and I'd go off and cry."

"She got so skinny and sick." It is Darlene now, leaning against the kitchen counter, her eyes widening at the memory of her mother diminished by this death. "Our mama's a strong person. A very strong person."

Sharon says, "The kids told us years after they graduated that they would go out to the cemetery."

And Darlene: "They still ask me all the time, 'How's your mother?'"

The night is growing outside, I can feel it, the way I used to be able to when I was a kid, when it changed from something simple to a place that held every secret ever kept, and I think now that secrets told here where the light spills yellow across the room where Ronny once stood belong to this pregnant night. The women have all gone back to that time ago with Ronny and then tempted it right here so that we can feel it on our skin, one world sliding against another, and Darlene says, "This memory always comes. I see Ronny standing out in the yard eating an apple, and I see him and Sharon cutting up, and I see him blowing smoke rings. And I see y'all blowing smoke rings. And I remember how Sherry didn't want him to smoke."

Memories fall out of them like change onto a countertop, and we watch them spill and turn and catch the light.

"Mama knew we smoked," Sharon says. "Mama always knew everything before we did."

And I think that it is a line both prophetic and sad and that it is time for me to go. As I stand, so does Mae, and as I move toward the door, saying my thank-yous, she moves to meet me, and we stand now face to face, the windowed door to the dark carport at her back. She puts her arms around me and holds me close for a moment, and I can smell the talcum scent on her skin and her fresh hair. "We love you," she says as she steps back and holds my shoulders tightly, and it is then that I see the quick light through the carport door, perhaps the wild arc of headlights, and then it is gone.

CHAPTER TWENTY-TWO

PETER BOULETTE WAS TEN YEARS OLD when the Candle-stick Tornado hit South Jackson. He is now forty-four. He says that the storm is in his blood. The day after I visit the Hannis family I take a wild ride with Boulette, the unofficial tornado tracker of South Jackson and a radio DJ who goes by the name Peter Christian. I have not heard Boulette on the radio, so I do not know if the surname Christian refers to an ecclesiastical leaning or simply to the fact that he frequently yells out, "Jesus!" as an exclamation. I never see Boulette standing because he stays glued to his command post, the seat of his Jeep that rides high and bounces higher on the uneven Jackson streets as we make our way back to tornado country. His quiet wife rides shotgun as we run the route out to where Boulette says the tornado first made its dark entry, talking all the while of his obsession and of what began to grow in him after that afternoon in March.

It is the back of his dark-haired head that I stare at most often, but sometimes he turns and takes his eyes from the road to emphasize a point, and then I see a face that is not unfamiliar, a kid I may have seen running the streets of Oak Forest when I was a kid, a face that may give way to jowls in a few years, a Mississippi-boy face with maybe some Cherokee or Choctaw blood, rough and open at the same time. Boulette's voice is good-ol'-boy liquid smooth, deep and vibrant, and I can tell that he would sound impressive on the radio. He plays parties often, at the country clubs, at private functions, but he was first a kid from South Jackson and the mark is still there in the way he remembers the place with a sentiment that surfaces at odd times and of which he seems only partially aware. I tell him as we head into the woods that flank the still-rural roads near Forest Hill School that I understand obsession, particularly an obsession with Candlestick.

"I mean, I had dreams," he says as we bounce along, "for two, three, four years, who knows how long, where I'd be in a tornado and I couldn't run, you know, that type thing, and it took me over to a point. I'd like to chase 'em now!"

The sheer glee he expresses at this idea is almost disturbing, and I get a quick, ridiculous picture of Boulette atop a galloping horse, his quarry twisting in the distance as he raises one arm in the air and yells, "Jesus!"

"Jesus!" Boulette says, almost on cue. "Now, you know it bothers me, it really deep down bothers me when I tell everybody and they don't remember the tornado and I say, 'What do you mean you don't remember it? How can you not remember it?' It was just so vivid to me that it couldn't have been any other way."

Boulette talks about how when he ran from the back door of his house to see what all the commotion was about, the wind was coming at him so strong that he could not hold his eyes open.

"I can't honestly say I heard a train, like they say," he tells me, "but what I heard was fascinatin'. I remember holdin' my hand up and I couldn't see. The wind was just blowin' profusely, and my mother says, 'Get back in the house, get back in the house.' This power was comin' from the back, which would have been facin' Cooper Road, southwest, and I looked up and there was a sycamore tree right on our property line, and when I looked up at it that's when I saw what I considered to be a tornado, in my mind, you know, bein' a ten-year-old, what's a tornado? But I saw bricks, boards, what have you, but it couldn't have been *the* tornado, it was no way it was *the* tornado."

It was the evil spin-off, I tell him, the miniature second tornado that Karei McDonald and Larry Swales saw, the spiral that my friend whose mother killed her father watched roar up the creek. No one else has mentioned it in the creek, but I see now, according to where we are and what Boulette is telling me, that there was maybe a moment when the smaller funnel moved along the creek bed and then slipped into the main vortex behind Liberty. It has become detective work, and Boulette is a willing gumshoe, looking for motives, patterns of behavior, broken brush in the woods.

We are winding along the upper end of Cooper Road now, thick into the trees and the honeysuckle that still spills from fences almost to the road, and then to the fork where Cooper meets Forest Hill Road and the woods crowd in closer still, the way I remember it being when I was a kid, riding the careening bus to school, the driver a cocky boy of eighteen who could get the bus up on two wheels when he took the curve. The screams of the kids leaning into the windows come back to me now as Boulette takes the curve sharp, but not as sharp as the boy, and memory floods in full in a hundred different ways, how I chipped my tooth on the seat in front of me when the boy slammed on the brakes, how I had held a science project—a Styrofoam replica of molecules—close on my lap in the narrow seat while the kids behind me gawked, the way the woods looked as we raced past, the light that filtered through stuttering in flashes, the smell in spring, when the windows were rolled down, of red clay and cornfields and the slender white-flowered wild onions, and the wrecking-yard smell of the bus itself, oil and gas and transmission fluid and rust, and then the sight of the school as we broke through the trees, a brick stronghold, ancient-looking, untouchable. I remember Donna Durr shining blond at the chalkboard, and then in her Volkswagen seventy feet in the air like Dorothy in the Kansas farmhouse.

"This is Forest Hill," Boulette is saying. "The tornado didn't even mess with it."

It is not the old school. The old school is gone, torn down in 1987 and replaced with another brick building, now just a high school, modern brick with wide, mortared seams, a clean, tall monument. The amphitheater-like field that drops from the woods is now a parking lot, but the overall sense is the same.

"I got a brick from it when they tore it down," Boulette says, his voice excited as a two-year-old's. "And I also got a piece of the old gym floor. I remember my mother used to drop me off up there and I would play basketball in the old gym, and when I got that piece of wood, I told everybody that's one of my prized possessions that I love, and I said, I guarantee you, I bounced a basketball on that piece of wood, don't care where on the floor that piece of wood was, I bounced a basketball on it. She'd drop us off Saturday mornin', my mother, at eight and come get us at four, and I bounced, no doubt about it, I bounced."

Basketball was our game at Forest Hill, I think as I stare at the gym that was built when I was still there, a small domed building later dedicated to Shelby M. Bailey, the former principal, who is in his nineties now and still eats once a week at Hudgie's restaurant. I see the old band room, too, where I played clarinet and Ronny Hannis played cornet. I think of how he missed band practice on March 3 and wonder if it would have made a difference if he had gone, if maybe he might have noticed how bad the skies were and might have waited to go to work. I think of all the games played in the old gym that is gone now, the bleachers splintery where I would sit and wait out a foul. I think of all the out-of-town games we played in junior high, of the pine resin in dispensers bolted to the walls of the gym and how it smelled like creosote on your hands, the way it made the grip better on the ball. I covet Peter Boulette's piece of the old gym floor. I would pocket it if he showed it to me.

"We used to come down here when we were kids, right down here where this light is now," Boulette says as he points to where Forest Hill makes a T with Raymond Road. Raymond was nothing but country then, and I see that now there is a convenience store across the road, but it is still country.

"We'd go and hunt shark's teeth," he says. "They would take us in science class, yep, right in there, in these woods. I don't know how, I don't know why they'd be there, but we would find 'em. And then out at Oak Forest Elementary, out where Mr. Mosley taught that died, we used to dig up arrowheads."

It was what we looked for in the bed of Caney Creek, arrowheads and stone tools, chips and pieces of the past, the bottom of the ravine paved in a thousand different shapes of chert, but the arrowhead among them the prize as great as Peter Boulette's piece of gymnasium floor.

Boulette points off toward Raymond as we turn around and head toward Candlestick.

"Now, listen up," he says, a cop's voice, the man who knows the M.O. of the killer, "the first time somebody recognized it, that tornado had to come out of Raymond. It had no option, see what I'm sayin', it had no option, because that's the only place it coulda come from. They didn't have any weather warnings back then, really, until it was on top of 'em, and then it's like, 'Oh, my God, what is *this?*'"

Boulette drives now to the house where he and his family moved a few months after the tornado hit. It still looks like rural subdivision, no matter how people say it has been built up, the trees still outnumber the houses and the roads are wide and winding. Boulette points to the southwest as he stops the vehicle, and says, "The tornado came from that direction, directly that way. Had we been living here then, like we ended up doing, I woulda had a bird's-eye view because it hit, and I'm gonna show you, anywhere from three hundred to five hundred yards directly back in these woods."

I look into the dark woods where he points, remembering the

suffocating green of them, how no light filtered through, but still how hot and damp it was in there, and how you could come upon a wood's pond as dark as the air beneath the leaf canopy where albino catfish swam, and where snakes crawled in to cool themselves.

"As a ten-year-old kid," he says, "what you're gonna do, you're goin' to the woods, and I explored those woods, and all of a sudden I said out loud, when I was out there deep in 'em, right out in there, I said, 'This is where the tornado came through!' I mean, trees were just demolished back in there, there was no doubt of what it was."

I look again toward the woods and think of the resistance the trees would have given, and of how a tornado maybe takes on a mind at that point, where it meets with something aimed to slow it down, and how it would leave the path of greatest resistance for the Tinkertoy fodder of houses slapped together with drywall and weak foundations. I think, too, of how it could have hidden itself in there, a murderer in the woods, and that three minutes away on a direct line, over at Candlestick, no one would have known yet what would burst from this thicket. I imagine myself as Boulette, far into the woods, coming upon the twisted trees with roots pulled out of the clay showing like the handbones of a corpse, and I am afraid in the same way as when I have seen the trunks of trees submerged in reservoirs. It is like a graveyard with all the graves still open.

"And I'll show you right where it came out," he says as he settles his foot back on the gas. I look to his silent wife, her debutante profile, and give up worrying whether she will speak.

We are back in Boulette's old neighborhood now, as he turns onto the street where he and his family moved months after the tornado. What is left of the green in winter swallows us up again, the light through the car windows turns to shade, and Boulette says, his voice wistful now, the softest I have heard it, "Now, this is Broadwater. I hadn't been down in here in . . . *Jesus* . . . I don't know how long."

He looks around, separated for a moment from our mission as he slows the Jeep at landmarks only he recalls, stopping to look at certain trees, at how the houses have been kept up, whispering to himself about how one person lived here, another there, wondering out loud what became of them.

His reverie is broken quickly when, several streets later, we pass a fire station, and Boulette tells me that this is where the tornado emerged from the woods. He is looking for trail marks now, certain trees that still bear the sign of the tornado more than thirty years later. I am unconvinced that in the tangle of trees he can find the sentinel that has stood all these years, but he slows the car repeatedly and points anxiously out the window.

"See that tree that's leanin'? That's one of 'em. It bent a tree that didn't die. There was a tree back there leanin', and here, look here, here's another one!"

I peer studiously out the window at trees—oak, sweet gum, maple, sycamore, some with broken branches, others with double trunks, some gouged by disease—but I do not see the tree Boulette wants me to see. Still, I give a mild affirmation, nod when he slows and points. It occurs to me that we are looking for a witness tree, for the one that stood and watched and might speak of what it knew of that day if we could find it.

Perhaps sensing my disbelief, Boulette says, "I used to could see a tree occasionally that was, you know, bent-like, and I know just where one used to be, and I'll see if we can see it. Well, here, right here, that tree right there."

His voice trails off, and his own disappointment begins to show. "Naw," he says, "maybe that idn't it. I can't say for sure it is, but that one back there definitely was, it was leanin' all right."

We are aimed on a southwest diagonal, as near as we can be, moving slowly through a series of roads until we emerge onto Cooper again.

"Now we're comin' up to Cooper, we're comin' up on the Bowlen house," he says with an excitement that is a mixture of boy and war fanatic.

"Yeah, yeah, yeah," he says, his breath constricted now. "This is *it*, we're comin' up to the Bowlens', right there it is. Now, near as my recollection is, the tornado's on the right side of the road at this stage, so it had to make a U-turn, and it just de-*stroyed* the Bowlen house. De-*stroyed* it."

I stare at the cathedral-like, exaggerated A-frame of Wayne Bowlen's old house, the house we stared at from the bus on our way to Forest Hill each morning, not only because it reminded us of a church and because it was a handsome house, but because this was where the heartthrob of our class, Wayne Bowlen, got on the bus, his hair pushed back in a Marlon Brando sweep even in the sixth grade, the tough, chisel-featured boy every girl wanted to go steady with.

"Now, this neighborhood over here to the left, Windsor Forest, if I remember, was like a cornfield," Boulette is saying now. I think quickly of the absurdity of Windsor Forest springing from a cornfield. There is still a wide expanse of mown green field at this juncture of Cooper and Forest Hill Road, and I tell Boulette that, yes, it was a farm field then. There is still a low depression along the road, and I know, before Boulette says it, that this is where the Reverend Mosley died.

"Right there's where it threw Mr. Mosley, the teacher, and he died, right up there. He was comin' up here, he was in a little ol' Volvo. I don't know from which direction. Died out in the field. Now, look—*look!*—see that tree that's leanin'?"

I nod and stare at the run of green field with houses set far back and far apart and think that it does not look so unchanged through here, and that it was maybe a kinder, softer ground that Lewis Mosley hit than Joe Bullock did out on Highway 13, but the thought makes little sense. It had to be a hard death either way.

"Now, there's the Bradshaw house," Boulette says. "The Bowlens', then the Bradshaws'. Jimmy Bradshaw said it took the house across the street entirely off its foundation. The story goes that there was so much pressure built up inside the house that somebody threw a chair through the window and that their dog died from pressure, from internal injuries, his internal organs just exploded."

Here, I remember, is where the baby was thrown into the field, its arm broken, and I look upon it momentarily as one of those sacred grounds where the babies who survive these storms fall like water-weighted balloons, resilient and lucky and one of a legion of babies carried this way to some sort of lifelong, oft-repeated tale of the survivable. I remember what Jimmy Bradshaw told me when I asked what he had taken away from the experience, that tornadoes were "survivable." I think now, jaded, that he should ask Lewis Mosley about that, and that it is nothing more than the luck of the draw.

"So it makes a U-turn," Boulette is saying, "and turns left. Now, I can't imagine it going to the stop sign and waiting for traffic."

I roll my eyes at this one, hoping Boulette is kidding, and see his thin smile in the rearview mirror.

"Now we're on the front line now, we're still goin' on a front line, absolutely, we're headed on the path," Boulette says, and I again note his military take and begin to worry a little for him, he is so worked up.

"Yeah, still goin' on a front line, but we're gonna make a little detour, and I'm gonna show you where I lived when it hit, right here in this black brick house, this is Westway, and there is a tree, now, I don't know if that tree's back there still or not, I think that's it right there, or maybe not. It would be one of the bigger trees. I mean, this has all grown up tremendous."

The quiet street runs through a jungle of trees, and the houses they shelter are going fast to seed. We are back in the old neighborhood now, mere blocks from where I lived on Cherrywood, and I think about how busted up the place looks. There is trash in the yards, the paint on many of the houses is peeling, the weeds have taken over the short Saint Augustine grass, and a block over I know that the creek is running wilder than it ever has.

"Now, what the hell has happened to this neighborhood?" Boulette says, reading my mind. "Just what the hell has happened? What houses used to go for in here was a decent price, now they go for thirty thousand. You could have a house here for thirty thousand dollars, but who'd live here now, tell me that?"

Something comes up in me quick, a defensiveness, and I want to say, "I would," but even as I think it I know it is a lie. I feel the sense of doom here, now, the knowledge that the bright hope we once held in the golden age of Candlestick has become this decaying thing, and that once hope was broken here it was broken for good, and that those who still live here from that time have maybe given up. It is a small piece of history with the shellac worn off, and the worms have eaten through. I see a small face peer from behind a curtain as we pass; a young boy alone, poking a stick in the dirt in one yard. I wonder where the other kids are. These streets used to be filled with kids.

"Now, here I am at the house," Boulette says, "and I'm out the back door, so I'm pretty close, close enough I'm hearin' some kinda noise which I can't identify. I was like, *Jesus*, can't hold my eyes open, and I think to myself, I gotta call Lloyd. Now Lloyd, I know, is gotta have a bird's-eye view."

We drive on up a low hill to Lloyd's old house, and Boulette points to it, saying, "Now, Lloyd lived in that house right there."

He is silent for a long while as we sit staring at the simple house with the requisite carport. Boulette's wife looks to him, waiting.

"Yeah, my old buddy Lloyd," Boulette finally says. "He lived in that house right there. He died. Lloyd Carrol."

I run down the list of the dead quickly in my head and tell Boulette that there was not a Lloyd Carrol who died at Candlestick.

"No, no, no," he says. "Naw. He didn't die in the tornado. No, he became a bum. I never could believe it. He died out on the streets or somethin'. I don't know. How does that happen? This is Palm Circle. Yeah, Lloyd lived here, had a bird's-eye view, but you know, I can't remember what he said about it, can't remember us talkin' about it. He was my best friend."

Peter Boulette's life, I can tell, is far removed from bumhood. He's trying to wrap his mind around this altered picture of his boyhood friend, the boy he ran the woods with, seeing him as some broken-down drunk on the streets, and he still sees the boy in him, he can't help it.

"Yeah, Lloyd and his brothers. Lloyd, Boyd, and Floyd."

I laugh out loud, the timing couldn't be worse, but I see that Boulette is amused, too, at the memory of the rhyming names. "Yeah," he says again, his voice reflective. "It was, like, 'L' for 'Large,' Boyd for 'Between,' and 'F'—Floyd—for 'Final,' that's what his parents used to say."

We drive on up to Candlestick now, just two blocks away, but I turn my head and look out the opposite window, hoping Boulette will not notice, as he talks about the Dog 'n' Suds being gone, the power station blowing up, how there was part of the sign with the candles still left after the wind had died. I do not want to look yet and am thankful when Boulette pulls up to the bridge that spans the creek and turns left on Longwood. The boy I had the crush on lived on this street. Boulette tells me that the boy's mother, Sarah Parker, was his—Boulette's—mother's best friend. He wants to show me the house, but they all look so much alike that he cannot pinpoint the exact address. But I know it as I pass it and do not say. I know it because in the winter when the leaves thinned out, I would watch from my window on Cherrywood and see the back of the boy's house lit up yellow, and when the lights went out, I would imagine he was stealing along the dark streets to meet me by the creek.

"Well," Boulette says, giving up on finding the house, "Charles Parker, Sarah's husband, left wherever they lived through here to go get Sarah. He got to the bridge, the bridge was out, blown up, and he had to circle back a different way, and he was one of the first people there. Course, Sarah was dead. Now where she was at, at the time, was workin' at the Laundromat, she was like, you know, back then they'd have an attendant, well, that's what she did. She attended to the clothes, take 'em out of the dryer, fold 'em, that kind of thing. My mother usually went and visited her on Thursday afternoons, but she told me, she said it was interesting, because that day, for whatever reason, I can't remember why she did, she went on Thursday mornin' instead, and they would just sit down and talk. They were good friends."

Boulette tells now of how he and his brother and mother made their way to Sarah Parker's house through the wreckage and that it seemed to him as if it took hours, and that once they were there young Alice Parker, Sarah's daughter, was crying and asking if her mother was alive. Boulette says that he seems to remember that his mother was coming to tell Alice the news of her mother's death. He does not remember the boy being there.

"And on the way there," he says, "I thought I saw, seems like I saw, a picture of Jesus. An open Bible that was in perfect shape, lyin' on top of something, open to a picture of Jesus, and I thought, you know, that's pretty cool."

From others I have heard this story of the picture of Christ lying in the wreckage, untouched, after the storm. Sometimes the Bible is on top of a broken crossbeam from the five-and-ten-cent-store, other times it is in the burned rubble of the power station, some have said it was on top of Donna Durr's Volkswagen when it fell to earth. True or not, I recognize the mutability of the miraculous, how it fits itself to the dimensions of faith and shores it up.

We are back at the bridge now. Across from it the rebuilt power station stands. I see the creek flowing beneath the bridge and think about the Parker boy who became motherless, and I wonder, too, why he has become anonymous, why so few remember him or what became of him. Peter Boulette is saying that this is the end of the line.

"Now, this is where my knowledge of that tornado stops," he says. "Right here. This is as far as it takes me, and then it lifts back up and goes on to Rankin County."

He asks me what time they are saying the tornado hit, and I

absent-mindedly give him an incorrect time, and Boulette explodes at the error.

"They are wrong!" Boulette turns full around in his seat and delivers this news to me eye to eye.

"What time did you say they were sayin'? Three thirty-three? They're wrong, they're wrong, *they are wrong.* I was saying to myself, I gotta call Lloyd, sayin', check this out, buddy, and I picked up the phone and it was dead, and I remember, I'll never forget this, ever, I remember lookin' at the clock and it was four thirty-three exactly. *Exactly.* No, no, no, no—*no!* That is something I'll never forget, lookin' at that clock. I can still see it. Now, you tell them Peter Boulette says it was four thirty-three, and that they are *dead* wrong."

It is idiocy, I think, carelessness, to have forgotten the exact moment of apocalypse. Sacrilege. I know the time, have known it, have told others when they have asked. I tell Peter Boulette that I will tell them, those fools, whoever they might be, that they are wrong, wrong, wrong. I will tell them that not pinning this event to the entire history of time makes it all worth nothing, because if we do not know when it happened, how could we ever mark time again?

Boulette takes a slow route back, and I watch the countryside out the window and think that I see little difference in then and now if I squint my eyes and do not look too carefully. The smell is the same, the dirt is the same, the trees are the same, the slow, drawn-out accent of the people I am with is the same, we are just all wearing bigger clothes and our faces are streaked with fine lines, but when we're back out here, in the old neighborhood, we're just kids again. For a long while we are stuck waiting for a train to pass, and Boulette and his wife and I watch as the freight moves slowly along the tracks, gaining speed at one point so I can almost hear what it might sound like, a locomotive coming at you, and then it slows and it is just another rusty string of boxcars in a dusty southern town. Boulette is in no hurry. He looks out the window at the sky.

"It marks you," he says. "You don't forget it. Now, when the sky around here turns an orange color—well, I actually predicted a tornado that happened between '86 and '88, out in Flowood, when the sky turned that color. I remember wakin' up that day and I saw that tint, and I told people, I said, this is 'tornadic,' as I call it. It's got a burnt orange, kinda weird haze, a glow almost, and I said, "This is *'tornadic.'* And later that day we had a tornado. And I've seen it before and since. Whenever you see that weather, we don't always have a tornado, but inevitably we have some bad-ass somethin'. Now, I don't know if it's a talent, I just know when I see that look. It just registers in my head, and it always will."

CHAPTER TWENTY-THREE

LINDA FLOWERS IS THE RED-DIRT GIRL of my childhood, the tomboy I was, the ravine urchin, the kid who never played with dolls because they were sissy stuff, the girl who ran with the boys and rode wild on horses across the hot pastures and deep into the cool woods. She was the twin I never knew I had whose sensibilities were dirt bound and sky high and all that was in between, and if we had met up when we were young we probably would have hated each other because we were the rulers of our respective worlds and each pledged allegiance to the rocks and dirt and mud and leeches and fireflies and craw-dads of our country-rough neighborhoods, and neither of us ever really believed, until we were grown, that there were others whose affinity for this place where we grew up was as strong or as natural as ours, and we would have shouted each other down as to who could climb higher, swim deeper, and run faster. But there would have been a grudging respect, and ultimately there would have been a bond.

In my search for those who were at Candlestick that day in

March so many years ago, it was Linda Flowers who appeared first with her description of the sky. "Yellow hell," she had written to me. "It was like the anteroom to Hell." At that description a remembered fear had surfaced in me, of the sky gone wrong, washed in an unnatural light. From the picture window on Cherrywood Drive I had watched the sky re-form itself in a light that was not really light at all but the chemistry of light, ions linking up in an atmosphere gone haywire with the burn of static. Not the yellow of sunlight but the pulsing yellow edge of Hell before the pit of fire shows itself. She had nailed it.

I recognize her without ever having seen a picture. She stands leaning casually against the cheap front desk of the motel, her feet crossed at the ankles, reading a book, one hand tucked into the pocket of her jeans. It is an easy pose, self-assured, unconcerned, and she is unaware of me for a moment even as I stand beside her, her hair a wild Medusa fall of black and silver curls pinned up, her cheekbones high and high in color, her frame strong and slender. As she moves to close the book, I notice her hands, broad and elegant—Cherokee hands, she will tell me later. And the term "sloe-eyed" comes to me as she looks up finally and smiles. Here is the girl who has lived on past that day, middle-aged now, still lovely, still a tomboy.

This day, for the first time in more than thirty years, Linda Flowers is going back to Candlestick.

In the car she hands me a foil-wrapped package that is warm, and when I look at it, puzzled, turning it over in my hands, she says, "Cat-head biscuits and sausage, girl. Mama thought you might get hungry, so she made you some sausage biscuits."

It is a gesture not to be denied, this I remember. The South will feed you and feed you good, and if you say, "No, thank you, I just ate," then you might as well have spat right in the person's eye. It is an offering, a tradition of gracious plenty, bound over from a time when plenty was scarce. I open the package, and the Sunday-morning-breakfast smell floods the small car, Linda hits the gas with her bright white sneaker, and I eat gratefully, tasting the burn of hot peppers in the sausage, the butter-milk in the biscuits.

We have had long conversations by telephone. We are not strangers in that sense; we have talked about where we grew up, we've traded a few secrets, but never having laid eyes on each other until now, we give each other the once-over, curious.

"I've got a surprise for you," Linda says as she taps her index finger on the steering wheel and then takes a sharp turn with the same finger.

"So give me a hint," I say, comfortable with her already.

"One word," she says. "A one-word hint is all you get."

"Shoot," I tell her.

"Albino."

I stare back at the receding industrial area we have just passed and then at Linda, driving, a smug look on her face.

"That's the hint?" I say.

"That's the hint."

"What're you, nuts?" I ask her. "What kind of hint is that?"

And then it dawns on me that she's referring to the albino catfish pond deep in the woods where the eyeless mutants swam, their bellies glowing like birch bark in the muddy water.

"The pond," I say, delighted that this is where we are going first.

"The pond," she says back. "And I'll tell you something I bet you don't know. It's the headwaters to the creek we played in."

I think about it for a minute, remembering the ignorance of childhood, how I never thought about where creeks began but only that they were there and how they changed with the sea-sons. It made sense now, of course, that from the huge sinkhole in the woods that was always full, always level, there would be runoff.

Linda looks at me hard now as we enter familiar territory, Cooper Road again, a path that is becoming well worn.

"This place is still way in you, isn't it?" she asks. Her smile is a knowing one. She nods her head before I answer.

"I'm *rooted* to this state," she says. "This state, I *love* it. Go back to when we were growing up here, in the fifties and sixties, Jackson was not what Jackson is now."

I say, "Amen," take another bite of sausage biscuit, and praise her mother silently.

"And amen again," Linda says. "Jackson used to be a big ol' country town, with Highway 80 as the dividing line. North of Jackson were the bluebloods, south of Highway 80 were the country folk. And Jackson now has gotten too big, too sprawling, too corrupt, too dirty, too unkempt, too dangerous, and it no longer fits the memory of those of us who grew up here, and you can't go home again, things change, and it has changed so dramatically."

I look out at the slow, tree-lined streets we are passing through now, a more gentle version of my ride with Peter Boulette the day before, a more familiar version. I recognize houses now, the layout of the old neighborhood. From the looks of it, I think that the neighborhood has changed only to grow older, greener, a bit more run-down and settled. I know that this is not what Linda is talking about, but the whole of the city itself and how that badness has spilled out even here.

"You know," she says, as we drive at a creeping pace through the streets, each of us craning our necks to see, "you don't see kids playin' on foot like we used to. I heard a country song on the way in today, it was a gospel song, country gospel, and it was something about G-rated kids in an X-rated world. They just don't get out and do what we did when we were kids. Any of that look familiar to you?"

She asks the question as we pull into a clear-cut area where the houses and the yards have thinned out, and beyond the clear-cut an expanse of woods, an old barbed-wire fence closing it off, and I forget about the houses for a moment, imagine the trees less tall and dense, imagine a hill of red clay pushed up on one side at the entrance to the woods, and I see it then the way it looked the day I found it years ago. It is hard at first to imagine, impossible almost, but I know that this is the place. I feel it more than see it, and look to Linda.

"This is it," I say. "Right out there, the albino catfish pond."

"In heavy rains," she says, "the water funnels up and gets, well, you can see it right there . . ."

I peer beyond the barbed wire and catch a flash of sunlight reflecting on the dark water. It is a place I never expected to find again.

"And it funnels up bank high," she continues, "and goes on . its merry way, and feeds into Big Caney Creek in Oak Forest."

It is a moment of reverence for me, and I stare past the barbed wire again, feeling suddenly old, brittle. It was the place where we gathered in silence when we were kids, stricken into dumbness by the mystery of it, the white bodies sliding through an underwater world, the haunted feel of the old trees so close in, the quick rustle of snakes through the leaves, the whine of the cicadas moving in. In those woods, beside that pond, the clean, vinyl-tiled floors of our homes were things of fancy, our mothers' faces became blurred, and we could not even remember the name of the school we attended. Here was where we forgot and remembered at once. Here, though we did not know it then, was the source of everything that drew this place where we grew up deeper into memory. Here was the birthing pool of Caney Creek and the home where the fish gods lay in cool opulence, too fat to follow the thin reed of water on its course to the widening gully beyond. Here, overlaid in green, was the collective unconscious of our home, our sense of place, the waterborne seed of our remembrance.

"Wanna go see it up close?" Linda asks, and I tell her no, that what I see now is enough, that knowing it is still there is enough.

"Remember," she is saying, "how we played in that creek, crawdads and leeches. We'd come out and leeches would be stuck to us and it was fun to pull 'em off. Catchin' fireflies in mayonnaise jars and pokin' holes in the top, playin' under willow trees."

I nod in silence, still staring toward the pond.

"And do you remember," she says, the excitement rising quick in her voice as she backs the car away from the barbed-wire fence, "do you remember the—now, are you ready?—the *fog machine?*"

I actually squeal. I try to remember if I have ever squealed before.

"THE FOG MACHINE!" we cry out in unison, giggling.

"The fog machine was the best-o, wadn't it?" she asks, and I nod fast, nearly bouncing in my seat.

"God knows what we did to our brains riding behind that thing," I say.

It is a remembered, delightful horror, knowing what we know now, that the chemicals spewed out by the fog machine could have caused respiratory collapse and brain damage.

"You think we're brain-damaged?" I ask.

"Of course!" Linda cries.

In summer, at dusk, the deep-bellied truck with the mosquito poison would make the rounds of the neighborhood, pumping out in a rolling white cloud the foul-smelling, toxic spray, and we would converge like a wild nest of hornets behind the ghastly thing, riding our bikes close in the "fog" that billowed out behind, weaving in and out drunkenly, closing our eyes against the sting of the spray. To my recollection I do not recall one child being told not to do this—that it could be dangerous to inhale insecticide. We were idiots then, dumb as sticks when it came to such things, kids and parents alike, and it was not until years later that we would all shake our heads and cringe at the memory. The fear then was yellow fever, not brain damage. Still, it was adventure.

"Fire ants!" I scream, and now it is Linda's turn to squeal.

What couldn't be blasted on the ground could be bombed from the sky, and I remind Linda of the planes that flew low over the neighborhood dropping poison on the fire-ant hills, little orange-brown pellets that we would gather up and eat because they had a nice crunch, manna from the crop dusters. I remind her, too, of a baby who fell into a fire-ant hill and died, its body stung thousands of times, and how it looked like a cherry red balloon, burnt bright and swelled beyond recognition, as if it had been boiled. And with our diet of noxious gas, fire-ant pellets, road tar, and wild onions from the fields, I tell her, it is a wonder that we did not become, like the albino catfish, mutants, and then I think to myself that perhaps we did and that it is this place that is our affliction.

We pass over a bridge now that spans a wide stretch of Caney Creek, and I look down the deep, dug-out gully that is half in shadow, cottonwood and honeysuckle and willow trees running the edge of it, and my breath catches quick in my throat because it is a picture out of time for us both, and it is as wild and as beautiful as I remember. I ask if we can stop awhile.

"Makes you want to go back, doesn't it?" Linda asks, and I nod as I pull my camera out and aim at the expanse of woods and creek. All day long I will snap pictures, trying to capture a feeling lost, a memory, a particular cast of light, the specific color green that is the green of these woods in summer, and I will fail because the camera, on this day and this day alone, does not record one still frame out of the dozens I shoot, and I will later question the oddity of this.

"Get that picture," Linda says. "Posterity at a glance. Our heritage. Our inheritance. Right there."

The camera screeches with an absurd Donald Duck sound, and I am pleased with what I think I am capturing. I imagine already how I will line the pictures up end to end and stare at them, remembering.

"You remember what it was like here then," Linda says. "There was an incredible innocence here, in South Jackson, in the country, and even though you might say, well, in 1966, that was the hippies and Vietnam and riots and killings, well, not here, not right here on this spot. Here it was Frankie Valli. It was so safe, everything was so safe. You'd play in the rain. It would start to rain, and you would go in the yard—I did—and hold your face up to the sky and just get pelted with raindrops, freeze to death, come in and strip down naked, and then run and jump in a tub of hot water. And the God that we loved was a living God, who made your garden grow, who painted skies, and who kept your children safe in tornadoes, and there was a strong sense of what's right and what's wrong, and what's fittin' and what's not fittin'."

But He didn't, I think, as Linda takes a long breath, He didn't keep them safe. And then, as if she has heard part of my thought: "And the memories I have of growing up down here, freedom, animals, and oddly, *good* wind." She laughs now, throws her head back, and then looks on to the creek. "The kind of wind that when you ride your bicycle, the fresh air's blowin' in your face and your hair is flyin' behind you, or you're on a horse's back, racing across the pasture, and the wind is cool even when it's hot, and that freedom, that nonpretentious freedom, it was good, it was the best, it was the *best*, and ours was a house that everybody wanted to be there. My parents made that possible. My earliest memories of them as a couple is helping people who were down and out, and they were the stepladder for everybody around them, family members and non–family members. And it was a good life, and we had a garden and I had chores. I had to pick and shell beans, cooked, cleaned. Mine was not a family of financial leisure, mine was a working family, but we were spoiled, insofar as their means could spoil us, with food, with attention. From the time I could walk, I was parked on top of a horse's back, from a rockin' horse to a Shetland to a Welsh to a quarter horse to runnin' horses. So what was on my mind was never bad things, never that the world could hurt me. And what was on my mind on March 3 was just horses and gettin' some orange juice for my mama. That was it. I was oblivious. I was oblivious because this was my world."

I look at the old world now through the window of Linda's car, deceptively the same, a world where it still rains and where kids still ride horses across pastures, but I know that it will never be the same for us. We cannot mold it from the clay again. We cannot raise the dead.

"We don't have that anymore," Linda says. "That innocence. The adults then were far more determined than the adults now to make a better world. Now it's what's in it for me, don't bother me, don't infringe on my time. People are becoming isolates. Even here."

We are not far from Candlestick now, just a few blocks, and I ask Linda if she is ready to go. We take the long way over, up Cooper to Forest Hill, to McClure, to Rainey. I see that the small farmhouses that were there when I was a kid have remained, the home of a friend set far back on three acres that I used to call "The Farm." Linda talks about her father as we drive.

"My daddy is my heart," she is saying. "He is my hero." She draws the last word out, *hee-row,* and I look at her profile in the stuttering shade that moves through the car window like wind on water, and I see the Indian in her clear as the creek on a good day. "Daddy was a marine, fought in the South Pacific, Okinawa. Chesty Puller was my daddy's C.O. You've got to understand, my father was John Wayne, and nothing hurt John Wayne. His arms were as big as watermelons, big, thick fingers. And as long as he was around, nothing hurt me. But he knew I was scared to death of tornadoes after that day, and anytime there would be a tornado watch he would call and say, 'Weather warning. Come up to the house.' And I would immediately gather my cigarettes and whatever project I was working on and go. And we'd watch the sky together. When I was with him, nothing could hurt me."

Linda's father has been dead three years. The mark this has made on her is clear. She mentions his advice as if it was just given yesterday.

We drive and smoke as Linda watches for the spot where she first saw the tornado. The ash on her cigarette grows long and threatens to spill into her lap.

"I was in my shiny new red car," she says, "and I drove right through here on Rainey. None of these houses were here. It was woods 'cause we used to ride horses on the side of the road. These little country-looking houses were here. There was a barn right here with an arena. And it was back there that I looked up, at my second stop, and said to myself, 'Oh, look, that looks just like the tornado in *The Wizard of Oz.*'"

It is an image that can always be called up, the bleakness and inevitability of that tornado bearing down, but I have to erase the pale blue sky I see now to imagine it, and not just a tornado on the horizon, but feeding from boiling clouds that cast a yellow pall across the countryside.

"I was looking west," Linda is saying now, "right at it, and it was coming right at me, and I did not even consider what this meant, did not even consider, because I lived in a world with my daddy and my mama and my horses and my brother and my new red car."

We turn right now, back onto Cooper, finishing the loop.

"I drove about the speed we're driving right now," Linda says, "about twenty miles an hour, and it wasn't far I had to go from where I first saw it. Turned into Candlestick with its flaming candles, and all these diagonal spots were taken, right in here."

We are at Candlestick now, and I look around for the first time, unable now to turn away. It is a ghost town. It is what a ghost town looks like, it is what a ghost town feels like. Ours is the only car in the lot. I look to the sign with the candles that was damaged in the storm and replaced. It looks the same except that the candles have gone pale from the sun. The strip of stores that Homer Lee Howie rebuilt looks the same, but they are empty now except for a post office and a barbershop. The old Liberty supermarket, after it failed, became a YMCA for a while, but now it is empty. The letters on the window here, too, are bleached by the sun. The field still fans out beyond the parking lot, almost white with late-blooming wild onions. Across the lot an exact replica of Dog 'n' Suds sits small and old and peeling. Empty. Next to the specter of Dog 'n' Suds a narrow, rickety row of bleachers looks onto a go-kart track dense with weeds. A rusted go-kart lies on its side. A liquor store stands where Polk's once stood. Nineteen sixty-six was still a prohibition year in Mississippi. The service station is still across the parking lot from Polk's. The power station has been replaced. It is as if a movie set has grown up where the old world used to be, but the actors are long gone, and it is just Linda and I in the car now, surveying silently, each avoiding the other's eyes. It seems as if dust has settled thick on everything we see and is still sifting slowly in the afternoon light. Homer Lee Howie said they had begged him to rebuild, and he said that what had been rebuilt had never taken. For a while, people had come back, tried to make it work, but soon they had just stayed away, not wanting to remember, believing in a curse. Linda is moving in her seat, looking uncomfortable, and I wonder about the prudence of re-forming the ruined to look exactly as it did before, dressing up the corpse and flooding it with lights, how it is like tempting fate. We sit atop a burial ground, I think, paved and repaved so the ghosts stay still. But they won't, they can't, they never will. I remember the parking lot here full, kids all over, the paint on the Dog 'n' Suds still bright, and now there is no one and everything feels rusted out and hollow. Weeds have grown up through the tar and gravel; the high grass in the field bends in our direction.

There's your barbershop," Linda is saying. "California Concepts."

I look up to the small windowed front of the barbershop next to the old Liberty store and see the ridiculous name, and think of how it was probably meant to draw customers when everything was rebuilt. It is one of those sad, telling statements of small, out-of-the-way places. I think that maybe South Jackson is still thinking of the Beach Boys and surfer shirts and California-style hair, and that the place to get all three is here in this deserted, weed-choked lot. I think of how old the barber, Bobby Grant, must be now. I wonder if the new name for the shop came to him in a moment of desperation. I think of Homer Lee Howie listening to the World Series when the inspiration for Candlestick Park came to him, and of what a redeeming place he had imagined it would be.

"Right in there, there was a beauty shop," Linda says, pointing to a vacant store slot. I get the sudden, disturbing sense that none of this is real. That the tiny strip mall has appeared just for us and will dissolve into the long shafts of sunlight splayed across the field.

"That's where I saw the woman running out with her hair in curlers," Linda says, "with the pink plastic cape on, screaming, and I looked up and I thought, 'Oh, I wonder what's going on?' and I parked very near to that shop."

We get out of the car after Linda pulls up to the place where she parked that afternoon. She is trying to re-create each move she made that day, walking quickly toward the Liberty.

"And I walked down here," she is saying as we move on a diagonal toward the wide plate-glass windows. "And when I walked here the fellow was running out, and I think he said, 'Take cover!' and I just went straight into the store as fast as I could and I dove underneath the checkout counter and covered up as we were trained to do in the bomb drills, covered my head, and I heard it then. You know, people describe it as sounding like a train or sounding like a jet engine. That's not what it sounded like to me. It sounded like a guttural growl. You know, I've been at railroad crossings and have heard trains flying by. It didn't sound like that. I've been in a jillion airports, and it doesn't sound like a jet engine. It sounds like something from the bowels of Hell. It was guttural. A deep, angry raging. And I didn't hear it until it was right on me. Oh, it was living all right, and I knew, I just *knew*— and this is what maybe made me block it—I *knew* it was going to get me."

We are standing next to Liberty now, and Linda is looking at the palms of her hands. There are little dots of moisture on them, and her fingers are trembling. She closes both hands quickly into fists, clamps them to her sides, and sighs. I look off across Cooper Road, straight down the wide, tree-thick chute of Cherrywood Drive. Down at the end of the street, although I cannot see it from here, is the house with the big picture window where I once lived. Where we are standing now is where we stood as children thirty-three years ago, but it is a mirage. It is not the same cement, it is not the same storefront we stare at. It is a fake, put up fast so people wouldn't have to look at the empty field, so they wouldn't have to be reminded each day of what had happened. That is why they wanted Homer Lee Howie to build it back quick. And I think now, who can blame them?

Linda stands silent with her fists still at her sides. I ask if she is okay, and she does not speak. I walk to the field and look around the back of the old Liberty, to the west, try to imagine the sky that day and realize that I will never be able to fully see it, no matter how many times they tell me the color and the sound and how great was the force of it, I can never fall back in memory to what they have witnessed. But I can feel it here, ground in deep below the fractured pavement, in the echo of our voices off the storefronts, in the silence that follows, and in the abiding recollection I have of this place full with people, mothers and children into and out of each store, a hopeful stream, a grateful stream, buying and primping, getting their hair washed and cut, having a hamburger at Dog 'n' Suds, picking up a prescription at the pharmacy, dropping quarters and dimes down the bright slots at the Laundromat where Sarah Parker smiled and folded, "attending," as Peter Boulette had said, my friends and I stalking the sidewalks for green stamps, and what is left here now is the white-hot mark of an iron held too long to the fire, burned in so that anyone who comes here feels it, not just those who know, not just me. It is a nothing little place, I tell myself, it was a nothing little place in the scheme of all places, but it was our place, and we never knew it was nothing.

"Hey!" I call to Linda from the field where I stand deep in the wild onions. I bend to pick one and bite the white flower from the stem the way I used to. "Hey!" I call again when she does not answer. She turns slowly in my direction and waves me back.

"Chiggers!" she hollers out to me. "You get out of that chigger grass, girl!" And I remember then the tiny red bugs that looked like specks of cayenne pepper burrowed under my skin after a day in the tall grass. I realize that I am no good at this anymore, kidhood in the Mississippi wild. I have forgotten too many cautions and all the ways there are to live through a day here. The aftertaste of the wild onion is nice. I meet Linda back at the car.

As we get in, she points back to the Liberty. "I do remember that there was no roof," she says, "and that there was dust, dust all over, from the cinder blocks, and the wires wrapped around my leg, and blood, and then the rain. It had gone from yellow to jet black and rain, and then I ran out into the parking lot, and it was darker than any thunderstorm I've ever been in, and I have this heavy memory of what it felt like, so dark with all that dust, this heavy memory, and I cannot quite bring it up. It's there. There were live wires everywhere. I remember exactly what I was wearing. I remember what my hair looked like. And the wires from the banners that the circulars from the store hung on, the advertisements, they had gotten wrapped around my legs, and I reached with my right hand, and this I remember clearly, and just pulled these wires and when I did I cut beneath my knee, just sliced through, like you're cutting cheese with a wire cutter, and there were shards of glass everywhere that were causing little rivulets of blood. I realized I was not dead. I did realize that."

We are in the car now, and Linda is shaking as if she is cold. I think to myself that she is the first person I have talked to who was there that day who has not cried.

"I have physiological responses to it now," she says. "If there's a warning my heart races, I get sweaty, my hands get sweaty. If I let myself, I could hyperventilate and pass out."

I worry now that this will happen, but I see that she is shutting down hard, trying to rein in the panic.

"Suck it up, girl," she says suddenly in a booming voice, and I realize as the flesh rises up on my arms that these are her father's words, his tone, his volume.

"It's just sheer terror," she is saying now. "Just sheer, unadulterated terror. If I'm just where I can go away, remove myself, physically, mentally, emotionally, and protect my psyche, I'll go there. I can leave now. We can drive outa here right now."

I tell her that yes, we can. The light is beginning to fade and the sun is spilling yellow across the field.

"But you know," she says, still not making a move to leave, "you can never do that without damage. You're still there. On some level you're still there, you're still attending, because everything that goes into the psyche, into the brain, is coming into the senses. So it's still there, the memory, the experience, everything, it's just for the moment that it's happening that you don't have to pay attention to it. Then you just act. I never went back here. I never drove by here."

Linda stares out at the empty parking lot, runs her gaze past the Liberty store, the barbershop, and then she turns in her seat to look at the Dog 'n' Suds. There is astonishment on her face, as if she has just been asleep in her bed and woken up in the rain.

"I will tell anybody of the mercy and grace that's been shown me and mine." She speaks these words as if in prayer. "It came over me the other night just to start counting my blessings. To go as far back as I could remember, to where I was delivered and from what, and I just started clickin' it off, and it became so awesome that there could be no reason . . ." She leans forward quickly now and pounds her fist on the dash with her next words. *"There would be no reason I wadn't killed in that tornado!* Five seconds, *two* seconds, just two seconds had I sat in my car, I woulda been dead. TWO SECONDS!" She screams the last words in my face, and I feel myself flinch. She is right. I know what happened to her shiny red car, the body of it folded and creased, her purse that she had left on the seat found in a tree in Florence, Mississippi. I tell her I know.

Her eyes look feverish, and she is agitated. The day is coming back to her, and her daddy is not here.

"I think of my father's war service," she says, trying to take deep breaths every few words. "Most soldiers, large numbers of soldiers, didn't make it in on one beach landing. It was unheard of to do two. My father did *three*. *Why? Why! Why!* And the only thing that I can come up with is that God had a plan. Had my father not survived those, I wouldna been born, my brother wouldna been born. That's not to say my father lived so we could have life. It may be our children, it may be his great-grandchildren or great-great or somewhere way down, but that *had* to be preserved, and he had to come with my mother to start this line, because there's a plan, there has to be, I know this, and I don't know what it is, I don't know, I can't think that it's me, because I just don't think it's me. I think my service . . . well, put it this way. I like prayer closets, not street corners."

She laughs gently, the fever in her spent for now, and I think that Linda's is a better reason than believing that we are all just fools, waiting each day to die for no cause, no reason, without mercy.

"Then," I say, "there is no reason that Ronny Hannis died." The words fall out of me. I hadn't wanted to say them, but they are there. It is what I am thinking as I look at the replica Dog 'n' Suds, the lie that says that March 3, 1966, was sunny and beautiful and the wind blew fair.

Linda looks at me firmly, but there is kindness there, too. I look beyond the window to where a cardinal has lit on the parking lot and think that he is as bright as the candles on the sign once were.

"Those who lived," Linda begins, and there is a long, long pause before she speaks again. "Those who lived, I believe God allowed it. I believe that the people who survived, there's a reason, they weren't done yet. And the flip side of that is, well, does that mean that the people who died were done? I'm a Christian, Lorian, I believe that God knows our days before we're born, before we go into our mother's womb, so the answer to that is, yes, they were done. And the young man who died, who was helping to dig out bodies . . ." She thinks for a long time now, and for a moment I do not think that she will finish. She sighs and places her palms together as if she is praying, leans her chin on her fingertips, and sighs once more, long and hard, and when she speaks again it is slowly and deliberately.

"If there can be any joy for Ronny's mama and daddy, then it is to know that he loved so selflessly, and to know that they brought up someone to be that loving. Isn't that a wonderful thing?"

But they'd rather have him back, I think, and when I turn to look at Linda I see that she is smiling almost beatifically. My thought seems harsh in the face of that smile, and I think that it looks like every Sunday sermon ever preached and like every vacation Bible school class rolled into one, and I think that I have seen that same smile on Mae Hannis's face and that there are saints who have smiled that way, too.

We do not talk as we pull away from Candlestick and sit with the motor idling by the service station with its flat canopy. It was a rusted-out heap when I was a kid, a perfect country gas station with oil spots leaked all over as big as the chassis of a car. It smelled good then under the canopy where the gas fumes collected and the oil steamed up from the dirt.

"When I started running," Linda says quietly, "here is where I saw the first live person, the first human on his feet. It was a black man, and he looked very dazed, and he had his hand up and there was blood, and I asked him, please, if I could use the phone, and he just looked at me, dazed, and said, 'There's been a tornado. There is no phone.'"

We drive back up Cooper now, the seven tenths of a mile Linda ran that day across downed wires and through the rubble to Woodville Heights Baptist Church. The church had been hit, the pastor's wife and child inside, but they had lived. Linda vaguely remembers debris filling the church and then a man and his wife pulling into the parking lot.

"I was just standing there screaming," she says as we stare at the rebuilt church, an octagonal addition that wasn't there before. I remember how grand the church had been with the cathedral sweep in front, the cross atop the modern spire. "I was just screaming and this man, he slapped the pee-turkey outa me, slapped me as hard as he could, and I snapped out of it and they took me home, but I don't remember any of it until I walked into my mother's house, and I said to her, 'There's been a tornado,' and her knees buckled and she caught the kitchen cabinet and she went white as a ghost and white-knuckled, and she just started shakin'."

I think of what Linda had to cross to get to the filling station and then the church, the parking lot mounded with sheared-off metal, broken walls, telephone poles and wires down all over, trees uprooted and fallen across the roads. She says she remembers lifting her legs high up over the wires, but not much else, just freeze-frames, she says: the man at the gas station with the bloody face, the couple in the parking lot at the church, a memory here and there and worry that her father would hear the news and have a heart attack, but when she got home someone had already radioed him to say his family was alive, and she says that she knew then that everything would be all right because her father wouldn't die.

As we sit in the quiet church parking lot, she shakes her head back and forth, still mystified by what she cannot recall.

"A friend of mine told me that I came to school with my arm in a sling. I do not remember that. I asked him, 'Are you sure?' And he said, 'I am positive.' Another friend told me that I had handed a candy bar to a little boy in the store because he was cryin' for his mama. I just reached out from under the counter and grabbed a candy bar from those racks they have, and handed it to him. She told me that I said this happened. I don't remember it. I have never read the reports of the tornado. I never saw it on TV. I never looked at a photo. I never saw a newspaper, and I guess I want to. I want to see how I'll react to that, see if it can make me remember. But there's one thing I'll tell you, I don't want to remember gore. If I saw gore, I don't want to remember it."

The likelihood, I think, is not good. Of all the structures broken and fallen, there were as many bodies. More. There is no pristine memory locked away in Linda Flowers, I think. How could there be? What she has remembered is the thing that moved her forward that day, and nothing else. The rest of it is dug in deep, and for her sake I hope it stays there.

"That's it," she says. "That's all I know. My daddy said shake it off, go on, like he did when I fell off a horse. He said, 'You pick your butt up, girl, and get back on that horse.' I shook it off, but you can just shake off what's outside, you know?"

We drive away from town now, toward Byram to the south, toward the Pearl River. Caney Creek winds on down out of South Jackson and feeds into the red-brown waters of the Pearl, and I think to myself, as we take the Old Byram Road out to the river, that it is always good to know where a creek ends up.

The wind through the trees is warm and buoyant as Gulf Stream water as we pass huge pin oaks and gullies filled with kudzu that winds thick up the telephone poles and along the wires. Everything grows to excess here, I think, as we pass the drying reeds of cornstalks high as saplings, a field of cotton here and there not quite picked clean, errant snowfields in the waning light, the hard, heaped-up rows of dirt distinct as arrows pointing back toward the river. Cotton grows well near a river, in the flat floodplains where the minerals have gone in deep, in dirt that always holds the hope of water, even in a dry season. What keeps people here? I had asked Linda once. "It's the dirt, girl," she had said, and it always goes back to the dirt, I think, no matter what you put in it, no matter what you build on top of it. And here the smell of dirt never leaves. Dirt along the windowsills, the dust from dirt in the trees, mud, clay, the parking lots and roads that smell like dirt, the fields that take in whole families and give them back when they're done, the dirt that covers them when they are. Dirt, like a flood, like food, hand-picked and deep-fried, and still dirt no matter how it runs, no matter how it tastes. The dirt that binds arrowheads for decades and then gives them up on a whim, the dirt where the war dead are buried, the dirt that mixes with water and runs red as blood in the gullies. The same dirt, given up, scored and divided and scarred a dozen ways, and then the scar covered in more dirt, so you never quite know the mark of the wound, but you know the nature of it. You know there has been some damage done.

"Look at that," Linda says as we pull up to an old rusted bridge that spans the Pearl. She is pointing through the open sunroof of the car, at the sky. We get out and stand, shading our eyes toward the horizon.

"I've never seen this," she is saying, still pointing. "This is not a rainbow. I have never seen anything like this. Never."

Above us, on a diagonal from the horizon, is a perfect rainbow-colored cross made by the setting sun. But it is an odd light, yellow and turquoise and purple in distinct bands, the bands distinctly a cross. I am not necessarily a believer in signs from God, and I tell Linda so.

"Fool!" she says. "Just look at that. Rainbows disappear, girl. Do you see this disappearing? This is strange. Look at it."

I look again, and the cross has grown even brighter, saffron yellow and pink now, and I think that it is the most extraordinary thing I have ever seen. No meteor I have seen blazing a trail at twilight comes close. I hear the low hum of the cicadas rise up behind us from the trees along the river, and then the frogs along the bank, signaling dusk. And I hear the river, too, the washboard sound of water against the small stones in the clay. Arrowheads, maybe. I think that it is magic here.

"Now, the day my daddy died," Linda is saying, "this color yellow was in his room." She points again to the cross in the sky. "It was not an ominous yellow, like the day of the tornado. It was that late-afternoon Mississippi sunshine yellow, like here, like right now."

The cross is washing out now, melting across the sky in a burn of yellow, and we turn our backs to it, heathens, and walk to the old bridge. We stand on the rotting planks, wrap our hands around the rusted struts, and peer into the water that is rusted, too, running dark red in the fading light to a bend in the tree line along the bank that our eyes cannot negotiate, and it looks from here as if the trees just take the river in. I imagine that photographers, looking for the rustic, looking for something that says *this* is Mississippi, have taken pictures of this bridge. I find myself wishing one would come along so I could throw his camera in the water.

"What're you thinking?" Linda asks, and I laugh.

"Forget that," I say. "What are *you* thinking?"

She looks as thoughtful as she has looked all day.

"I was thinking," she says, "that we never really know what to pray. That we might think we know what to pray, but we really don't."

And if we did, I think, then we would pray ourselves wise.

"Then make a wish instead," I tell her as I pick a piece of rust the size of a silver dollar from the flaking bridge support. I smell it first, thinking it smells just like the dirt, just like the air, and then toss it high above the river. We watch it spin and wink like a coin and then catch high in a cottonwood branch and hang suspended in the warm light before it falls, fast as a stone, into the deep water.

CHAPTER TWENTY-FOUR

MY LAST DAY IN JACKSON, I return to Candlestick alone. It is a day that is warm for winter, but not uncommon. Even in winter the gulf air presses north, and as I travel Cooper Road once more the heat rises up from it in waves, making a mirage of small lakes on the hot pavement. I am reminded of days like this when I was a kid, when we would run barefoot along the hot tar road as far as we could stand it, and then we would take off screaming through the high grass to the creek, where we would hold our feet beneath the opaque water, nearly as warm as the road, until the sting went away. Storms are forecast before midnight, a cold front will be moving through, but by my amateur estimate and the still benign look of the sky, I will be on a train heading north by then. I think of how deceitful the sky can be, a blue bowl of nothing that can suddenly fill with snakes, and I wonder, idly, if there is any way to calculate how many skies there are between the ground and Heaven.

The Crawford Nursing Home sits far back in the trees off Cooper Road. It is the place the tornado bounced over, on a whim it would seem, the only shelter between it and the back wall of Candlestick, the narrow ribbon of Rainey Road and a pasture where a drugstore now stands. In looking for the mercy inherent in that moment, people often mention how the nursing home was spared, as if God, charmed into awareness, said, sure, let the old folks live, and for ten reverent seconds pulled hard on the leash of the beast and yanked its head skyward. Those asleep, those too far gone from consciousness to know what was happening, never heard a thing. But somewhere, perhaps, just like the deaf people in the storm of 1916, they must have felt it, they must have known what hammered overhead, the dim-witted, the aged, the crippled, and who is to say they understood it not as mercy, but as penance?

I am reminded of Faulkner's Rowan Oak in Oxford as I drive the long, tree-lined road up to the nursing home. The light beneath the canopy seems old as starlight, held tight in this fist of green, pulsing long after the star is dead, having reached across time to this exact spot where light is absorbed and then given back in a chlorophyll haze. Out from the tree line a pasture opens, defined at its periphery by a thicket of honeysuckle and blackberry vines. There is a sentinel here: Faulkner's Benji bumps along the uneven road in a wheelchair, a young man with a simple face damp in the heat. He waves to me slowly as I pass. I wave back. He smiles crookedly and rolls on toward Cooper Road.

The nursing home is a cluster of bungalows at the end of the long road, set in a circle of gravel and dirt and thick vegetation. There is no direct light here either, and it is cooler. I stop the car and get out for a moment. No one stirs in the doors of the bungalows, I see no one at all, just the faraway blur of the boy in the wheelchair down the road. It feels safe in here, a sense of comfort that pushes up for an unknown reason, perhaps the absence of light, the long shade of all this green, the antiquity of the place, its settledness, the fact that it bears no scars, or simply because it reminds me of the old neighborhood, how it was dug in long before the '60s, long before any of us came here, and it stays on. Maybe because those inside the bungalows do not hurry outside to peer at the stranger standing in their open circle, not only because they cannot but because the world out here no longer exists for them. I wonder if they would find it comforting to see that it has not changed.

I drive back down the road that could be the hard-packed, clean-swept road of a plantation, on into the hot, rusted smell of the afternoon, and pass the boy once again, heading toward the bungalows. He waves once more, and I wave back and think that there must be a rhythm to his days, that its very repetition will keep something quiet in him and free of fear, if nothing is disturbed here, if his world keeps on growing darker and more secure.

I turn right on Cooper Road, then go up the few hundred yards to Candlestick and park in the lot next to the only other vehicle, a police squad car. Inside California Concepts, Bobby Grant's renamed barbershop, I find Grant with a customer, the cop whose car is outside. There is no one else waiting in the small shop. The walls are covered in inexpensive paneling; there are two barber chairs, a wall of mirrors, a small cubicle of a bathroom, and the Miller Beer clock that hung in the old shop the day of the tornado. It is dim and cool inside.

"Clock still works," Grant says as he catches me staring at it. It is a '60s memorabilia hunter's dream. The clock's face is lit from behind the yellowing plastic, and there is a scene of a running mountain stream and then the Miller Beer logo in red cursive script. It is the same clock I have seen in a dozen roadside joints from my childhood, and there is something vaguely comforting about the moving water that is always clear, always on a level, and always moving toward a place you never see.

"Same clock," Grant says now. "Had it all along."

The term "California concept" does not apply to Bobby Grant, I think as I turn to study him for the first time. He is wearing a plaid shirt. His face is broad and fleshy, his thinning, oiled hair combed back carefully from his wide forehead. His hands, too, are broad, and he concentrates almost completely, except for occasional beneath-the-eyebrows glances at me, on the haircut he is giving. His fingers, despite their thickness, move quickly. I wonder how many heads of hair Bobby Grant has tended in his life and how many secrets he has heard. There is one thing certain, he will not be telling any of them to me. Grant does not seem to be annoyed by my being in his shop, but I can tell that he is not pleased either. I am the only woman in the good-ol'-boy bastion of the barbershop, and this alone makes me suspect.

"I'm the tornado lady," I tell him, as if this needs to be announced. His wife had called me several months back, wanting to tell Grant's story. She has since passed away. I have talked to Grant on the phone once, asking if I could come out to the shop.

"Suit yourself," he had told me. "I don't know anything new I could tell you." And we left it at that. I figured if anything would work with Bobby Grant, it would be the element of surprise. I was wrong.

Grant clicks along professionally with his scissors and reaches into a drawer with his free hand. The cop sits stone-faced.

"Here you go," Grant says, holding out a yellowed newspaper. "Read this, and then see if you have any questions."

I take the paper and climb into the empty barber chair. It has been cranked up high, and my feet do not reach the footplates. It is the first time I have sat in a barber chair, and I am certain that my stupid delight at this shows on my face because Grant gives me a quick, disapproving look.

I study the newspaper. It is material I have read before, a story written on the twenty-fifth anniversary of the tornado with a picture of Grant standing beside the Candlestick sign and then a picture next to it of the sign the day after the tornado. The tall base is bent in a "V" windward, the face of the sign is missing, all but for the three letters "ICK." The fractured candles blaze above.

It is a retrospective of that day, of people who have not forgotten. There are pictures too, of the cars heaped and mangled in the parking lot, of twisted rebar with the concrete peeled away, of a field of unidentifiable rubble that was Candlestick.

In the article Grant tells of how the red-haired boy came running in, out of breath, yelling that the storm was coming. The shop went dark then, the pounding of the tornado was heard, and the boy curled up in a corner, tucked into a fetal position with his hands covering his head. Grant braced himself against another corner, and five others ran into the bathroom. Then the walls came down and the roof fell in, but the bathroom still stood. Grant says that when people ask about it happening again, he tells them, "We're probably as safe here as we'd be anyplace else."

I know now, finally, what became of the red-haired boy on his mad run the length of the small shopping center, after his cry went up and he was certain that everyone believed him. He must not have left much ground uncovered, I think, as I add up the number of people who have mentioned seeing him, hearing him, that day. His is an indelible face in the panic that barely had time to take hold. He had always been such an odd boy, a know-it-all whom kids instinctively picked on, with his bright hair and freckles and old-man glasses, his shortness. Those who saw him that day described him as a young boy or a little boy. The child was thirteen then, at least, a shrimp, the taunted runt of the neighborhood, but he had news that day that would carry across decades, and it would always be the same news, delivered in the same high-pitched, warning voice, and it would always have the same end to it. I try to imagine him now as a man in middle age, and I cannot.

I read now about the "legacy of Candlestick," as the paper calls it, about the ghost town it has become. A woman who owned a business here briefly says that when people called her up and asked where she was located, and she said "Candlestick," they would grow silent, or just say, "Oh." There is the word, I think, and then the image, never again the bright suburban Valhalla of Homer Lee Howie's dream but instead a graveyard. They built it back just as it had been, the paper says, before the year was up, and people stayed away. Businesses failed one by one. No one comes to buy hope in a graveyard.

I swing my legs in the high chair, look out the small storefront window of Bobby Grant's shop onto the empty parking lot, and feel exactly what I felt here with Linda Flowers. Dread. Incalculable dread. The day is still sunny. And I hear Bobby Grant's scissors stop, see him whisking the hair from the policeman's shoulders with a soft brush. He takes the cape off, brushes the man's shoulders again, and slaps some tonic on his neck. It smells like limes, like fresh-cut grass, like summer here.

I ask Grant the only question I can think of, the only one that really matters anymore because I am at the end of the chain now. I am here on death row, in the chair, staring out at a place where people were buried alive, and I can feel it crawl up in me *how* they died here, and I know it in a way I have never known it, and it makes me sick. And I want to stand up and shake my fist at God and holler, "You bastard, you ever-loving lying bastard, *why?*" Because I look back at the way the years have turned since that day, and I see how they have spilled out into this empty place where everything is dead and dry and where the humorless barber has become the ghost of Candlestick Past, and for all I knew he died that day along with the rest of them and has been waiting here in this airless mirage, a place we would have claimed was real before it was pulled, heaving, from the pins that held it tight, just waiting to say, "Here, here's the way it was, now read about it, tell me if that tells it all. Look—nothing out of place, nothing changed, same clock, same time on the wall, same moving water, same barber chairs, same layout, same story for everyone who comes in here. No one died. Not here. They lied. Not a scratch. No one hurt. Just as safe here as anyplace else, I guess. You can never know about these things. Just as safe."

But it isn't true. It isn't safe here. It will come again. Five years.

Ten years. Three months. Two hours. Once a mark is on a place you can see it even in the dark, no matter how you put a cover to it. I know it this time. If there were money in my pocket, I would slap it flat on Bobby Grant's tonic-slick palm and make a coward's bet. If there were a Bible on Bobby Grant's long, cluttered counter, I would put my hand to it.

So I ask him, "You know the Hannis boy?"

He doesn't answer me directly. He swims beneath the question and surfaces like the ghost he is.

"I'll be," he says. "His folks still live up on Ridgeland?"

It is not his fault, I think, that he is a ghost.

"Same place," I say. "Still there. Nothing changed. Same house."

He smiles then. Hearing what I have told him, I wonder if it makes him feel less alone here, but I cannot know for sure. It is a lonely place no matter how you look at it.

I slide down from the barber chair, hand Grant the old newspaper, thanking him, and follow the cop out the door into the oppressive afternoon. Off to the west the sky is still clear.

THEY WERE THE BOYS OF SUMMER in our world, the upperclassmen of Forest Hill School who had matured before the eyes of the young girls who wanted them for their own, Mississippi boys with the country still in them, the dark smell of the dirt still on them, boys with value systems handed down from God, boys who could tease and flirt, but who would also defend and protect because in doing so they became men before the age of men was upon them. They had the sense of manhood in them early on, understood the boundaries it drew clear. And by action, by commandment, by bearing witness to each, it had been taught to them. Fixed in the heightening yet unmoving aftermath of a war that no one knew was coming, a war that in time would have a name but never a purpose, they became resolute and silent in their duty, bending to the task, not looking to the sky, they and their fathers, they and all the men who answered the call to Candlestick that day. They did not ask at that moment why or how when they saw what death could do. They did not ask that it be undone. And for those who crowded behind the rope of the demarcation lines, there was comfort in knowing that men will go to war, but no comfort when they heard that the war had taken a son and the mother grieved.

They were the boys of summer, too, in the creek where I now stand, Larry Swales and Ronny Hannis, a dozen others, fit and young and made light with incaution. This creek was their training ground, their boot camp, and we looked on from the eroded shore, down the steep bank that held the rushing chute of water, and watched them as they rode the torrent from pipe to pipe, their wet faces bright in the sun, their forearms brown and taut as they held on against the current. If they looked at us, the dirt-smeared urchins, bank maggots come to dream that we could be like them, we beamed back, waved our muddy hands, jumped up and down, called them by name, and on they rolled in the swell of the tide, barely noticing. But had we fallen, pitched forward into the deep water, they would have seen, they would have saved us, and this we knew.

The water is past flood season now, no more than knee high in most places, filled with red clay silt so it runs orange past my bare legs and forms a small tidal chevron on the surface of the fast water. I watch water bugs ride the current, the hard-shelled ones tumbling in the small riptides, the surface skaters poising on the taut skin of the backwash pools. As I move against the stream, the chert rattles beneath the water like bones. It is sedimentary rock, clay turned to stone, the rock of tomahawks and arrowheads, the rocks we piled high for dams to divert this current when it could be tamed.

Each year the walls of the ravine that hold the creek grow steeper. Flood season carves the creek bed deeper, smooths the high edges of the bank that acts as a natural levee. But there were times when the streets lay vacant in water, when the creek fell past its banks, the flash floods that came not in the midst of rain but when all the rain had been gathered up, the belly of the creek so full it spilled its guts in a dark rush, carrying snakes to the high mark of the tide that lay the reedlike grass flat as the water sought the low-lying world and the hollow skins of houses. We would play then in the streets waist deep in water, against our mother's pleas, against the warning hum of mosquitoes, which laid their eggs in the stagnant lake. The fog machine could not reach us in flood season. And then the water would recede and the yards would shine slick in red mud, the road now a soft canvas upon which we would press the hieroglyphs of hands and feet and knees, indelible until the next pounding rain.

I stand facing the headwaters of Caney Creek, the deep sowbelly slough of the albino catfish pond, far into the woods past the barbed-wire fence where the water world begins. I cannot see it, but I know now that it is Mecca. Up the high bank to my right runs the long, pine-shaded yard of the girl whose mother killed her father, the girl who stared across this creek, not remembering I had gone, as she watched trees and walls spin by. And up the high bank to my left, one weed-choked yard removed, is the house with the big picture window where I had lived, and less than a block away, Candlestick, where Bobby Grant is sweeping the floor of his barbershop, turning off the lights, locking up, and walking out the door into the level empty lot.

Twenty feet ahead of me is the pipe that spans the two shores, a long black conduit of cast iron, joined together in a coupling with bolts big as a fist, the one road in that day for the long march of those who came to unbury the dead. I remember the sharp burn of it beneath my feet as I crossed it barefoot, trying to ignore the blur of water and rock beneath, the tilt of the sky above, the cries of the kids onshore. Karei McDonald had taken the length of pipe in a bound, on his way to help, but he had remembered it. All those who crossed it remembered, and by that acknowledgment it has entered into the history of that day, it is a monument that survives. I look upon it now as an altar of sorts, with Mecca to the south, Hell to the west, and the past rushing straight at me down this corridor of clay.

Here, I think as I push my feet deep into a smooth wallow of mud where there are no rocks, is where I was born, on a summer night when the moon was full and I slipped beyond the confines of the house, out into the air that moved in great wet clots, down the fissured banks of the ravine in the platinum wash of light to perhaps the very place I stand now.

The summer gown I wore drew up the creek water like a wick as I knelt beside the potholes, plunging my hands in deep, feeling for the soft mounds of tadpole eggs, the filmy, sheathlike skin of tiny bass, and all around me the night had a voice and a smell and a sense of time that was bound back to the very genesis of time and smell and sound, and so I came to know, by the scent of clay and the dragonfly hum of cicadas and the density of rock, where I belonged and from what, as Linda Flowers said, I had been delivered. This was home before I ever spoke its name, before I had been born. And it did not hold affection for me as I did for it. A place does not love you, only people do, but a place gives up what it is made of in an elemental rush, so that once you breathe it in, the chemistry in you changes. And then there are the things that it will not give up. And there are the things that it will claim for its own. Lives. Hearts. Souls. Those who stay on when it has taken these things from them understand that home is where you die.

It was this place that formed us, I think, as I watch the mares' tails now riding in from the southwest, so high and thin and icy up where the war begins. Change in the weather. If we had been able to read the sky the way we read the dirt, then we could have sown cotton on the wind.

In here Ronny Hannis's '56 Oldsmobile lay with boulders of concrete, shattered wood, the deep roots of trees with the dirt still attached. Headstones set loosely in mud and water, pried free, carried out, but the haunt of them remains, the afterimage burn of things where they never belonged. I wish he had not died. I wish none of them had died.

Here lives the religion of memory and its sacrament: scars in the dirt, scars on the soul, and from those scars the undeniable meaning of place. To this place, then, is owed the story of its tragedy and the mortal price of its endurance.

I stare back down the long canyon of the ravine. It is a place of echoes now.

Printed in the United States
By Bookmasters